About Island Press

Island Press, a nonprofit organization, publishes, markets, and distributes the most advanced thinking on the conservation of our natural resources— books about soil, land, water, forests, wildlife, and hazardous and toxic wastes. These books are practical tools used by public officials, business and industry leaders, natural resource managers, and concerned citizens working to solve both local and global resource problems.

Founded in 1978, Island Press reorganized in 1984, to meet the increasing demand for substantive books on all resource-related issues. Island Press publishes and distributes under its own imprint and offers these services to other nonprofit organizations.

Support for Island Press is provided by Apple Computers, Inc., Mary Reynolds Babcock Foundation, The Geraldine R. Dodge Foundation, The Charles Engelhard Foundation, The Ford Foundation, The Glen Eagles Foundation, The George Gund Foundation, The William and Flora Hewlett Foundation, The Joyce Foundation, The John D. and Catherine T. Mac-Arthur Foundation, The Andrew W. Mellon Foundation, The Joyce Mertz-Gilmore Foundation, The New-Land Foundation, The J. N. Pew, Jr., Charitable Trust, Alida Rockefeller, The Rockefeller Brothers Fund, The Florence and John Schumann Foundation, The Tides Foundation, and individual donors.

Environmental Disputes

Environmental Disputes

Community Involvement in Conflict Resolution

James E. Crowfoot and
Julia M. Wondolleck

ISLAND PRESS

Washington, D.C. • Covelo, California

The authors are grateful for permission to include table 3.1 from *Breaking the Impasse*, by Lawrence Susskind and Jeffrey Cruikshank. Copyright © 1987 by Basic Books, Inc. Reprinted by permission of Basic Books, Inc., Publishers, New York.

Crowfoot, James E.
   Environmental disputes: community involvement in conflict resolution/ James E. Crowfoot and Julia M. Wondolleck.
        p.   cm.
   Includes index.
   ISBN 0-933280-74-2.—ISBN 0-933280-73-4 (pbk.)
   1. Environmental policy—United States—Citizen participation. 2. Conflict management—United States.   I. Wondolleck, Julia Marie. II. Title.
HC110.E5C76   1991
363.7'058'0973—dc20
                                                                    90-47863
                                                                    CIP

Printed on recycled, acid-free paper

Manufactured in the United States of America
10 9 8 7 6 5 4 3 2 1

*To those individuals and organizations
working for environmental change*

Contents

Preface

Citizen groups are typically on the fringe of governmental decision-making, frequently having neither the power and resources of business and industry nor the political and strategic skills so critical in influencing decisions. Hence, citizen groups usually resort to the courts or administrative appeals processes for recourse after the fact against decisions they feel are inappropriate or that seemingly ignore their legitimate claims. Pursuing these other avenues can, at times, be an effective strategy, both empowering the citizens and setting important precedents for future decisions. But they are not *always* fruitful and, moreover, are frequently quite costly to the organization's resources and general well-being. As a result, some citizens are lobbying for a more proactive role in decision-making processes, one that might avoid the sort of reactive battles that are now so prevalent.

Not surprisingly, government and business representatives are frustrated as well by the inability of current policy and decision-making processes to reach effective and timely outcomes. They, too, seek change.

In the environmental arena, citizen, business, and government representatives have for almost a decade been successfully experimenting with alternative decision-making processes, at both the policy and the site-specific levels (Bingham 1986). These processes are designed to manage the inevitable conflicts that arise in making complex environmental policies and in allocating scarce resources. They acknowledge the value differences underlying many conflicts, yet try to resolve the resulting disputes by cooperatively seeking a common ground between the different interests at stake and then building upon this common ground. In many instances, these processes are able to satisfy creatively the basic concerns of participants and, as a result, are preferred to the uncertainties and delay of more traditional administrative and judicial processes.

Quite often, proposals for including citizen groups more directly and collaboratively in governmental decision-making raise fears of co-optation and concerns about the ability of citizens to participate as equal partners with other parties in ensuring that their interests are indeed represented. Such concerns have been raised as well about the abilities of other groups—government agency representatives and individuals in business and industry—to participate in forums that differ from their past experience and established "standard operating procedures." However, the role of business and government in these processes has been explored in depth (Clark and Emrich 1980; Emrich 1980; Harter 1982; and Kuechle 1985), while the involvement of citizen groups, the difficulties they encounter and lessons learned have been but touched upon by a few (Amy 1983; Crowfoot 1980; and Susskind 1976).

Little research has been done on questions such as: What has been the experience of citizen groups with environmental dispute settlement processes? What promise do such processes hold for citizen organizations? What are the problems that they have encountered? Are these problems surmountable? If so, how? What are the benefits derived by citizen groups participating in these processes? Can these benefits be increased? If so, how? How should citizen groups evaluate whether or not participating in an alternative process makes sense for them? What options are available to citizen groups? It was with these questions in mind that the Joyce Foundation funded the Environmental Conflict Project at the University of Michigan's School of Natural Resources. Its mandate: to undertake a two-year study probing citizen involvement in environmental dispute settlement processes.

Environmental Conflict Project staff chose a case study method to begin their analysis of these issues, expecting that an in-depth understanding of how and why citizen groups behaved as they did in seven selected cases would yield valuable new information. The comparative case study approach taken in this research permitted an in-depth examination of the experiences of the involved environmental and citizen organizations.

A case selection process was initiated in which the key issues currently confronting environmentally oriented citizen groups, as well as those most likely to arise in the near future, were identified: protecting groundwater resources; managing forest and parkland; coping with rural and urban economic decline; harmonizing industrial and agricultural development with environmental quality; and protecting natural areas. Next, a range of different alternative processes in which citizen groups frequently become involved was identified, including: formal mediation; facilitated problem-solving processes; informal collaboration on specific issues; consensus-building in the legislative arena; and ad hoc negotiations. A search was then begun for cases that would represent both the range and relevant issues and the environmental dispute settlement processes most likely to involve citizens in the future. After preliminary interviews with individuals who participated in acceptable cases, seven cases were selected for in-depth analysis.

The cases were all quite different, illustrating a range of diverse issues, citizen organizations and coalitions, environmental dispute settlement processes, level of sophistication and outcomes. The data were gathered using in-depth phone interviews with all the major parties involved as well as with the third party intervenors when present. Other supporting materials were gathered and used as appropriate to supplement the phone interviews.

The purpose of the case presentations and analysis in this book is *not* to serve as an argument for why citizen groups should turn to alternative processes. Rather, the intent is to help develop a framework to be used by citizen groups in evaluating when and how a dispute settlement process might best serve their interests and how to participate in these processes when appropriate.

The cases illustrate a range of problems as well as benefits to citizen organizations participating in these environmental dispute settlement processes. While many of the long-held fears about citizen weaknesses ring true, others seem open to question.

Citizens participating in the dispute settlement processes analyzed here felt they had used their organizational resources more efficiently than would have been the case had they pursued a more adversarial approach. They believed their organizations were strengthened as a result and that, as individuals, they had gained valuable new skills. Additionally, the outcomes were designed more creatively to respond to the specifics of the issues involved, solutions that probably would not have arisen in the traditional process. Furthermore, the processes bestowed some long-lasting benefits on the citizen organizations. They opened doors for continuing dialogue with both business and government representatives and, in at least two cases, actually modified the existing administrative process, thereby allowing for continued direct citizen involvement in future decision-making. The processes increased the credibility, legitimacy, and trust between what had before been traditional adversaries. In at least two cases, citizens gained a role in implementing and monitoring the final decision.

There *were* problems, however. Most of the processes analyzed entailed a tremendous time commitment for all participants, one taking a particularly heavy toll on the citizen participants. There was, in addition, a resource drain on the citizen organizations, which encountered difficulties in keeping their constituencies abreast of, and interested in, the progress of the environmental dispute settlement process. Citizens believed they lacked adequate skills when entering the processes, although most "learned by doing" and, by the end, felt more or less on a par with the other parties involved. Even though the citizens never gained as much leverage in the processes as they had hoped to, in most cases, they did think that they had achieved more than they would have in a more traditional forum.

The purpose of this book is to present an in-depth, if limited, look at citizen group involvement in environmental dispute settlement processes. The conclusions and recommendations reached here represent but the first step toward a full understanding for guiding citizen groups in future processes. Because the cases are limited in number and are each, intentionally, unique, they obviously do not serve as a comprehensive base from which to make generalizations about other cases and situations. However, because of the detail with which they're described, and because comparative analysis of them is based on an understanding of other cases, the conclusions and recommendations reached can be taken more broadly. The cases shed important insight into how citizen organizations might in future processes avoid specific problems, increase their skills and effectiveness, and maximize the potential benefits of participating in an environmental dispute settlement process.

The research on which this book is based was funded by the Joyce Foundation, of Chicago, Illinois. Their deep commitment to improving environmental conditions in the Great Lakes region, which includes enabling effective citizen action, provided ideal support for the work we report here.

The research project was greatly assisted by an advisory board made up of citizen leaders experienced in environmental advocacy and citizen-initiated process/change. We thank the following individuals for their input and their support of our research work: Bonnie Anderson, East Michigan Environmental Action Council; the Reverend Clifton Bullock, Washington Heights United Methodist Church; Dr. Robert Ginsburg, Citizens for a Better Environment; Tom Klein, Sigurd Olson Environmental Institute; Sue Lacy, Ohio Public Interest Campaign; Sally Von Vleck, Northern Michigan Environmental Action Council; Steve Sedam, Ohio Environmental Council; David Stead, the Ecology Center; Grant Williams, ACORN; Peta Williams, Connections, Inc.

Dr. Patricia Bidol and Dr. James Crowfoot were the principal investigators for this research and were joined early in the effort by Dr. Julia Wondolleck. These individuals, along with Lisa Bardwell, Kristen Nelson, Sharon Edgar, and Nancy Manring, were the core staff of the project, joined by Martha Tableman, who developed a significant case study. Dr. Mark Chesler assisted the project at the stage of comparative case study analysis by advising us on qualitative data analysis.

Dr. Bidol, in addition to sharing in the leadership of the project, led the development of a comprehensive manual—*Alternative Environmental Conflict Management Approaches: A Citizens' Manual*—directed to citizen organizations participating in environmental dispute settlement processes. John Ehrmann and Dr. Michael Lesnick contributed to this manual by helping develop ideas and the proposal that led to the funding of the research.

While this research project is responsible for the case studies, it was assisted in developing and revising the cases by individuals directly involved in the environment conflict management efforts described.

We are grateful to the Project on Conflict Management Alternatives at the University of Michigan, which supported us in the writing of this book. This project is funded both by the Hewlett Foundation and by the University of Michigan.

It is at the University of Michigan School of Natural Resources where the research reported here was carved out and where the co-authors have their academic appointments. The school's commitment to developing courses and expertise in environmental dispute settlement processes provided a very hospitable setting in which to do this work.

Unless otherwise noted, information and quotations in the case studies are from authors' interviews with the various participants.

The writing of this book has been assisted by the editorial expertise of

Barbara Dean. Her patience, creative suggestions, and interest in the topic have been a continued source of invaluable support. The draft manuscript was reviewed by Michael McCloskey and Dr. Michael Lesnick, who provided us with valuable feedback.

References

Amy, Douglas. "The Politics of Environmental Mediation." *Ecology Law Quarterly* 2, no. 1 (1983): 1–20.

Bingham, Gail. *Resolving Environmental Disputes: A Decade of Experience.* Washington, D.C.: The Conservation Foundation, 1986.

Clark, Peter B., and Wendy M. Emrich. "New Tools for Resolving Environmental Disputes." American Arbitration Association, 1980.

Crowfoot, James E. "Negotiations: An Effective Tool for Citizen Organizations?" *Northern Rockies Action Group Papers* 3, no. 4 (1980): 24–44.

Emrich, Wendy. "New Approaches to Managing Environmental Conflict: How Can the Federal Government Use Them?" American Arbitration Association, 1980.

Harter, Philip J. "Negotiating Regulations: A Cure for the Malaise." *Georgetown Law Journal* 71, no. 1 (1982): 1–118.

Kuechle, David. "Negotiation with an Angry Public: Advice to Corporate Leaders." *Negotiation Journal* 1, no. 4 (1985): 317–30.

Susskind, Lawrence. *Citizen Involvement in the Local Planning Process: A Handbook for Municipal Officials and Citizen Involvement Groups.* Cambridge, MA: MIT Laboratory of Architecture and Planning, 1976.

1   Citizen Organizations and Environmental Conflict

James E. Crowfoot and Julia M. Wondolleck

Using the natural environment and protecting it directly involves many societal groups. These groups are sometimes composed of concerned citizens, sometimes of government officials or industry representatives. Conflicts between the groups over the use of the environment and natural resources are now common occurrences and are growing in number and importance as the human population grows, technology changes, and as pressures to use the environment increase (Gladwin 1979). These conflicts are intensified as humans become more aware of the need to achieve changes to ensure protection of the environment for future generations.

Since the early 1970s, new approaches to managing environmental conflicts, particularly environmental negotiation and mediation, increasingly have been employed to help resolve some of these disputes. These processes are new to citizen groups, and are very different from the established strategies and tools with which most environmental and citizen organizations are comfortable. The techniques include collaboration among contending interest groups instead of adversarial relationships; they involve consensus decision-making rather than judgments by authorities. Consequently, dispute resolution processes require new, different skills and perspectives on the part of citizens.

Often the mediation and negotiation has been promoted by government, business, or interests sympathetic to government or business. This support by traditional adversaries can further heighten the suspicions of citizen organizations that these strategies and tools will help other interest groups more than they will help them. Historically, citizen organizations involved with government or business groups have seen their interests co-opted through familiar techniques: appeals to common values, requests that citizens put their trust in government or in business, and participation processes in which citizen interests have been overwhelmed by the expertise of *other* interest groups. This history contributes to citizen organizations' skepticism toward environmental dispute resolution processes.

Carpenter and Kennedy, two pioneers in these new approaches, have observed that "public disputes are commonly fought by people who are unfamiliar with negotiation and are compelled to negotiate" (1988, 225). Furthermore, "negotiation of public disputes is carried on with few accepted

guidelines and without established traditions" (242). Therefore, citizen organizations, as one of the major parties in these disputes, need information
about environmental negotiations and mediation. They need to understand
the structure and dynamics of these processes, how they might most effectively be involved in a dispute settlement process, and when participation
may not be in their best interests.

This book describes some of the experiences of citizen groups that have
participated in environmental dispute settlement processes. Our purpose is
to begin responding to the concerns and questions of citizen organizations
about the advantages and disadvantages of these new means of settling
environmental and natural resource disputes and how they might use these
processes to advance their interests. While this approach to environmental
decision-making is still young and much remains to be learned about both
its positive and negative impacts, these early experiences can provide useful
insights to other citizens contemplating involvement in dispute resolution
processes.

Chapter 1 is divided into two sections. The first section describes the
defining characteristics of environmental and citizen organizations. It then
identifies the key challenges to these groups that arise from new processes
of dispute settlement. This section includes questions citizen organizations
must answer in deciding whether or not to become involved in a dispute
settlement process.

The second section provides information on the sources of environmental
conflict. While the evidence of environmental conflict is quite clear, the
interpretations of both specific individuals and groups concerning the extent
of this conflict and what should be done about it are often very different.
This section draws upon research on environmental values to illustrate the
differing values and views that give rise to specific environmental disputes.
It then provides a framework of three distinct perspectives that capture the
different understandings of environmental conflict and what should be done
about it.

Citizen Organizations and the Challenges of Environmental Dispute Settlement

Conflict is an integral element of the change processes that are the lifeblood
of citizen organizations. These groups are not strangers to either internal
or external conflict. They frequently find themselves adversaries of other
organizations advocating different decisions and competing for some of the
same resources.

The Nature of Environmental Citizen Organizations

Citizen organizations—those focused on the environment and natural resources—organize when people become dissatisfied with the decisions and

values of government, business, and other interest groups. These citizen organizations want something different from what these other powerful societal actors may want. To achieve their goals, citizen organizations face three major tasks. They must: (1) determine what they want; (2) obtain resources and create influence to achieve their goals; and (3) act to influence the decisions and actions of other organizations.

Each of these tasks is a major challenge. Each presents a conflict for the organization, and that organization must have the ability to settle the resulting disputes.

To determine what they want requires choices about a group's objectives. Members inevitably bring different preferences and priorities into an organization, and the resulting discussions and decisions involve conflict. The individual citizen organization cannot be all things to all people; to be effective, it must limit what it seeks to do.

Citizen organizations cannot be maintained without resources. They often must acquire these resources in competition with other associations that need the same contributions, members, media attention, volunteered time, and leadership skills. Sometimes acquiring these resources involves conflict. When the group converts these resources to effective influence, structures are created and leaders are selected—which also at times involves conflict. Again, the organization must possess the ability to settle these disputes sufficiently so that it can function.

The final activity in the citizen organization's triad of major tasks is influencing the decisions and behavior of other organizations that have the ability to meet citizens' needs. To exercise influence requires a coherent plan (usually referred to as a "strategy") and specific actions (usually referred to as "tactics") for carrying out the strategy. Employing these tactics in hopes of influencing others requires decisions, discipline, evaluation, and adaptability; conflict is a partner to such activity. Furthermore, the actions of citizen groups in exercising influence encourage similar actions by competing organizations, leading to interorganizational conflict. It is this conflict that is the chief focus of our environmental dispute settlement analysis.

Citizen organizations are most often the least powerful party among the multiple parties seeking to influence a specific environmental policy or management decision. These organizations function with fewer dollars and staff resources than do other interest groups. They rely on volunteer contributions, rights accorded by laws and regulations, public sympathy, and the traditions of a pluralistic and democratic political culture. They do not have the specialized resources of government and business, nor do they command the same access and influence with the media, legislators, and other constituents that generally support established institutions, leaders, and policies.

Citizen organizations are effective and survive by engaging in conflict to gain the attention, resources, and influence they need to meet their goals. They acquire these critical resources by distinguishing themselves from other groups. As they do so, they are dependent on the differences in values and attitudes found in society among citizens and leaders. These different values and attitudes will be discussed later in this chapter.

The Challenges of Environmental Dispute Settlement Processes

Citizen and environmental organizations face difficult choices in deciding whether or not to participate in environmental dispute settlement processes and how to proceed if they decide to do so. Environmental and citizen activists are often more familiar with adversarial strategies of change in which pressure, coercion, and unilateral decisions are key features than they are with dispute settlement efforts. In fact, as Carpenter and Kennedy note, "It is the nature of public disputes that some of the participants have never before been involved in formal negotiation, and some are unlikely to be negotiators again after the principal issue is settled" (1988, 233). These differences in experience and skills can be threatening because they carry the risk that important environmental goals will be ignored and citizens' needs will not be met. Also, these new approaches can be seen as lowering the visibility of citizen organizations and reducing their ability to attract the resources that are critical to their survival and effectiveness. Carpenter and Kennedy have observed, "Citizen groups contending with powerful government agencies or large corporations often must take the hardest possible line—total victory—to keep the support of their members and maintain their momentum" (1988, 2). Strategies stressing collaborative problem-solving, negotiation, and consensus decision-making confront many citizen organizations with unfamiliar options and requirements for information and skills they may not possess.

Douglas Amy, who since the 1970s has studied environmental negotiation and mediation from the perspective of environmental organizations, offers this advice:

> . . . This process should be approached carefully and skeptically. Environmental mediation should not be accepted at face value and should not be entered into quickly. Potential participants must be careful to see through the myths of mediation—the illusion that it is a simple and easy process, that all participants around the table are equal, that the process is inherently fair, that compromise is always reasonable, and so on. . . . Given the many pitfalls of this process and the absence of significant procedural safeguards, only the intelligence and vigilance of the participants can insure that it is a mutually beneficial process. (1987, 197–98)

To exercise this intelligence and vigilance requires that citizen organizations pay careful attention to their key tasks and to other critical choices confronting them. One set of choices focuses outside the organization and concerns the strategy to be used by it in seeking to influence different societal decisions and plans. A second set of decisions focuses internally on how to develop and use social change tools or tactics in relation to factors like the organization's leadership, structure, member commitment, and communication processes and, additionally, to its values and goals. Both sets of choices, while having a specific focus, must nonetheless take into consideration the total circumstances of the organization.

Making such strategy choices requires that attention be paid to alternative actions that could also be pursued to achieve the changes desired by the citizen group. Gail Bingham, an experienced mediator and evaluator of environmental mediation, makes this comment about the choice among alternative strategies:

> Although voluntary, environmental dispute resolution processes are often characterized as alternative to litigation—with the presumption that litigation is bad—they are better viewed as additional tools that might or might not be more effective or more efficient in particular circumstances. Litigation and other traditional decision-making processes remain important options. (1986)

These judgments of whether or not to be involved in environmental negotiation and mediation require relating these tools and their proposed use to the organization's basic understanding of conflict and how change occurs. Also, attention must be given to identifying alternative strategies for a specific situation in light of the other parties involved and the organization's objectives and resources. Perhaps litigation or direct action would be more effective in a given situation.

Judgments concerning whether or not to participate in environmental dispute settlement processes cannot be made without attention to the other parties that need to be involved in ending the dispute. Are all the other important parties willing to be involved? Will they be seriously committed to the negotiation process and willing and able to bargain in good faith? In some instances, there are other groups with which the organization would have to be in coalition for the negotiation to occur. Sometimes, this coalition-building is workable and can save the organization's resources, while other times it is not possible without sacrificing core objectives.

Turning to internal and more tactical considerations brings another set of concerns and issues into the determination of whether or not to be involved in environmental negotiation, and if this decision is yes, how to be involved. These considerations are important, because, as Gerald Cormick, an experienced environmental mediator, has observed:

> This is a hard, tough process, full of pitfalls and dangers. It takes work, organizations, clear thinking and stamina. Groups that don't have a clear idea of the process, of what they want and how much they can actually get, are in for a disappointment. Those that are together and know how to stay that way have the best chance to succeed. (1977, 10)

To become involved and to be effective in environmental negotiation and mediation require that an organization's leadership and membership understand these processes, support their use, and are skilled or willing to become skilled in using these tools. Members' time and energy and organizational communication processes must be such that they can regularly receive information on the negotiations from their representatives and provide them with reactions and directions as to what the organization will and will not accept.

The organization's immediate objectives in the environmental conflict at issue must allow for some give and take and compromise. Sometimes, objectives are based on principle and are not negotiable. If the issues potentially to be negotiated are not of high importance to the organization, then involvement might be a highly questionable use of the group's resources and could be ineffective because of insufficient commitment by leaders and members.

The organization's resources and power must be examined in relation to a possible environmental negotiation. Does it have the power to make an impact and do other parties perceive this power? Is the organization willing to use its power on these issues and in this negotiation? Is there adequate time, money, and information to become involved? Is the organization willing to use these resources in this forum as opposed to applying them to other potential issues and/or strategies for bringing about change to meet stated objectives?

Environmental and citizen organizations must constantly build their membership base, increase the level of donations and other support, and develop their leadership. How will involvement in environmental negotiation and/or mediation affect these vital needs? Sometimes, the answer to this question is that these needs will be negatively affected when examined from the perspective of other issues that the organization could be pursuing. In those instances, different strategies should be adopted.

Citizen organizations either implicitly or explicitly select a strategy as they undertake actions in pursuit of their goals. This choice of strategy requires that assumptions be made about how environmental conflict might be used to bring about change. It is essential that an organization understand different perspectives on environmental conflict and change and adopt the one that best reflects its values and goals. To make sound judgments on whether or not to be involved in environmental negotiation and mediation requires relating these tools and their proposed use to the organization's basic understanding of conflict and how change occurs, and to its goals.

The Sources of Environmental Conflicts

Environmental conflicts are rooted in different values of natural resources and environmental quality. Some individuals perceive an intrinsic value in things that are wild and natural while others do not. Some see a societal obligation to protect species and preserve habitat while others do not. Some place priority on maintaining biological diversity and environmental integrity for future generations while others place priority on harnessing nature's resources to service the needs of today's society.

Environmental conflicts are also incited by different stakes in the outcome of environmental and natural resource management decisions. The threatened loss of a resource with particular significance to a group—whether it is a wilderness area, a local park, or a neighborhood's serenity—causes people to organize and protest; so does the immediate monetary threat of a delayed development and lost investments should a governmental decision run contrary to the economic interests of particular groups or individuals.

Similarly, the uncertainty surrounding various environmental actions, and the different assessments of the risks associated with these actions, cause conflicts. How many people will contract cancer as a result of a new power plant or industrial facility? Is this risk one that is "acceptable"? All groups assess such risks differently, reach different conclusions about appropriate decisions, and therefore find themselves in conflict.

Before moving on to chapter 2 and a discussion of the structure and dynamics of environmental dispute settlement processes, and chapters 3 and 4 for a look at issues that citizen groups must consider in participating in these processes, it is important to step back and explore the causes of environmental conflict and hence the reasons why these conflicts will inevitably persist long into the future. It is vital as well to understand the implications of different values and perspectives on conflict for a group or individual's perceptions of dispute settlement processes. What bearing will these perceptions have on how, or whether, a group will be involved in efforts to resolve a specific dispute?

For citizen organizations to make intelligent choices in relation to processes aimed at ending disputes, it is essential that they understand these different dimensions of environmental conflict. Why do environmental conflicts exist and persist? How do other groups in society look upon environmental conflicts? How do other groups—groups that the citizen group will likely find itself across a table from in a dispute settlement process—perceive the appropriateness of collaboration and negotiation in settling disputes? Where do different citizen associations fit in this scheme and how should they respond to opportunities to participate in a dispute settlement process?

The remainder of this chapter will probe these questions and provide the larger societal context of environmental conflict and dispute settlement.

Differing Views of Environmental Problems

Understanding public perceptions of the environment and environmental problems is a key ingredient in an organization's efforts to influence environmental decisions. These perceptions are the basis of an individual's commitments to an organization and its goals and they are major influences on the behaviors of both members and leaders.

Widespread public concerns with environmental problems emerged in the late 1960s. Since then, researchers have been continually assessing public opinion regarding a variety of environmental and natural resource issues. While public concern declined somewhat through the decade of the 1970s, and many wondered if it would further decline and possibly disappear in the 1980s, researchers found that "by the early 1980s it was common for public opinion analysts to describe environmental quality as an 'enduring concern of the American public' " (Dunlap 1983, 59–60).

Data gathered by public opinion analysts indicate that while moderately declining during the 1970s, public support for environmental protection again began to rise in the early 1980s, not long after President Ronald Reagan took office (Dunlap 1983). This increase in public support was a result of perceptions that environmental problems were becoming more serious, that the government should reduce these problems, and that in the Reagan years at least, government was not providing the desired level of environmental protection. As Riley Dunlap, a public opinion researcher, concludes:

> Public support for environmental protection has not only survived Reagan, but has apparently been strengthened by the challenge posed by his administration. While its electoral importance remains ambiguous, the public consensus behind environmental protection nonetheless constitutes a significant political resource for lobbying and, more generally, influencing public officials. (1983, 36)

The same public opinion data show that individuals are generally more concerned about basic economic conditions than they are about environmental quality. This greater emphasis on the economy is often seen in voting behavior. However, Dunlap speculates that "environmental problems will probably become more potent political issues as they become increasingly viewed as threatening to public health" (1983, 36).

A large number and variety of environmental conflicts have accompanied this heightened public concern because of major differences in environmental values and attitudes among various groups in the society. These differences, along with the above described commitment to the importance of environmental problems and the maintenance of environmental quality, result in widespread environmental conflict. To better appreciate the sources of this conflict, it is necessary to examine current research on differences in environmental values among individuals.

Lester Milbrath's research (1984) lends insight into some of the sources of this conflict. He systematically surveyed both citizens and representatives of leadership groups from across the country. He found clear evidence that conflicting belief systems concerning environmental problems help distinguish these groups. His research identifies three key beliefs that separate these fundamentally different perspectives toward the environment.

One of these key beliefs is the degree to which the world environment is perceived as a problem. Some respondents indicated the world environment is a very important problem, while others perceived it to be a problem of lesser importance when compared with issues like economics, peace, and drugs. A second key belief that distinguished fundamentally different perspectives toward the environment concerned what kind of change is most needed to solve our environmental problems. Some respondents saw the necessity for greater scientific and technological development, while others indicated the need for basic change in the nature of society. The third distinguishing belief discovered by Milbrath was whether or not there are limits to growth; some respondents indicated that such limits exist, while others believe they do not.

When evaluating his findings for these three ideas, along with numerous other values and attitudes, Milbrath concluded that two fundamentally different perspectives are now present in our society. One is held by "people who believe the environmental problem is small, that it can be solved by technical fixes, and that there are no limits to growth . . ." (Milbrath 1984, 44). According to this research, between 18 and 19 percent of the U.S. public hold this view. We refer to it as view A. The other perspective is maintained by people "who believe that the environmental problem is large, that it can be solved only by basic change in society, and that there are limits to growth . . ." (Milbrath 1984, 44). Based on the 1980 survey, 18 percent of the U.S. public held this perspective. We refer to it as view B. Milbrath's findings also show that the balance of people who are the majority hold a mix of elements from these two fundamental perspectives toward the environment and do not fully agree with either one of these basically conflicting perspectives. He concludes that this data "demonstrates the reality of sharp divisions over these fundamental beliefs in modern society" and "these sharp divisions on fundamentals imply continued conflict for some time to come" (1984, 61).

Milbrath further discovered that most business leaders and a majority of public officials, labor leaders, and media gatekeepers hold view A. Environmental leaders are for the most part strong adherents of view B, but the research data showed a substantial minority of the other leadership groups also hold this view.

The average age of people holding view B is much younger than those holding view A. As Milbrath states, "Since people tend to retain beliefs developed in their formative years, we can expect further increases in the proportion of people who accept view A."*

---

*At the same time as this research was being conducted in the United States, the same surveys were done in England and Germany. The results in these countries also show the existence of the two strongly conflicting perspectives that we described above. Interestingly, in England, 24 percent of the public are adherents of view B, and in Germany, 29 percent hold this view. With regard to view A, only 9 percent of the English public falls into this category; in Germany, it is only 5 percent.

Environmental conflict is widely present in the United States and is based on a continuing high level of public concern for the quality of the environment and fundamental value differences among groups and their leaders. It is not surprising that Milbrath's research concludes that these value differences will continue into the future, and hence so will the resulting conflict.

Three Perspectives on Environmental Conflict and Negotiation

Given the well-documented differences in perception of environmental problems, it is to be expected that different understandings of environmental conflict are also present. Describing and contrasting these views are necessary prerequisites to describing different evaluations of the usefulness and dangers of environmental negotiation and mediation. There is no single evaluation of these tools of environmental decision-making.

These various views of environmental conflict have been organized into three categories in the literature on social conflict. These three categories are known by different names, depending on whether one links these views to political ideologies or to sociological theories as the sources of information to describe and interpret these perspectives. As described here, however, the three contrasting understandings of environmental conflict are referred to by a number to avoid relying on short titles that can easily miscommunicate their meanings. Table 1.1 summarizes these three perspectives on environmental conflict and negotiations.

According to the first view, there is an underlying societal consensus that both the environment and economic development are important and compatible. This consensus is reflected in societal values and laws and, more importantly, in the attitudes and practices of leaders. Given the complexity of our economic and environmental systems, and given human nature, there are often misunderstandings between different groups about the relationship between the environment and the economy. Furthermore, given the ever-changing nature of both society and the environment, there is the need for an ongoing and slow readjustment between society and the environment. This adaptation to change must be reflected in either revised or new policies and management practices. As these adaptive changes are made, different groups and individuals will learn about them at different rates.

At any time, groups could experience differences and disputes that need to be referred to the basic societal agreements (embodied in laws, policies, and internal norms) about the environment and economic production. Education and expert information are very important in helping people adapt to change and to apply the basic societal consensus to specific and practical problems over which there may be disagreement.

On rare occasions, there are individuals and organizations that break the basic societal consensus and closely related laws and norms about the environment (e.g., by dumping toxic wastes in unauthorized places). These people are in conflict with the basic societal agreements, and their deviant

TABLE 1.1
Three Perspectives on Environmental Conflict and Negotiations

	Perspective 1	*Perspective 2*	*Perspective 3*
View of environmental conflict	Basic consensus that the environment and economic development are important and compatible. Specific disputes grow out of ongoing need for adaptation, misunderstandings, and deviant behavior.	Both conflicts and consensus exist among disparate interest groups. Political pluralism exists to promote and accommodate differences.	Conflict is deep and pervasive in society, involving different economic groups and matters of principle. Established authorities deemphasize and "cool out" conflict. Contending groups emphasize and escalate conflict.
Preferred response to conflict	Educate leaders. Problem-solving assisted by specialized courts.	Legislation as supplemented by regulation and judication. Negotiation.	Use of power to force compliance. Use whatever will win and enhance power.
View of environmental negotiations	Supplementary tool. Collaboration to identify the common interests.	Extension and refinement of long-established practice. Differences exist on how it should be institutionalized.	Use as last resort. Sometimes use for delay and/or co-optation.

behavior must be stopped through the action of established and legitimate authorities.

As leaders and citizens receive education and updated information about the environment, their values and behaviors affecting the environment will change. Expert knowledge of the environment and environmental problems is the necessary resource for effective education along with the long-established, traditional values of the culture. These traditional values reflect the proven wisdom that slowly changes based on new experience, particularly as guided by expert knowledge and the judgment of societal leaders.

From this perspective on environmental conflict, problem-solving by well-educated leaders assisted by specialized experts is the most prevalent and preferred mode of solving environmental and natural resource problems. Sometimes, other tools will be needed. When expert information is still sketchy, scientists with different views will need to utilize science courts, so the most rational course of action in the face of uncertainty can be determined. In other situations where leaders differ and there is a dispute, problem-solving should be supplemented by negotiation and mediation to clear up the misunderstanding and to provide up-to-date information as a basis for consensus.

Douglas Amy maintains that this view is often presented by the supporters of environmental mediation and that it "assumes that environmental disputes are largely caused by misunderstandings and miscommunications rather than by basic conflicts of interests, and that therefore many of these conflicts are unnecessary" (1987, 165). He recognizes that "this view persists . . . because it corresponds to positions being espoused by some significant actors in environmental politics" (1987, 167). He has observed that a number of business leaders, government officials, and environmental leaders who take essentially this view also maintain that "conflicts of interest between developers and environmentalists have been greatly exaggerated." He attributes the theme of common concerns between business and environmentalists to what he describes as "the less adversarial and more conservative environmental groups like the National Wildlife Federation and the Conservation Foundation" (1987, 168).

From this perspective, disputes are an unfortunate side effect of ongoing evolutionary changes and the adaptations of institutions, leaders, and members to these changes. This dynamic gives rise to the need for problem-solving, information and education, and the once-in-a-while use of negotiation and mediation to settle a prolonged dispute.

According to the second view, there are in society both ongoing conflicts as well as underlying consensus about the natural environment. The ongoing conflicts arise from the different interests of societal groups. The groups that come from industry and government, and environmentalists, have different goals and responsibilities as well as different values; often these characteristics are in conflict.

In a political democracy, there are structures and processes that allow the expression and protection of these differences. These processes also promote decision-making when differences need to be resolved. All these structures and processes have been developed to accommodate conflicts among groups and individuals who want different things or who view what is meaningful or important in different ways.

From this second perspective, environmental laws and regulations are essential as reflections of the agreements among groups with differing interests. These agreements are also explicit rules of behavior for individuals and groups who are not in agreement nor expected to be in agreement about how the environment is to be used and protected.

The preferred means of settling disputes, including ones involving the environment, that are an inevitable part of ongoing interest group conflict is legislative decision-making by democratically elected representatives.

Within this process of decision-making, interest group advocacy provides the perspectives, goals, and values of the contending groups as they express their differences. Executive branch regulation utilizing expert information is an extension of legislative formation and implementation of laws.

An essential but secondary means of dispute settlement is provided for by judicial decision-making. The work of the courts rests not only on specific statutes, but also on the country's Constitution and Bill of Rights. These documents articulate agreed-upon values and beliefs of the society, including belief in a political pluralism that provides for the expression of differences in interests.

Negotiation occurs informally in the course of the operation of the legislative and judicial branches of government and, to a lesser extent, in the executive branch. As this occurs, a wide variety of nongovernmental groups and organizations are active parties in these negotiations, which are fundamental to the expression of different interests and working out of decisions in the face of differences. Many laws are the outcome of negotiations, as are the settlements of many lawsuits. Other important societal agreements, often embodied in contracts, result from negotiations.

Environmental negotiation and mediation are merely a recent extension and refinement of the long-established practice of informal negotiation among differing interest groups and individuals. These new tools of environmental conflict management and environmental decision-making are understood as supplemental in legislative, regulatory, and judicial processes. Douglas Amy maintains that "many environmentalists and industry executives would see this model as being much more accurate than the previous one" (1987, 173). Here the "previous one" refers to the first perspective described above, and the attribution of accuracy is a statement of Amy's values and choices of perspective on environmental conflicts.

Adherents to this second perspective on environmental and other social conflicts nonetheless do debate as to when and in what ways environmental negotiation and mediation should be used. For example, should such negotiations be under the supervision of the courts, as opposed to the current practice of "freestanding" or ad hoc negotiations? Should environmental policy consensus processes be used in developing legislation?

The third view of environmental conflict maintains that social conflict, including environmental conflict, is deep and pervasive in the society. According to this view, it is only the coercive power of government in league with the economic power of specific individuals and organizations that hold society together in the face of these basic differences. These interests exploit the natural environment as they proceed to create wealth and benefit from it. Industrialization and its attendant scientifically based technology exploit natural resources and pollute the natural environment.

Schools and other societal institutions such as the media and the church provide experiences and ideas that persuade citizens to accept such environmental exploitation as being in their own interest and as ultimately benefiting them. These institutions seek to promote the perspective that utilitarian use of the environment is justified (for example, God created humans to use the environment in this way) and, further, it is necessary for providing jobs and the economic standard of living to which workers have grown accustomed. The present pattern of environmental use—according to this view—does not seriously damage the environment because business is planning for the future as well as seeking to use the environment in ways that respect other needs for the environment.

Processes by which citizens participate in government (public hearings, for instance) are designed to elicit support for the decisions and plans that those in power are promoting. From this perspective on environmental conflict, citizen participation is highly desirable as long as those in power retain control of goals, values, and decisions.

One element of this view is that some individuals and citizen groups seek to show that the policies and practices are not in the interest of those in the society who lack political and economic power nor in the interest of achieving a future that is environmentally sustainable. They maintain that the environment is harmfully exploited and will continue to be as long as the interests in power retain control. Sometimes, it is further argued that modern industrialization inevitably exploits the environment, and that a new philosophy and technology of social production, as well as new goals and expectations, are needed to insure long-run viability for the relationship between society and the natural environment.

From this perspective, environmental values and practices are matters of principle and all efforts should be pursued to insure the maintenance and/ or advancement of these ideals. At times, these principles are embodied in established authorities and at other times they are represented by challenging citizens who do not accept prevailing policies and practices as being in their interest. Douglas Amy points out that "there is a real difference between seeing environmental disputes as conflicts of interest or as conflicts of principle" (1987, 175). He notes that many environmentalists view them as conflicts of principles and observes: "This is especially true of the more activist organizations, such as Greenpeace, Earth First! and Friends of the Earth . . ." (1987, 175).

In this third perspective, mediation and negotiation are tools of delay or co-optation or of cutting possible losses that could occur by utilizing other means of continuing or settling the dispute. The objective here is twofold. First, to use strategies and tactics that will insure that one's own perspective prevails while maintaining and enhancing one's power. Second, and at the same time, to defeat or suppress challenging perspectives while reducing the power of the group that is advocating these challenges.

These perspectives embody three very different understandings of environmental conflict. The importance of environmental conflict ranges from a minor and temporary perturbation of basic societal agreements to a major and permanent element of pervasive and fundamental societal conflict. All three views are prepared to recognize the existence of environmental negotiation and mediation, but they evaluate these tools of dispute settlement quite differently. The first and third perspectives, for different reasons, relegate environmental negotiation and mediation to a very small role in environmental decision-making. In contrast, the second perspective gives negotiation a more major, yet still debated, role relative to other more established means of settling disputes.

In seeking to understand and relate to the new process of environmental dispute settlement, it is important that citizen and environmental organizations determine their own view of environmental conflict. Doing so will help guide them in using these new tools of conflict resolution. It will also clarify their analysis of other organizations' orientations toward these new means of conflict resolution.

Conclusion

Widely differing views of environmental problems by U.S. citizens and leaders are the reality that citizen organizations face and use as they seek to achieve new adaptations between our society and the natural environment. The different and conflicting understandings of environmental conflict, change, and negotiations form a basis for the strategy choices made by citizen organizations. These choices are also influenced by internal organizational considerations. Such strategy choices determine whether or not a citizen organization decides to initiate or participate in an environmental negotiation and, if it participates, what it tries to achieve.

To better understand citizen organization behavior in relation to environmental negotiations, knowledge is needed of this means of dispute settlement and the wider field of environmental conflict management. The next chapter provides an overview of this relatively new set of processes for environmental decision-making. It provides examples from our research on citizen group involvement in environmental dispute settlement to illustrate the structure and dynamics of these new processes for resolving disputes.

References

Amy, Douglas. *The Politics of Environmental Mediation.* New York: Columbia University Press, 1987.

Bingham, Gail. *Resolving Environmental Disputes: A Decade of Experience.* Washington, D.C.: The Conservation Foundation, 1986.

Carpenter, Susan, and W. J. D. Kennedy. *Managing Public Disputes: A Practical Guide to Handling Conflict and Reaching Agreements.* San Francisco: Jossey-Bass, 1988.

Cormick, Gerald. "The Ethics of Mediation: Some Unexplored Territory." Paper presented at the annual meeting of the Society of Professionals in Dispute Resolution, 1977.

Dunlap, Riley. "Paradigm Conflict." *Bulletin of Atomic Scientists* 37 (1983): 36–60.

Gladwin, Thomas N. "Trends in Industrial Environmental Conflict." *Environmental Consensus* 3 (September 1979): 1–2.

Milbrath, Lester. *Environmentalists: Vanguard for a New Society.* Albany, New York: State University of New York, 1984.

2 Environmental Dispute Settlement

James E. Crowfoot and Julia M. Wondolleck

Since the early 1970s, new approaches to ending episodes of environmental conflict have been developed and implemented. These new approaches have been called by many different names: "environmental conflict resolution," "consensus-building," or the term used throughout this book—"environmental dispute settlement." In this chapter, we will describe what we mean by the term "environmental dispute settlement" and outline its connection to traditional environmental decision-making processes.

Environmental Dispute Settlement: A Definition

The phrase "environmental dispute settlement" (EDS) means different things to different people. There is no single description in the literature of these new approaches to resolving environmental disputes; to the contrary, numerous titles and explanations are invariably encountered. For example, we might find: conflict resolution, dispute settlement, conflict management, alternative conflict management, conflict intervention, negotiation, mediation, arbitration, special masters, regulatory negotiations ("reg-neg"), consensus-building, alternative dispute resolution, and mini-trials.

Why have we selected "environmental dispute settlement" rather than some of these other terms? Environmental and natural resource disputes have special characteristics that distinguish efforts to settle them from processes used to resolve public policy disputes more generally. Because the focus of this book is specifically environmental and natural resource conflicts, the term *environmental* dispute settlement communicates this interest, one that is narrower than the entire area of public policy disputes.

Because environmental dispute settlement processes are not designed to end the ongoing environmental conflicts as discussed in the first chapter, the term "dispute" is used throughout this book to denote a specific conflict episode that is part of a continual and larger societal conflict. In the first chapter, environmental conflict was described as the fundamental and ongoing differences, opposition, and sometimes coercion among major groups in society over their values and behaviors toward the natural environment. Such conflict is very wide in scope and in part arises from the rapid change in human population, technology, social structures, and social norms. Within this conflict, there are many smaller and quite specific episodes

17

referred to here as "disputes." In making this distinction between conflicts
and disputes, Gerald Cormick (1982), an experienced environmental mediator, defines conflicts as occurring "when there is a disagreement over
values or scarce resources" and a dispute as "an encounter involving a specific
issue over which the conflict in values is joined." He goes on to state "the
settlement of a dispute is achieved when the parties find a mutually acceptable
basis for disposing of the issues in which they are in disagreement, despite
their continuing differences over basic values" (Cormick 1982, 3). Some of
these differences in basic environmental values were briefly described in the
preceding chapter. (It is important to note that while ending environmental
disputes is the focus of the processes explored in this book, valuable work
is being done by others in identifying and developing disputes through
advocacy.)

Because environmental conflict, as described above, cannot be resolved
or "ended," the commonly used term "environmental conflict resolution"
easily can give rise to expectations of ending societal conflict over the environment. This societal conflict is essential for bringing about the change
and adjustment of society to the natural environment; environmental conflict
is not going to end, and even to imply this is to give a misleading and false
impression. Hence, we use the word "settlement" to denote the ending of
a specific dispute or conflict episode and *not* the once-and-for-all disap-
pearance of conflict implied by the term "resolution."

The adjective "alternative" is used frequently as a basic descriptor of these
new approaches to dispute settlement. Use of "alternative" grew out of the
desire to stress that using these approaches involves a choice to do something
different rather than relying exclusively on the established and more traditional means of ending disputes (through litigation, legislation, or administrative review and regulation). In fact, as discussed later in this chapter,
these new approaches are supplementary to the traditional ones and not
substitutes for those more familiar means of arriving at environmental decisions (Susskind and Cruikshank 1987). For this reason, the adjective "alternative" is not used as part of the term "environmental dispute settlement."
Similarly, words like "negotiation" and "consensus-building" describe processes and behaviors that are found within traditional environmental legislative, administrative, and litigious activities. To use these terms in a title
for the new approaches to ending environmental disputes can connote that
negotiation and consensus-building only occur in these approaches, which
is clearly not true. However, it is important to understand that negotiation
and consensus-building are essential components of dispute settlement processes.

Some analysts and practitioners, for example Carpenter and Kennedy
(1988), favor the term "environmental conflict management." This term is
much broader than "environmental dispute settlement." Because conflict
occurs over time and involves other phases (initiation, engagement, esca-
lation, and so forth) besides the phase of settlement, people interested in

managing conflict are concerned with understanding and influencing what happens in other phases of conflict besides the settlement phase. "Management" is a term particularly suited to managers and administrators and others familiar and comfortable with management activities. From our point of view, conflict management is an important and legitimate area and one with which managers should be familiar. But conflict management is a much more general area and involves a somewhat different philosophy than does the focus of this book. Furthermore, while conflict management is traditionally directed toward managers, this book is intended for a broader audience, including, particularly, the leaders, members, and supporters of environmental and citizen organizations. Usually, these parties to environmental conflict include those who do not perceive themselves as managers and, at times, some who are even distrustful of what managers are doing to the environment and, by extension, the efforts of these individuals to manage environmental conflict.

Quite often, the term "environmental mediation" is used for these new approaches for resolving environmental disputes. This title denotes the use of a third party intervenor or mediator (that is, a person or persons who are not direct parties to the dispute but who utilize special skills in helping those involved arrive at a settlement). However, some environmental dispute settlement processes do not have a mediator present and, in fact, some of the cases in this book describe processes in which a mediator was not involved. Also, the term "environmental mediation" is narrower in focus than the ideas at the core of this book. By itself, "environmental mediation" does not connote a focus on ending disputes, which is an essential descriptor of these new approaches.

Characteristics of Environmental Dispute Settlement Processes

Three key characteristics distinguish the processes involved in environmental dispute settlement:

1. Voluntary participation by the parties involved in the dispute;

2. Direct or "face-to-face" group interaction among the representatives of these parties; and,

3. Mutual agreement or consensus decisions by the parties on the process to be used and any settlement that may emerge.

Gail Bingham, in her pioneering evaluation of these approaches, defines them as follows:

> The term "environmental dispute resolution" refers collectively to a variety of approaches that allow the parties to meet face to face to reach a mutually acceptable resolution of the issues in a dispute or potentially controversial

situation. Although there are differences among the approaches, all are voluntary processes. (1986, xv)

In the traditional arenas for resolving environmental disputes, participation often is not voluntary. For example, litigation requires all parties to be involved. Most commonly, those engaged in an environmental dispute do not interact directly with each other in these traditional arenas; when they do, it is not a group discussion or consensus-building effort as in environmental dispute settlement. When they meet with legislators (in the course of lobbying or a legislative hearing, for instance), agency administrators (perhaps in a public hearing concerning a site-specific development proposal or establishment of an administrative rule), or judges (in a court proceeding), the discussion is usually one-way advocacy, placing the groups involved in adversarial positions and not in a consensus-seeking mode. In none of these typical processes of environmental decision-making do the parties sit down as a total group for a discussion of the issues in conflict and potential solutions. In these traditional means of environmental dispute settlement, decisions generally are not made by the parties themselves, and when the parties are involved, decisions are not determined by mutual agreement. For example, legislators use voting to determine how a dispute will be ended and agency administrators and judges individually and unilaterally (within explicit guidelines and constraints) make their decisions ending specific disputes.

Environmental dispute settlement processes have been developed and used in two quite contrasting situations: the policy-making process and site-specific decision-making. Despite the differences in scope and degree of abstraction of these two levels of decision-making, the same basic environmental dispute settlement characteristics are present, as are most aspects of the process described in the next section.

Basic Environmental Dispute Settlement Processes

At the heart of an EDS process is the collaborative problem-solving effort of all parties to a dispute. In pursuing a more cooperative process, the hope is to save time and other resources, arrive at a decision that makes better use of available information and is more acceptable to the parties, and to do this decision-making in ways that result in deeper commitment to implementation by all those involved. The fundamental plan is to settle disputes "through cooperative, consensus-building processes rather than in the traditional, adversarial manner that current processes often encourage" (Wondolleck 1988, 212).

For an EDS process to be effective, all groups with a stake in the conflict must be identified and involved. For an environmental dispute settlement process to go forward requires that each affected group must agree voluntarily to participate. Such agreement implies that, from the perceptions of the different parties, the disputed issues are at least potentially negotiable and the EDS process is preferable in comparison to other available avenues for arriving at decisions to end the dispute. Sometimes several groups enter into coalitions and are represented by a single person. If the coalition maintains effective communication with all member groups, each affected group will still have a means of input to decision-making and a means of registering support or nonsupport for any potential agreement.

In an EDS process, interaction between the parties is designed to be one of mutual problem-solving and negotiation in pursuit of the interests of all the involved parties. As described by Carpenter and Kennedy:

> Traditionally, each side in a negotiation takes a position knowing that it will not get all that it asks for. The positions become realities in themselves separate from the original issues. The positions, not the problem, determine the direction of the bargaining. . . . An alternative way to find solutions is to persuade the parties to . . . talk with each other about their interests — what they need in an agreement for it to be acceptable. (1988, 60–61)

To accomplish such an interest-based problem-solving and negotiation process requires the parties (sometimes with the help of a skilled neutral) to develop and agree upon a process for discussion and decision-making. For example, in the Common Ground case presented in detail later in the book, the participants all agreed at the outset on their roles and objectives, how information would be exchanged, and how to communicate their task force's results to their own organizations and to government agencies. They used a professional facilitator to help guide them through brainstorming, interest identification, issue clarification, and discussions. Early agreement must be reached on the scope of the problem-solving (that is, what problems will and will not be considered), as well as on the schedule of meetings to address the problem. Process guidelines specify when all representatives will work together and when subgroups will be used. Norms or rules for communication and related behavior are usually part of the agreed-upon process. For example, it is usually specified at the outset of an EDS process how the groups will deal with the media, that representatives are required to show respect in their interactions and not impugn the motives of one another, and that all participants or their substitutes must attend meetings regularly. Provisions also are made to specify how the groups will agree upon a final settlement, if reached, and how all parties will be bound to the agreement. For a group participating in an environmental dispute to shape such a process and agree to it requires that it conduct a thorough conflict assessment at the outset (Bidol et al. 1986, 69–73).

In developing and agreeing upon the tasks comprising an EDS process, the representatives must be concerned about information and expertise necessary to decision-making. Agreement should be reached among all parties establishing guidelines for sharing information. Sometimes provisions must be made for obtaining experts to gather additional information, to interpret the meaning of existing data, and/or to educate representatives and interested others who may be unfamiliar with parts of the information, theories, and/ or techniques being used.

To the extent that the dispute settlement process requires finances beyond those each party will use to cover its own participation, the sources of these funds and provision for their distribution also become part of the partici- pants' agreements on the basic process of dispute settlement at the outset.

Environmental Dispute Settlement Processes and Traditional Decision-Making

The major differences between traditional and environmental dispute set- tlement (EDS) processes are really rooted in two different conceptions of "public involvement." In the traditional process, public involvement is limited. It is, for the most part, public input to decisions, inputs that are multiple and often conflicting. Constructive criticism and offering of alter- natives by citizens are certainly permissible; whether or not action is taken on these suggestions, however, is the decision of the authorities in charge of the relevant areas.

In the environmental dispute settlement processes, in contrast, a citizen group's role in processing multiple inputs and in decision-making is much more direct. Issues that a citizen group raises are acted upon (or purposefully not acted upon) with the citizen group participating. Data are acquired and analyzed and trade-offs made with direct participation of the citizen group. Alternatives are developed and evaluated collaboratively. Additionally, through strategically participating in an alternative process, a citizen group can become involved in implementing whatever decision is eventually reached, thereby expanding its influence on a particular issue.

This difference between alternative and traditional processes is rooted in the structure of the process itself: who is involved, how they are involved, and how issues are framed and then acted upon in making and then im- plementing decisions. Consequently, the major difference between the tra- ditional and EDS processes is the level of true collaboration and involvement of non-decision-makers with the decision-making authorities.

While we might advocate EDS processes in various situations, we should not expect a governmental decision-maker—an authority—to easily or wholeheartedly set aside the traditional, established procedures in favor of "alternative" processes for several reasons. First, the established processes are the ones that have been institutionalized: they have elements of legislative mandates in them as well as regulations that have been codified in different ways. These institutionalized processes have some level of public acceptance and, in addition, are supported by existing patterns of power among groups and organizations.

While there are certainly discretionary points in each established process, the skeletal structure is seldom flexible. At the federal level, there is a Federal Advisory Committee Act and an Administrative Procedures Act that limit the direct interactions that can occur between an agency and its client groups. There are similar legislative mandates at most state levels. While these statutes, for the most part, were enacted to prevent collusion between government representatives and private interests and the resultant domination of a single interest group, they also frequently inhibit nontraditional processes that would bring all interest groups together to address collaboratively a common concern. At the state and local level, there are established procedures for when and how "the public" is to be involved in decision-making. Hence, a decision-maker would be violating his or her responsibilities if he or she were to set aside the prescribed process in favor of an "alternative" one, let alone to then implement whatever agreement is reached in that "alternative" process.

The second reason EDS processes are not immediately and warmly embraced by governmental decision-makers is that there are long-held values and paradigms in agencies and other "authorities" that frequently run counter to the notion of nontraditional dispute settlement. The natural tendency of decision-making organizations is to oppose this type of process: they do not want to show weakness or to relinquish power or authority, particularly to those outside the group. Hence, it is a rare organization that welcomes an alternative process with open arms . . . unless, of course, it has something to gain by so doing.

Other powerful interest groups besides governmental decision-making organizations care about whether government authorities become involved in EDS processes. These interest groups have shaped the policies and procedures of the agencies, in some cases captured the agency's programs, and they do not want these arrangements changed unless it will be to their benefit. These groups monitor what government authorities do and informally influence emergent changes.

From the perspective of citizen organizations, therefore, the interesting questions on this topic are less "How and when are traditional processes receptive to dispute settlement?" and more: (1) "What are the different ways in which citizen groups might encourage a traditional process to evolve to an EDS process?" and (2) "What are the different ways in which the decisions made in a traditional process might be influenced by an EDS process?"

It is difficult to generalize from one case about this link between traditional and nontraditional EDS processes. Each case is unique, with the exception, however, that each is linked in some way to established, decision-making authorities. For the purposes of analysis, the cases do seem to fall into two broad categories framed by the above two questions: the first category involves those EDS processes that evolve from and then fold back into the traditional process (case studies: Pig's Eye, Sand Lakes, Wisconsin groundwater, Fitchburg, San Juan); the second category comprises those EDS processes that are structured separately, yet in such a way that they will in turn influence the traditional process (case studies: Common Ground, Malden).

Connections Between EDS and Traditional Processes

Each case study forming the foundation of this book is summarized briefly below, highlighting the reason an EDS process came to be and explaining what link the alternative process had to the established traditional process. Following the case summaries is an analysis of what lessons the cases have for citizen groups interested in encouraging and/or participating in nontraditional dispute settlement processes.

San Juan National Forest Mediation

The impetus for this case was dissatisfaction with U.S.D.A. Forest Service decisions and the agency's decision-making process. While citizen groups and individuals felt that they had provided input to the Forest Service decision and had commented on proposals, they did not believe that their concerns were ever addressed adequately. There are two reasons an EDS process was instituted: (1) the citizen group's attorney was familiar with the concept and active in the San Juan dispute and felt that a common ground did exist; (2) the forest supervisor was receptive to the idea. (If the decision-making authority had not been receptive to the idea, we would have seen a very different outcome.) However, the forest supervisor was only receptive to the idea because he originally viewed the dispute as being between different user groups, with the Forest Service professionals providing technical expertise and procedural guidance. As the process evolved, though, it became clear that the Forest Service was indeed a party to the dispute and had to participate more actively.

This process clearly evolved from the traditional and then folded back into it. The Forest Service had control over the process in that the agency could halt the process at any time simply by issuing its final decision notice (which, in the end, is precisely what it did). There was reason for the agency *not* to issue this decision notice, however, because the citizen interests had organized themselves in such a way as to be in a very powerful position. If the Forest Service hesitated, an appeal and lawsuit were likely (which, even if eventually unsuccessful, would be harmful to the Forest Service's public image and timber production needs). The citizen group had an incentive to avoid litigation, too. In the EDS process, the citizens could much more influentially suggest new solutions and focus on precise interests of concern. They could also potentially be involved long-term in implementing the final agreement. If the EDS process had not succeeded, the citizen interests were prepared to pursue the more traditional avenues for intervening: the appeals process and courts. In the end, even though the final agreement was not 100 percent of what the citizens would have liked, they thought it was better than what they would likely have achieved in the traditional way. (This case is presented in detail following chapter 2.)

Fitchburg Water Supply Mediation

The impetus for this case was the unsolved water problems of the small town of Fitchburg, Wisconsin. It was not quite clear who had the responsibility for repairing the water system, but it was obvious that it had to be done soon. The traditional process was going to take years to resolve this issue and its outcome was very uncertain in any event. In the meantime, the water supply problems would only persist. As a result, the homeowners mobilized to try to encourage an earlier decision. Their persistent effort kept the issue alive. Through continued pressure, the citizens were able to get the appropriate authorities (the state environmental agency, local government, and involved private developers) to a nontraditional "bargaining table" to hammer out a solution. While the citizen group was not a direct party to the negotiations, their presence kept pressure on the authorities and kept them at the table until a solution was reached. (This case is presented in detail following chapter 2.)

Common Ground Consensus Project

The Common Ground process was a policy dialogue involving environmental and agricultural interest groups in the state of Illinois. It did not address a specific dispute, but rather explored several common issues of concern (where there were certainly differences of opinion) in a joint problem-solving effort. While it did not evolve from a traditional process in the sense that our other cases did, it nonetheless did arise partly from acknowledged problems in reaching satisfactory legislation because of the differing opinions of the various interests at stake. The process did not evolve from this legislative arena, however. It was established independently and did not directly include those in position of authority over the issues being discussed.

While Common Ground did not involve the traditional process decisionmakers, neither was it completely separate. The processes were linked in three ways:

1. Key legislators and agency representatives were kept informed of Common Ground process;

2. The intent of this dialogue was to develop proposed legislation that then would obviously be interjected into the "traditional" legislative process; and,

3. As the issues were being discussed and agreements constructed, participants always kept an eye on the legislative arena in which such agreements would need to be debated and acted upon for them to

become a reality. This reality obviously affected their choice of issues to pursue and the way in which they structured their agreements.

For the final Common Ground agreement to be realized required legislative adoption. While the final agreement itself may be something that the traditional process would not likely have reached, by developing the EDS process appropriately, and by keeping an eye on implementation potential in the traditional process, the result was that the legislature "ratified" many aspects of it. (This case is presented in detail following chapter 3.)

Malden Negotiated Investment Strategy

The Malden negotiated investment strategy was a proactive, joint problem-solving process that was partly an evolution from the traditional city administrative structure and partly interjected from outside the traditional structure. In this case, Malden's mayor realized that his city had some critical problems that needed attention, that the existing processes were unlikely to foster the change that was necessary to address these needs, and that instead the change could most likely come about through coordinated attention on the part of all public and private sectors of the city. Moreover, the mayor was familiar with the NIS concept and had a willing facilitator in MIT professor Lawrence Susskind. Hence, while the process itself was then developed separately from the ongoing city administration, it nonetheless had very strong ties to this administration. It included a "city" team representing the traditional "authorities" as well as the business and citizen teams. It maintained communication with city agencies with responsibility over some of the issue areas and acquired needed information and technical assistance. Finally, the process objective was to develop realistic recommendations, many of which would need to be ratified and implemented by the city government. Unlike the Common Ground process, this dialogue was encouraged and supported by a key authority, thereby lending potentially greater influence and viability to its eventual recommendations. (This case is presented in detail following chapter 3.)

Sand Lakes Quiet Area

The Sand Lakes Quiet Area dispute arose when the Michigan State Department of Natural Resources (DNR) began considering a use for the area that local residents deemed inappropriate. The citizens, with the support of an individual with major political clout and familiar with both DNR administration and agency managers, as well as with EDS and other conflict intervention concepts, were instrumental in having the traditional decision-making process evolve into a nontraditional process. The citizen group's persistence encouraged the DNR initially to set aside their formal proceedings to meet with the citizens. As issues of concern were raised and discussed, the DNR agreed to address the proposed oil and gas exploration in the

larger context of the area's management plan. By so expanding the boundaries of this analysis, there was additional room for developing and evaluating alternative outcomes. With their "foot in the door" because of the
initial dialogue with DNR officials, the citizens strengthened their influence
by maintaining their forceful and persistent involvement. They developed
alternative proposals in the planning process to which the DNR responded.
Eventually, these interactions evolved into a somewhat informal issue-based
negotiation wherein the citizens had considerably more influence than they
would have had through traditional public input channels in the agency.
(This case is presented in detail following chapter 4.)

Pig's Eye Mediation

The Pig's Eye mediation was very much a part of the traditional planning
process for the Mississippi River around St. Paul. It did not evolve (the use
of the term "evolve" is not even appropriate in this case) from the traditional.
It was a process instigated by those in authority because of the level of
contention that plagued the traditional process. In fact, the administrative
authority in this case purposely tried a dispute settlement approach after
the traditional had failed. It was much like the out-of-court settlement model
of dispute resolution. A professional mediator was called in to try to help
the city more harmoniously complete its planning function. The city's hope
was that the adversaries could come to some agreement on the river plan
that would be acceptable to planners and not be contested at the state
Environmental Quality Board's hearings. However, this dispute settlement
process was a mediation only in name.

The Pig's Eye EDS process was linked to the traditional process in several
ways: (1) It was originally advocated by the city planner and supported by
the mayor. (2) It was linked to St. Paul's earlier negotiated investment
strategy (NIS) by a common mediator. (In fact, it may be that the NIS
experience paved the way for this process. Because the city had recently
been involved in an NIS process, the notion of consensus-building and
collaboration was not unfamiliar.) (3) If agreement were reached in the
alternative process, this agreement would then become part of the river plan
and be approved at the state level, and (4) the dispute encompassed two
decisions being made in the traditional arena: the Critical Areas Plan and
the Port Authority's barge permitting decision. In the end, the "mediation"
failed and the traditional planning efforts were resumed. (This case is presented in detail following chapter 4.)

Wisconsin Groundwater Legislation

The Wisconsin groundwater legislation case is another in which the traditional process latched upon nontraditional concepts in hopes of "doing
better" (rather than a process that evolved through the influence of external

groups). The Wisconsin state legislature had encountered, when developing complex environmental legislation wherein trade–offs must always be made, that legislation was always being contested and blocked by interest groups. Therefore, some legislators deemed it more appropriate to bring these adversaries together earlier to have a hand in developing the legislation at the outset. Their hope was that proposed legislation would then be accepted and supported rather than contested.

The process was a hybrid one, gleaning the most critical components of a collaborative effort but skillfully (and strategically) merging them with the realities of a political process. An outside third party was not called upon for assistance, but rather the process was orchestrated by a powerful individual in a significant position of authority. This process is much more institutionalized than our other cases, although it did not formally change the institution. Rather, it came about by an individual stretching the bounds of normal behavior, although not enough to confront tradition.

This "hybrid" consensus is little different from the traditional process. By participating in it, the different groups were participating in a traditional forum with the same recourse as the traditional should they be dissatisfied with the eventual outcome. This process combined characteristics of both traditional and alternative processes. However, it was not truly alternative because it did not really operate in a collaborative manner. Instead, a core group seemed to hold all the cards. The process paid close attention to the political realities of getting complex and controversial environmental legislation developed and passed and was, as a result, a very political process, albeit one that did try to bring the diverse interests together at the same time in the same place. (This case is presented in detail following chapter 4.)

Learning for Citizen Groups

It is critical for citizen group leaders to understand that these EDS processes do not operate in a vacuum, that the political realities of the traditional process persist, and that, as a result, these broader factors must be considered as they develop and participate in EDS processes. These brief sketches of each case study presented in this book illustrate a variety of ways in which alternative dispute resolution processes are linked to traditional decision-making processes. For citizen groups interested in the potential of alternative processes for addressing their concerns, it is important to understand what bearing this link has on how they might proceed.

Understanding the Traditional Process

In order to successfully encourage an EDS process to evolve from a traditional, a citizen group must understand the inner workings of the traditional's administrative management, review, and decision-making processes for those agencies having authority over issues concerning them. Citizen groups must find out who is to make what decisions, based on what information, when, where citizens may be involved, how to proactively encourage direct involvement, and what recourse is available should the eventual decision not satisfy their concerns. By understanding the traditional process in these terms, a citizen group can best determine what access points are most receptive to their direct participation and potential evolution to an alternative form. Additionally, this understanding will yield insights as to what incentives might be necessary to encourage decision-makers and other groups to adopt an alternative approach and stick with it to completion. In the Sand Lakes case, it was the familiarity of the citizen coalition with the DNR managers that allowed them to successfully encourage this process to evolve.

Similarly, it is important to understand the traditional process in order to ensure that whatever decision is framed in an alternative forum will be acceptable and hence authorized in the traditional and actually be implemented through established, traditional mechanisms. The Common Ground dialogue kept an eye on legislative implementation of the recommendations as well as maintained communication with key legislators and agency representatives. The Malden NIS process incorporated key city officials to ensure the viability of recommendations and to link itself with the traditional arena. However, in both cases, without these groups understanding the politics and the individuals in the traditional process, there would be little hope for influence from their alternative effort.

Incentives to Participate

For an EDS process to be successfully instituted, everyone, particularly the authorized decision-maker, potentially must have something to gain in pursuing it. If incentives to participate are not shared in this manner, the individual or group that can potentially gain more through the traditional process will likely not cooperate. Hence, the issue will be forced back into the traditional review and decision-making arena. For example, in the Pig's Eye case, the barge interests did not perceive that they had much to gain through the mediation; they felt they were much better served in the normal planning process. Hence, they walked out of the mediation midway and the process came to a halt.

As a result, should a citizen group believe that it has more to gain through nontraditional avenues, then it is incumbent upon that group to make the dispute settlement forum more advantageous for the other interests as well. As seen from these cases, there are a number of ways in which to do so. In the San Juan case, the citizen group had its petition in hand and was ready to file a lawsuit. The agency knew what would happen if they did not participate in the mediation; therefore, it was certainly worth a try. In the Sand Lakes case, it was much the same story. It was clear to the DNR that citizen concerns were valid. If the DNR refused to listen, bad publicity and potential lawsuits inevitably would occur. In this case, the perseverance of the citizens made the process eventually evolve into an alternative form rather than just a slight departure from the traditional process, one designed solely to obtain more "public input." In Fitchburg, the inevitable lawsuit, citizen persistence, and time pressures made an alternative forum more inviting to all parties.

Choice of Representative

The dynamics of the EDS process can be quite different from the traditional decision-making process. As a result, it is important that citizen groups select participants who have the appropriate skills and knowledge to represent them most effectively. In a negotiated investment strategy–type process, for example, it would most benefit citizen interests to have individuals familiar with specific issue areas be the group's representative to that particular committee. The Wisconsin groundwater legislation process was very political. Yet, the environmental group involved sent a representative who was most interested in the technical and scientific aspects of the groundwater problem and uncomfortable with the political aspects. His advisory and substantive orientation was not well suited to the political bargaining that dominated the process.

Conclusion

Environmental dispute settlement processes were a new experience for most citizen participants in the cases analyzed in this book. For the most part, the citizen organizations had to learn by doing in building their understanding of the new process and how they might most effectively participate in it. They had to acknowledge the link between these "alternative" dispute settlement processes and traditional decision-making arenas in order to build implementable agreements. It was through this conscious awareness that any decision reached in the EDS process would need to be acted upon within traditional arenas that made these processes realistic and guided most of them to both mutually acceptable and viable agreements. Moreover, in many of these cases, the citizen groups gained longer-term influence in the traditional process as a result of their participation in the EDS process: the involved neighborhood residents in Fitchburg became city leaders; the Pig's Eye Coalition gained credibility and respect in the public's eye; Malden citizens involved in the NIS process realized their potential for influencing city government; the San Juan interest groups now have a direct involvement in U.S.D.A. Forest Service planning.

The next two chapters and the case studies accompanying them present various strategic issues that any citizen organization must confront when considering the structure of an EDS process (chapter 3), and the potential organizational ramifications of participating in such a process (chapter 4). Before moving on to these chapters, however, it is helpful to have an image of the structure and dynamics of an EDS process and to understand the strategic implications of this link between traditional decision-making processes and an EDS process.

The two case studies that follow this chapter illustrate these points. The San Juan National Forest mediation case depicts the structure and dynamics of a "textbook" EDS process. In contrast, the Fitchburg water supply mediation presents the efforts of citizen groups to encourage an EDS process to evolve from a traditional decision-making arena that was making little progress in solving their water quality and supply crisis.

References

Bidol, Patricia, Lisa Bardwell, and Nancy Manring, eds. *Alternative Environmental Conflict Management Approaches: A Citizen's Manual*. Ann Arbor, MI: Environmental Conflict Project, School of Natural Resources, University of Michigan, 1986.

Bingham, Gail. *Resolving Environmental Disputes: A Decade of Experience*. Washington, D.C.: The Conservation Foundation, 1986.

Carpenter, Susan, and W. J. D. Kennedy. *Managing Public Disputes: A Practical Guide to Handling Conflict and Reaching Agreements*. San Francisco: Jossey-Bass, 1988.

Cormick, Gerald. "Intervention and Self-Determination in Environmental Disputes: A Mediator's Perspective." *Resolve* (Winter 1982): 1–7.

Susskind, Lawrence, and Jeffrey Cruikshank. *Breaking the Impasse: Consensual Approaches to Resolving Public Disputes*. New York: Basic Books, 1987.

Wondolleck, Julia M. *Public Lands Conflict and Resolution: Managing National Forest Disputes*. New York: Plenum, 1988.

CASE STUDY 1:
San Juan National Forest Mediation

Martha A. Tableman

The San Juan National Forest mediation case describes a site-specific dispute over logging and road-building in a scenic Colorado national forest. The process was mediated by two professional mediators, and involved representatives of the U.S.D.A. Forest Service, local businesses, federal and state environmental organizations, and timber companies. The dispute shifted to an environmental dispute settlement effort after escalating in the agency administrative decision-making and review processes. The proceeding was a flexible one that evolved as the needs of the participants changed.

Because the citizen participants kept their options open and were willing to develop compromise proposals, an agreement was reached that creatively addressed most concerns in a manner that the traditional administrative process was unable to do. The process uncovered several misconceptions among the groups about their concerns with agency land management and allowed discussion to thereby build upon the commonalities between them. Furthermore, the citizen influence in the process led to their ongoing involvement in implementation and monitoring of the final agreement.

This case study illustrates both the efforts of citizens to advance a conflict and then to use those efforts to encourage an EDS process to evolve. Moreover, the case sketches a "textbook" EDS process with details about its structure: who was involved and why; what ground rules governed the process; how the agenda was set; what function the mediators served; how ideas were raised and alternatives discussed; and, finally, how a final decision was reached.

Unless otherwise noted, information and quotes in this case are from personal interviews between the author and participants.

Background: Physical Characteristics of the Area

The Vallecito conflict focused on a mountainous area in the southwestern corner of Colorado located twenty miles northeast of Durango, and adjacent to Vallecito Lake. The lake—fed by the numerous streams that traverse the adjacent hillsides—is a large reservoir that provides resort activity, including boating, fishing, and hunting, and serves as a starting point for backpackers into the Weminuche Wilderness. Approximately 300,000 to 400,000 visitors come to the area each summer, primarily from Texas, New Mexico, and Arizona, to enjoy the lake, take trail rides, and hike and fish. The majority of the area businesses are locally owned and operated resorts or support the resorts (marinas, grocery stores, gas stations, and so forth). In addition to resorts, the east side of the lake has four national forest campgrounds, two private trailer parks, and numerous private residences.

The fall brings hunters seeking deer and elk. Close to a half million dollars is received each year from hunting and fishing license fees. The area provides calving areas for the deer and elk herds and is on the path of their seasonal migration route from the San Juan Mountains within the Weminuche Wilderness to New Mexico, where they winter.

In addition to its recreational uses, the area also provides range for cattle grazing, with their numbers controlled through the use of permits, issued by the U.S.D.A. Forest Service. Adjacent to the region, along the Los Pinos River and East Creek, there are private landholdings that are managed primarily as cattle ranches. Additionally, there are two resorts that provide lodging, guided hunting trips, and trail rides into the surrounding area.

The area is covered with four vegetation types: ponderosa pine/oak forest, mixed conifer with aspen, pure aspen stands, and grass/forb/sedge parks. Due to the area's high elevation and climate, much of the forest found here takes approximately two hundred years to regenerate.

The Environmental Assessment

The catalyst for the Vallecito conflict, analyzed here, was a draft U.S.D.A. Forest Service document titled *Environmental Assessment of the Transportation Planning Area Analysis for the East Creek–Beaver Meadow–Mosca Creek*. The EA was released in spring of 1983 and it analyzed a roading system that would provide access, primarily for logging, into the area east of Vallecito Lake. The adverse public reaction to the EA caught officials at the San Juan National Forest by surprise. When these officials had unveiled their draft forest plan in 1982, they had received very few comments from Vallecito area residents or organizations. In this draft plan, the area analyzed in the East Creek–Beaver Meadow–Mosca Creek EA had been allocated to livestock grazing, wood fiber production, and semiprimitive nonmotorized recreation. In 1982, the Vallecito Chamber of Commerce did not realize what these land allocations would actually mean to forest management practices on the land. As a result, they did not express much interest in the plan's details and instead turned their attention toward the local bug infestation problems. After 1982, however, the Chamber of Commerce's board of directors changed composition.

When they heard about the EA, with its image of what the U.S.D.A. Forest Service intended for the area, they opposed the proposal because they felt it would conflict with the primary profitable industry in the area— tourism. According to Vallecito Chamber of Commerce president Donna Carrington, "Logging would have a negative impact on tourism in the area" (Jackson 1983a). Her position was supported by Safari Lodge Resort owner Guenivere Marrs:

> Tourism and hunting is our livelihood. This timbering thing would knock the heck out of the tourist trade and this beautiful place. (McGaugh 1983)

The EA document presented seven alternative transportation systems that the U.S.D.A. Forest Service thought "would respond to the wide range of resource needs and management and public concerns" (U.S.D.A. Forest Service 1983). The alternatives varied along several dimensions, each having implications for how the area's management would occur:

1. The location of the road corridor;

2. The number of miles of road to be built;

3. The type of use planned once the logging was completed: constant, intermittent, or closed;

4. Whether the proposed roads would link the Vallecito area to the Beaver Creek area (east side of planning area).

Changes in any of the various dimensions would affect the area's management by determining which acres would be available for logging, the type of equipment that could be used to log, and the amount of public access that would occur after the logging. The decisions on any of these dimensions would affect the recreational opportunities available within and the wildlife management of the area.

Although not the EA's focus, within the document the U.S.D.A. Forest Service specifically identified its intentions to log many acres within the transportation planning area boundary. The implicit reason for building the road network was to enable the timber to be harvested. Within the next ten years, eight proposed timber cuts were identified with a date for the sales and with an estimate of the amount of board feet that would be removed.

The negative reaction to the EA's release arose primarily from concerns over the large proposed timber cuts and their impact on other resources, such as wildlife, water quality, and recreation.

The Conflict

Although the Forest Service had published in the local newspaper a notice of its intent to consider transportation system alternatives for the area, following standard agency procedure, it had gone unnoticed by the Vallecito area residents. The news of the U.S.D.A. Forest Service's proposed actions east of Vallecito Lake, as described in the EA, initially came to the attention of the local community through the efforts of Gene Bassett, a retired state game warden who had worked and now lives in the area. Bassett, who works part-time with Guenivere Marrs, the owner of Safari Lodge Resort, which serves tourists and hunters, told her and fellow worker Mark Audas about the management actions proposed in the EA. If the plan was implemented as originally described, Marrs would look out her living room window and see the proposed road cutting across a limestone ridge. It would be a road heavily used by logging trucks to remove timber. Both were dismayed at the news and immediately began to inform others in the Vallecito community. From there, the local response took two different paths, which eventually merged: one path went through the Chamber of Commerce, while the other went through legal channels.

Marrs, then Chamber of Commerce vice president, called Donna Carrington, Chamber of Commerce president, to inform her of the proposed roading system. Marrs then proceeded to set up a meeting, in mid-February, for the two of them with district ranger Tom Cartwright and Colorado Division of Wildlife representative Mike Zgainer to discuss the EA. The meeting was primarily an exchange of information, enabling the local interests to learn more about the details of the proposed project.

After the exchange, Marrs and Carrington scheduled a meeting, in early March, with forest supervisor Paul Sweetland. They informed Sweetland that they disagreed with the Forest Service's proposal and wanted to know if and how the proposal could be changed. The Forest Service was surprised at the negative local reaction. According to Sweetland, Marrs and Carrington left the meeting obviously dissatisfied.

Marrs and Carrington next called a Chamber of Commerce board meeting to present the Forest Service proposal. The board's reaction to the Forest Service plan was negative because they felt it would adversely affect area businesses. Carrington was surprised at the board's negative reaction and their willingness to fight the Forest Service. Her surprise was at their willingness to fight; it is not a response she would expect from the board members. According to Carrington, they are hardworking people who do *not* get involved in causes. They are even reluctant to sign petitions. The board members then asked forest supervisor Sweetland to come to a Chamber of Commerce meeting to provide additional information on the Forest Service's proposal and to answer questions. In mid-March, Sweetland and Cartwright met with the Chamber of Commerce board. The board members voiced their concerns and the Forest Service responded by suggesting possible mitigation efforts. The Forest Service's responses did not satisfy those present.

Some local residents had begun writing letters and making phone calls to state and national political officials raising questions about the Forest Service's plans and asking them to apply pressure on the Forest Service. Margaret Harper, a representative of the Homeowners Association, organized the letter-writing campaign. She and others distributed flyers that explained their objections to the Forest Service proposal and asked people to write the Forest Service and their political representatives to ask for a change in the plans. The letter-writing efforts succeeded in getting forest supervisor Sweetland to modify the EA that was being written.

In light of the negative public reaction accompanied by the letter-writing campaign, forest supervisor Sweetland decided to set up a formal public comment period during April and May. Having such an open comment period during the EA process is not standard procedure for the Forest Service. Although this procedure delayed the decision-making process, Sweetland felt it was necessary. He recognized that we "had a hot issue on our hands. [We] need[ed] to allow people to express themselves rather than just move forward with it."

Given the widespread public concern, Sweetland and the Chamber of Commerce board decided that he should come to Vallecito for a public meeting, which was scheduled for June 2, 1983.

The Issues

In the debate surrounding its proposed management actions, the Forest Service contended that it needed to log the proposed areas to deal with a spruce budworm and pine beetle infestation problem and to remove over-mature timber, especially aspen, to ensure the viability of the forest.

The road system was necessary to help achieve those goals. In addition, the Forest Service would be providing motorized recreational opportunities by creating additional vehicle access into the area.

Alternatively, those in opposition complained of the following:

- Incompatibility with the economic base of the area (tourism, scenic attractions, resorts, guide-outfitters).

- Impairment of the resource: scenic destruction that would be visible from the lake.

- Ability to protect elk and deer migration routes and calving grounds and streams and fisheries. Roads would increase access for poaching and hunting.

- Safety: proposed transportation of logs over the dam spillway, narrow county roads.

- The Forest Service had not adequately consulted and informed them, and hence had not sufficiently considered their views.

• Concern about the stability of the slopes and soils in some of the areas proposed for logging. (McGaugh 1983)

According to Carl Weston, San Juan Audubon Society representative: "From the beginning, the main issue was [that] roading superseded timbering. Roading is the tail that's been wagging the dog. Timbering is just an excuse for roading."

He felt that the Forest Service wanted to road the area to permanently remove it from consideration for formal wilderness designation. Others opposed to the Forest Service proposal did not agree, but they distrusted the Forest Service because of previous agency actions and claims that had not matched reality. A key incident in the Vallecito residents' minds was the clear-cutting of Middle Mountain, a finger of land sticking out into Vallecito Lake and visible from the lake and surrounding areas. The Forest Service had clear-cut the area in the 1960s. At that time, they had told the residents that it would regenerate quickly. They also had promised that they would only construct a primitive road into the area. Twenty years later, the Middle Mountain still looked barren, although under close surveillance regeneration was beginning to occur. The primitive road has been upgraded several times and is what Guenivere Marrs calls a "Cadillac road," implying that it is like a highway. It is her feeling that every road the Forest Service puts in eventually becomes a permanent improved road.

Prior to the first public meeting at the Chamber of Commerce, the anger of the Vallecito area residents became evident. Several newspaper articles were published with titles such as "Residents: Leave Primitive Area Alone" and "Vallecito Residents Fight Timber, Roads Proposition." In response to the public outcry, newspaper reporters interviewed the Forest Service representatives. Bob Lillie, from the forest supervisor's office, responded to queries by emphasizing "that no decisions have been made and that the Forest Service is in the process of writing an environmental assessment of the proposal" (McGaugh 1983). He also acknowledged that the Forest Service was surprised at the degree of opposition to the project, ranging from Vallecito merchants and residents to national conservation groups. At that time, the only letters of support had come from timber industry representatives and a few Vallecito residents (McGaugh 1983).

Prior to the June 2 meeting at the Vallecito Chamber of Commerce Building, Sweetland wrote a guest editorial in the *Durango Herald*. In the editorial, published on June 1, 1983, he noted his appreciation for the interest shown in the management of the area east of Vallecito Lake. He also gave an assessment of the breadth of comments received and his response to them:

Many area residents and even some individuals from out of state have taken the time and effort to become informed, analyzed the issues, and submit their comments either to me or to this newspaper. I not only wish to thank them, but also inform them that based on the comments received thus far, substantial changes have been made in the environmental assessment that is in the process of being prepared.

New alternatives are being considered, new routes for possible roads are being analyzed, harvest methods and schedules are being studied, and mitigating measures are being developed. (Sweetland 1983a)

Sweetland also expressed concern about apparent misinformation on the issues in conflict. He mentioned claims made in radio and newspaper editorials that referred to the area as "wilderness" or "former wilderness." The area is not wilderness; it was set aside for multiple uses in the 1980 Colorado Wilderness Act. If it were wilderness, then the Forest Service would be violating the law by roading and logging within its bounds. Sweetland stated that "comments based on misinformation cannot be constructively used in our analysis, in spite of our desire to consider all feasible alternatives" (Sweetland 1983a). He then issued an invitation to those concerned with the agency's plans to attend the June 2 meeting.

The other path of local response was initiated by Keith Graham, Jr., the son of a Texas millionaire who owned one of the large inholdings along the Los Pinos River that bordered the area in question. Some proposed clear-cuts would be visible from his property and some of the plans called for logging trucks to exit the area by crossing his land. In an attempt to determine how the Forest Service could be stopped, Keith Graham, Jr., called Sierra Club headquarters in San Francisco to ask for advice. They recommended he speak with the Sierra Club Legal Defense Fund office in Denver. The Denver office referred him to Luke Danielson, a Denver-based attorney whose practice concentrated on public land issues, and who was familiar with the Forest Service and its practices. After speaking with Danielson, Graham hired the attorney to represent him on this issue. Danielson asked Keith Graham, Jr., to send him a copy of the EA by Express Mail, since there were only three weeks until the decision notice was due out.

Danielson received and read the EA; he found numerous points that were questionable legally. He wrote Sweetland two letters, two days apart, listing his objections to the EA on behalf of the Grahams. In his first letter, Danielson provided the following introduction:

In general, we believe that the environmental assessment does not provide a legally adequate basis for adoption of any of the road building alternatives presented.

But even aside from the legal issues we strongly suggest that the Forest Service review the question of appropriate land use in this area. The area has a strong, dependable tourist and recreation-oriented economy. This will be injured by the proposed road program and timber sales, which will, in turn, provide only marginal benefits, while damaging fisheries, water quality, wildlife values, recreation, and other National Forest resources.

We thus suggest that "no action" is the best—and the only legally supportable—action to take at this time. Should the Forest Service desire to proceed with this program, a full environmental impact statement is needed. (Danielson 1983a)

Danielson then identified what he believed was the principal weakness:

[The EA] fails to come to grips in any significant manner with the real issue. That issue is whether historic, established uses of this area, which are the basis of a solid local economy of significant proportions, and which are important to tens or hundreds of thousands of visitors from all over the United States are to be sacrificed, and timbering to become the predominant use of the 23,000 acres subject to this proposal. In short, what will the dominant use of this area be? (Danielson 1983a)

Rather than focusing on the question of resource use in the area, Danielson argued that the EA assumed that this area would be predominantly devoted to timbering and that historical, established uses of the area would have to give way. The only real question looked at in the EA was "what kind of road system to build." He went on to state that the local people "deserve the opportunity to comment on the overriding issue of how this area is to be administered, and *whether*—not *how*—a massive, dense road network is really beneficial to the area" (Danielson 1983a).

After discussing in detail other specific objections to the EA, Danielson concluded his letter by summarizing three important issues:

1. The many concerned parties deserve a document which concentrates on *whether* timbering will be the dominant use of this area, rather than *how* timbering will be done;

2. The document fails to consider the cumulative impacts and unlawfully segments the proposed action into small pieces, only one of which is considered here; and

3. This is clearly a major federal action requiring an impact statement. (Danielson 1983a)

Two days later, Danielson submitted a second letter listing additional specific comments addressing wording and other technical issues in the proposal. For example, it noted the lack of a map, lack of definition and explanation of terms used, and the absence of other information that he felt would be helpful in making the decision.

Around the time of the first public meeting, Keith Graham, Jr., became aware of the efforts being made by the Chamber of Commerce and others in the area. The Grahams informed the Chamber of Commerce of their activities and their intention to fight the issue even if it meant taking the Forest Service to court. The Chamber of Commerce's board did not feel it had the money to fight the case in court, but agreed to join the Grahams as a party to their lawsuit if the following conditions were met: (1) they would be kept informed of what was happening at all times; and (2) they could back out at any time.

Carrington does not feel that the Chamber of Commerce would have ever gone with the case all the way to court. She thinks they would have backed out before then because of the costs involved and their natural reluctance to become involved in causes and to challenge the system.

The June 2 meeting was held at the Chamber of Commerce Building. Carrington expected about fifty people to show up; approximately three hundred people attended. Sweetland presented the proposed plan, using slides to illustrate the different alternatives analyzed in the EA. He also attempted to respond to comments received during the comment period. Because the meeting was scheduled just before the beginning of the summer season, most area businesses were only able to send one representative. The crowd represented more than the local business community. People from Durango and other surrounding communities came to express their concern. The district ranger was also present to answer questions and respond to concerns raised, since he had greater familiarity with the area in conflict. All comments made by those attending opposed logging in the area east of Vallecito Lake. People left the meeting outraged at the proposal and motivated to take action against the plan.

Based on the comments made and questions asked at the meeting, Bob Pontius, president of the Property Owners Association that represented homeowners at the north end of the lake, contended that Sweetland became aware that the Forest Service had a problem that had not been resolved. Because of the high level of public concern, Sweetland put off issuing the final decision notice for several weeks.

After the meeting, the letter-writing campaign was broadened, a petition drive begun by the Chamber of Commerce, and increased pressure applied to political representatives at all levels. Local businesses placed canisters in their shops to raise money to support their xeroxing, mailing, and telephone costs.

The 1,182 signatures gathered on the petitions were sent by the local organizers to Congressman Ray Kogovsek (D-Colo.), who represents the Vallecito area. The numerous letters and phone calls to federal legislators and the local Forest Service began to have an effect as they were translated into letters of inquiry and phone calls to Sweetland questioning what was planned for the Vallecito area. Sweetland received inquiries from citizens who had visited the area and from political officials representing those who vacationed there. Senator Cranston (D-Calif.) and Senator Tower (D-Tex.) and the governors of Colorado and Texas made inquiries questioning the Forest Service proposal. The petition, numerous letters, and phone calls began to have an impact on the Forest Service, and it began to make minor changes in the EA.

Part of the initial controversy arose from the two proposed routes for removing timber from the area. One route called for timber removal from the west side of the planning area to be transported around the east side of the lake and across the dam. The second proposed route removed the timber from the east side of the planning area. After many challenges to the proposed route that would involve transporting timber over the dam due to safety concerns, the Forest Service dropped that alternative. After the June 2 meeting, Sweetland agreed to rewrite the EA before issuing a final decision. His previous attempts to adjust the document had been insufficient to satisfy the local concerns.

As the summer season began, more people, particularly tourists and summer residents, became aware of and unhappy with the Forest Service proposal. Other governmental officials began to feel the pressure to stop the Forest Service plan. In addition to the petitions, Kogovsek's office was receiving letters and phone calls from residents of southwestern Colorado as well as other states. As visitors to the area returned home, they contacted their representatives and requested action. According to Ned Wallace, Kogovsek's representative in Durango, "This has taken on a different dimension. It's more than just some people opposing a decision made by Paul Sweetland. Our office is getting calls from congressmen in Oklahoma, Texas, and even a Senator. It's become a national issue" (Jackson 1983b).

In response to the petitions, calls, and letters, Kogovsek agreed to meet with the local residents at the Vallecito Resort Recreation Hall on July 30, 1983. More than 140 people showed up to express their concerns. No one at the meeting spoke in favor of the Forest Service proposal. Many asked Kogovsek to join them in their fight, citing ecological, economic, and safety considerations. Kogovsek informed the audience that he had been hearing from their congressional representatives:

> We've been getting calls from your representatives from California, Arizona, Texas . . . I want to assure you the letters you've been writing to your congressmen are getting answered. (Jackson 1983c)

He then pledged to continue his tradition of trying to resolve contentious Forest Service issues. He had been the individual responsible for developing the compromise that led to passage of the 1980 Colorado Wilderness Bill. He told those present that:

> whenever you have a tremendous amount of federal land in a county as you do here, and people live next to it, eventually, there's bound to be a conflict like this one. . . . I want to be a part of that resolution. I want to bring about a resolution quickly. (Jackson 1983c)

Kogovsek listened to the numerous speakers and promised that he would "talk to the Forest Service" to make sure that those opposed to the project would have adequate time to comment when the second EA was released. That assurance addressed a new issue that was mentioned frequently during the second meeting. It was the local residents' contention that, at the June 2 meeting, Sweetland had promised to allow a further comment period and was now saying that it was not possible. The apparent turnaround increased the local residents' mistrust of the Forest Service.

The second meeting was also attended by Donald McDonald, Senator Gary Hart's (D-Colo.) West Slope representative, and state representative Ben Campbell (D-Ignacio). Campbell spoke out against the Forest Service proposal:

> Any time the tourism here is off a little bit, it comes back. But if you cut down the trees here, they won't come back in your lifetime. I'm really concerned about that. (Jackson 1983c)

The Mediation

After the public hearing called by Congressman Kogovsek, which clearly illustrated the opposition to the proposed action, Danielson decided to talk directly to Paul Sweetland about the conflict; since it was a weekend, they met at Sweetland's office. It was clear that they were headed toward an administrative appeal and ultimately a court case. He suggested to Sweetland that it would be desirable to all involved if they could work out a solution at the local level. According to Sweetland, the fact that Danielson suggested using a mediation process made it a viable alternative:

> One reason the Forest Service went to the table is that Luke Danielson opened up the door for us. I [Sweetland] could never have suggested it in the arena we were in politically or in the heat of the issue either.

Danielson had previously participated in a mediation done by the Mediation Institute over the reclamation of Homestake Mine, a uranium mine near Gunnison, Colorado. Sweetland previously had used a process called a "charette," an intense problem-solving effort involving a large number of different groups. They agreed to hold a meeting to try to reach consensus at the local level.

Sweetland began to look for a neutral third party to help facilitate the meeting. He originally suggested Mr. Carol (Pete) Peterson, the chairman of the Public Land Advisory Committee. Peterson was not acceptable to Danielson, since he, Danielson, could not find out any information about him. Danielson suggested trying the Mediation Institute and Sweetland agreed to call them.

The Mediation Institute, located in Seattle, Washington, is a national center established to provide mediation and related dispute settlement services to parties in disagreement. Since 1975, its mediators have assisted in settling conflicts ranging from facility siting to regulation development to resource planning.

Before the Mediation Institute was contacted, Danielson and Sweetland put together a list of approximately twenty-six people to invite to the planned meeting. The list consisted of local interest-group leaders, including current users of the area, people who had been outspoken at the previous public meeting, and individuals suggested by Danielson. Sweetland wanted to ensure that representatives of all the multiple uses were present. Hence, off-road vehicle (ORV) users and cattle ranchers were invited, even though they had not participated previously. Invitations were sent out inviting these diverse representatives to participate in a two-day meeting sponsored by the Forest Service.

At the same time, Sweetland called the Mediation Institute and talked with them about the possibility of serving as mediators. He spoke with Orville "Ty" Tice about the conflict and its current status. He then asked Tice if the Mediation Institute would be willing to come to Durango to chair the two-day meeting.

The Mediation Institute initially was skeptical of becoming involved. It appeared to them that the conflict was, according to Leah Patton, a "classic wilderness versus nonwilderness, cut versus not, type of fight." If that was the case, they did not think that they could sit down with those involved and, in the two days planned, get them to "settle it" because the groups would not have time to move beyond their stated positions.

However, they continued to consider accepting Sweetland's offer because they had previously worked with Luke Danielson on the Homestake Mining mediation (Watson and Danielson 1982). They knew that Danielson was aware of what negotiations could and could not accomplish. Tice telephoned Danielson to get his assessment of the situation. Danielson encouraged them to seriously consider the case; he felt there was potential for compromise.

After some consideration, Tice telephoned Sweetland. He said that the Mediation Institute would take the case with the understanding that it would not be productive for them to just show up at a meeting called by the Forest Service. They would be uninformed on the positions held by different participants and it would appear as if they were there to work for the Forest Service rather than for everyone. From their experience, it was essential for the mediators to be neutral and to be perceived as being neutral. If they could come out earlier to meet privately with each individual invited to participate, then they would do it. In those individual meetings, the mediators would explain who they were, why they were there, and what reasonably could be expected from the meetings.

In addition, the Mediation Institute reserved the right not to chair the meeting if after their conversations with the individuals, it became clear that everyone was just going to restate positions. If the Mediation Institute reached that conclusion, they would contact everyone and explain why they were *not* going to chair the meeting. Reserving the right to withdraw from a conflict is a normal procedure for the Mediation Institute. It allows them to work only on conflicts that have some realistic potential of being resolved through the mediation process. It had even more significance in this case because the invitations for the meeting had already been issued. In most cases, the Mediation Institute becomes involved before participants are selected.

If these provisions were acceptable to the Forest Service, then the Mediation Institute would waive its usual fees if the Forest Service covered its expenses. The Forest Service agreed. The fee waiver used to be a normal practice for the Mediation Institute when they were funded by foundation grants: currently, they are primarily operating on a fee-for-service basis.

In this situation, they chose to waive the fee for several reasons. First, they were faced with a very short time period before the meeting. Its brevity did not allow them the luxury of looking for foundation support for the effort. Second, it was unrealistic to go to the twenty-six invitees and ask them to pay. The twenty-six individuals had received invitations; there was present no implication that they had sufficient stake in the meeting to fund it. Third, it was unclear at that point if the Forest Service could have paid them and it would have taken too long to determine. The Mediation Institute was also concerned that receiving money from the Forest Service would have caused them credibility problems with the participants who were skeptical about both the mediation process and its impetus. If they were not seen as "neutral," they could not be effective in their role.

As a part of the negotiation process with the Forest Service, the Mediation Institute made it very clear to Sweetland that, although the Forest Service was paying its expenses, they were working for everyone involved. Ten days before the two-day meeting was scheduled to occur, the Mediation Institute agreed to come. It did not give the mediators much time to prepare.

The Mediation Institute decided to send two mediators, Orville "Ty" Tice and Leah Patton, to work on the Vallecito case because of the large number of people invited to attend the meeting. Although they would have preferred to arrive earlier, the mediators did not arrive in Durango until five days before the meeting.

In their early meetings with the participants, Tice and Patton performed two tasks. One was to inform the participants about themselves and about the process: they introduced themselves and explained what their roles would be in the two-day meeting. As a part of their effort, they explained the ground rules for the meeting to each participant. The second task was for the mediators to gather information from the participants about the conflict. They asked the participants about the following:

- What were the real issues, not just the ones being appealed?
- What did they need out of this piece of land?
- How did they want the meeting run?

The first two questions were aimed at getting beyond the publicly stated positions to determine if there was potential for compatible solutions to the conflict. They also provided the mediators with some sense of the individuals' willingness to move away from their positions toward a mutually compatible solution. The third question was aimed at reassuring the participants that the mediators were truly working for everyone, not just the Forest Service, by providing them with an opportunity to express their desires and have them *heard* and acted upon.

Before ending the individual meetings, the mediators also tried to encourage each individual to think about specific needs and possible solutions. They advised the parties that it would be helpful if they came prepared to talk about their real interests and needs rather than restate positions held. The mediators also informed them that they had reserved the right to not participate in the meeting if the parties were only going to posture. They explained that if a settlement was reached, it would be the participants' agreement, not the mediators'; the mediators did not come in with an *answer*. The mediators also emphasized that the ultimate authority to decide the question continued to rest with the Forest Service. "However," the mediators did emphasize that "to the degree parties could unanimously agree among themselves on recommendations that met their respective needs, there was reason to believe their consensus would be given serious consideration indeed" (Tice and Patton 1983).

As explained by the mediators in the initial individual meetings, the final decision authority rested with the Forest Service. The agency would take the group's consensus, if the group could achieve one, as a recommendation. It would carry additional weight, though, because it was a consensus recommendation coming from so many different interests. As stated by Sweetland, "And if it is a consensus, these people have conveyed quite a message" (Jackson 1983f).

The mediators spoke with everyone involved either in a face-to-face meeting or by telephone. After the first round of contacts, as they worked on the agenda for the meeting, they made additional contacts with some participants by telephone to clarify statements or check on agenda items.

After their initial round of meetings with those invited, Tice and Patton concluded that they would chair the meetings. From their perspective, it appeared that it was possible to achieve a compromise. However, the mediators would not openly predict that a compromise was likely until after the parties had met and discussed the issues.

Based on the initial meetings, the mediators found the invitees willing to talk, but most had a "healthy degree of skepticism" over whether a compromise could be reached (Jackson 1983f). Vallecito Chamber of Commerce president Donna Carrington's attitude going into the meeting was probably representative of the attitude held by many of the locals:

> When we had all of the other meetings and they [the Forest Service] found out our viewpoints, we thought they'd cut off their plans right there. Since that hasn't happened, I'm not optimistic, but I hate to be pessimistic either.

Maybe we can come to some compromise. I'd hate to attend two days of meetings for nothing. (Jackson 1983f)

The twenty-six participants included a large logging company, several cattle ranchers, an owner of a motorbike store, Colorado Division of Wildlife, small timber operators, the Wilderness Society, Durango Audubon Society, Colorado Wildlife Federation, Colorado Open Space Council (COSC), Danielson representing the Grahams and two other ranchers in the Pine River Valley, the Chamber of Commerce, the Homeowners Association, the Property Owners Association, and a dude ranch. Eventually, everyone who had been invited participated.

Although the Forest Service had issued the invitations to the meeting, they made it clear to the mediators and those invited that they would be present primarily as a resource. Throughout the meetings, they would locate and provide maps, layouts, aerial photographs, and other information requested by the participants. Their presence would also enable the Forest Service to raise red flags when the group considered specific recommendations that would create legal, biological, or administrative problems for the Forest Service.

Just prior to the September meetings, the Forest Service released the second draft of the EA. In it, the Forest Service had tried to reflect many of the concerns voiced at the various public meetings. The second draft would be used as the basis for discussion at the meeting. The final decision notice was expected within eight weeks.

The mediators' skills were tested before the official mediation began. One of the established ground rules was challenged by a local reporter. The sessions were supposed to be confidential, which meant the absence of any press representatives. The local reporter had seen the meeting notice in the *Durango Herald* and wanted access to it. The Forest Service had published notice of the meeting, as was usual practice. Aware of the level of conflict surrounding the issue, the reporter wanted to be present at the meetings. The Forest Service took the position that it was an advisory group meeting, and, therefore, they did not have to admit anyone from the press. The mediators interceded in the discussion; they met with the reporter and worked out a solution satisfactory to all. Unsure of the participants' reaction to the presence of the press, they decided to allow them to discuss the question and decide as a group. At noon on the first day, the reporter could come to the first meeting to learn the result of the discussion. Even if the participants chose to close the meetings, the reporter would be able to interview the participants during the lunch hour and after the afternoon session.

The public notice also brought a few uninvited citizens to the meeting. As they were gone by mid-morning, it was assumed by Tice that they left once their curiosity about the meeting was satisfied.

The First Day

At the start of the meeting, Paul Sweetland introduced Tice and Patton. The mediators then spent the next hour to hour and a half elaborating on the following points:

- Who they were.
- How the meeting would function.
- Explained the goal of conciliation and compromise.
- How they would accomplish it (by reaching a solution acceptable to all).

In addition, they gave examples of other conflicts that they had mediated and how they had been resolved to illustrate that it could be done.

The mediation began with a discussion of the ground rules. The press issue was raised and the participants chose to close the meetings. According to Patton, the participants wanted them closed because they would not be comfortable having their words written down and reported on the newspaper's front page. However, they could talk to the reporters as individuals at lunch or after the afternoon sessions.

One ground rule that had been discussed previously was brought up again at the beginning of the meeting. Patton and Tice announced that the area's wilderness potential would not be considered. Although it had been discussed with them earlier, the announcement caught at least two participants by surprise, Chris Sanborn of the Wilderness Society and Mark Pearson of COSC. Sanborn was unhappy but did not feel she could challenge the edict. The rationale given for its exclusion was that the Forest Service had no control over that issue; the lack of formal wilderness designation had been decided in 1980 by Congress. Hence, this forum was not the proper one for its discussion. If the question of wilderness designation was to be reconsidered, it would have to be addressed by Congress.

Danielson supported the Forest Service on this point; it was felt that if the wilderness issue became the mediation's central focus, the loose-knit coalition composed of local residents opposed to timbering, the Chamber of Commerce, the ranchers, and local, state, and national environmental groups would have shattered. The Forest Service, Danielson, and some of the locals feared that the state and national environmental groups would use the meeting as a forum to raise that issue. The local resort owners and homeowners did not want to see the area designated as wilderness. It was their perception that a formal designation would result in limited access to the area for addressing fire and bug infestations. However, they did not want the area logged and roaded, with the resulting problems caused by increased access to the interior areas. Much to everyone's surprise, the environmentalists did not use the forum to demand wilderness designation.

Instead, they supported the local residents in their effort to maintain the area in a relatively pristine state.

Another topic of intense discussion the first morning was the absence of a representative from the Evergreen Lumber Company. The mediators had met with the president of the company prior to the meeting and they thought they had a commitment from the company to attend. However, when the meeting began, the lumber company representative was not present. One reason for their concern arises from the rule of thumb that all stakeholders should be present at a mediation. Additionally, the absence of the timber company, representative of large commercial timber interests in the area, was problematic since the Forest Service had based its previous arguments supporting the road network on the commercial needs for timber. It might be assumed from the timber company's absence that they did not care about the timber on this specific tract of land. If that was the case, it undermined the Forest Service's proposal. However, the interests of those who wanted to use the timber were not absent and several local, small timber operators were present.

The group discussed what could and should be done without a representative from the large timber interests present. Sweetland telephoned the timber company and determined that someone would be at the meeting on the second day. Given that assurance, the mediators and the meeting participants decided to move ahead with their discussion. Although the meeting eventually evolved to a highly collaborative problem-solving effort, initially the participants saw themselves entering a forum in which they were surrounded by supposed enemies.

At the beginning of the meeting, the conflict dynamic placed the Vallecito group, consisting of the Chamber of Commerce, the Grahams, the local property owners accompanied by Danielson and supported by the local and national environmental groups, against the Forest Service and the other user groups (for example, grazers, loggers, ORV users). The "we versus them" image was clearly established within the minds of the Vallecito group and the environmental groups. According to Mark Pearson (COSC), despite the fact that the Forest Service proposed the roading, they came into the meeting presenting themselves as impartial observers. They portrayed the conflict as one between different user groups. Including the ORV users and the ranchers in the mediation process set up a dynamic of the pro-wilderness/dude ranch/resort interests in opposition to the two- and four-wheel drive and logging interests. Prior to the Forest Service proposal, the ORV and logging interests had not asked for access to the area. Steve Bloemeke, Colorado Wildlife Federation, and Mark Pearson felt that the Forest Service's proposal had created the demand.

After the discussion of ground rules, the mediators had everyone introduce themselves and identify their needs and concerns for the area. This list of needs was written on a blackboard in the front of the room. Everyone complied except the Forest Service. According to Sweetland and the mediators, the Forest Service did not see itself as a participant at the first set of meetings. They saw their role as the providers of information on the area and on the restrictions that governed their management. Paul Sweetland began the meeting stating and then continually reiterating that he would take their recommendations on advisement. The Wilderness Society representative, Chris Sanborn, asked the mediators why the Forest Service had not told the group what its needs were from the area. With the omission pointed out, they asked Paul Sweetland to tell the group what the Forest Service wanted from the area. The Forest Service responded by saying the timber was overmature and bug infested, hence needed cutting. Although Sweetland responded, many of the participants feel that the Forest Service never revealed its true needs, its bottom line. They believe the agency's real need is to increase roading and timber cuts because of alleged demands by the Forest Service's Washington Office.

The following needs were identified during the discussion:

Party	Needs
Division of Wildlife	Protection of elk migration routes and calving areas.
ORV users	Public access.
Cattle	Access to their permits.
Environmental groups	Protection of resources in area. Support for local residents.
Chamber of Commerce/dude ranches/homeowners	Tourism, aesthetics, safety, protect lifestyle.
Small timber company	Access to timber in reasonable quantities. Protection of the area. Avoidance of building roads to Forest Service standards.
U.S.D.A. Forest Service	Cut trees since overmature and bug infested. Roaded recreation activities. Provide feed for wildlife. Maintenance of aspen stands.

Although not revealed the first day, Evergreen Lumber Company identified its needs from the areas as being only one: access to timber. With everyone's needs disclosed, the mediators had the participants break into small groups to talk. By having the meeting participants self-select into groups of people with similar viewpoints, the small groups presented a way to narrow differences so they could work toward consensus. The discussions also allowed individuals an opportunity to get better acquainted. Each group talked about the similarities and differences between the positions and needs of the individuals comprising the group. One of the small groups contained those individuals who supported the Forest Service proposal. It consisted of Gary Wilkinson (ORV shop) and Carl Brown (local logger and rancher). The grazing interests represented another group who seemed to support the Forest Service's position. The group consisted of Steve Pargin, a local rancher, a representative of the county grazing association and a representative of the San Juan National Forest Grazing Advisory Board. Another group consisted of Keith Graham, Donna Carrington, Luke Danielson, Bob Pontius, and Meg Harper. Another group was made up of the environmental groups: Chris Sanborn, Mark Pearson, Carl Weston (Audubon) and Steve Bloemeke (Colorado Wildlife Federation).

Once each small group understood what its members' concerns were, people began to move about to get additional information about the other groups' needs. According to Keith Graham, Jr., the first group he entered consisted of himself (a landowner), a member of the Chamber of Commerce, and a representative of the homeowners' group. First, they talked among themselves. Once they had reached agreement on their own needs, they moved on to talk with another small group. They engaged next with the cattlemen. Much to their surprise, it turned out that the cattlemen did not want roads in the proposed area either. Before entering the mediation, the Vallecito group combined with the environmentalists, hereinafter referred to as the Vallecito Coalition, and had assumed that the grazing interests would support additional roads since it would increase access to the acreage included in their grazing permits. When Steve Pargin stood up and said he had one mile of existing road on his permit and that it was one mile too much, the Vallecito Coalition could not believe what it heard. Although additional roads would facilitate the cattlemen's livestock management, it would also provide easier access for rustlers. Given a choice, the cattlemen would do without the roads. This unexpected response began opening up the possibilities for resolving the conflict. With that understanding, the two groups joined and approached the small timber operators and finally the recreation users. While the participants met in small groups, the mediators circulated between the groups to listen and then to inform the other groups of what was being considered so there would not be any surprises.

By the end of the first day, everyone had decided that the group was too large; with so many people involved, it would be difficult to move toward resolution. For the next morning's meeting, they established a smaller working group. The participants, assisted by the mediators, spent the latter part of the first day sorting themselves out by interest area, determining where there was overlap, and then identifying who should be in the small group. Each small group selected a representative; the mediators made sure that all interests were represented. The delegates selected were:

Steve Bloemeke	Colorado Wildlife Federation
Carl Brown	Rancher/logger
Donna Carrington	President, Chamber of Commerce
Robert Curry	Geotechnical expert
Luke Danielson	Attorney
Keith Graham, Jr.	Private rancher
Margaret Harper	Homeowners Association
Steve Pargin	Rancher
Mark Pearson	Colorado Open Space Council
Robert Pontius	Property Owners Association
Gary Wilkinson	ORV shop
Mike Zgainer	Division of Wildlife

Others present at the morning meeting were:

Forest Service Representatives
  Tom Cartwright
  Paul Sweetland

Mediators
  Leah Patton
  Orville Tice

In addition, before the meeting adjourned for the evening, the mediators identified where the interests differed and where they had agreement. Everyone seemed surprised at how little difference there was among the interests. The mediators told the participants they were doing a good job. Progress had been made; they had been able to reduce the size of the working group and had made movement on their positions.

According to Tice and Patton, by the end of the first day two major changes had occurred. The group as a whole had unified around an overriding concern for the area as a unit rather than their individual interests. They could agree on their concerns but not on how to address them. According to several participants, the Vallecito Coalition had changed their position the most. They had entered the mediation asking for no changes and were now willing to acknowledge the need for access from the west side. They also seemed to be moving toward supporting and advocating small-scale timber operations and low-impact recreational uses. However, these ideas were still different from the Forest Service's proposal.

Despite the comments made by the mediators, many participants did not feel that much progress was made the first day. Gary Wilkinson from the ORV shop thought that the mediators were being excessive with their praise. Some participants left with an increased awareness of each other's positions and thinking about where there were possibilities for compromise. Although they had that increased awareness of the other's points of view, many could not see evidence of significant movement toward a resolution to the conflict.

The interests represented by Danielson, the Chamber of Commerce, dude ranches, and property owners, almost fell apart at the end of the first day. During the course of the day, the various members had presented many different reasons for opposing the Forest Service proposal. Prior to the mediation, the coalition members had never fully explored all reasons individuals were involved. To deal with the dissension within the group, they held a meeting that night at Safari Lodge to work out their differences and to come up with a concrete proposal to present the next day. As they tried to work out internal differences, individuals voiced their concerns and worked toward clarifying their own positions. For many of them, they felt more comfortable explaining their positions in this small group than they had at the mediation meeting. They worked out their internal differences, then turned their attention to drafting a proposal. Given the specific needs raised at the meeting in Ignacio, they studied their maps of the area to see if other areas could satisfy those needs. They decided that all of the other needs identified could be met on other parcels of land in the San Juan National Forest.

The Second Day

With their proposal in hand, the Vallecito group entered the second day of meetings determined to get a consensus. Many group members felt and still feel that the Forest Service suggested the mediation because they never expected it to work. They feel that the Forest Service assumed that if all the different interests were brought together in one place, they would end up fighting rather than resolving the dispute. As a result, the Forest Service would then have to decide the question by default. Part of the coalition's determination to reach a consensus arose from their desire to thwart Sweetland.

The Forest Service, particularly Paul Sweetland, disagrees with that interpretation. He says he entered the mediation process because it was offered as an option to him by Luke Danielson. When Danielson suggested the following, it allowed Sweetland to alter the conflict dynamic:

> Instead of us shouting at each other, let's see if we can get a group that will reasonably sit down at a table and talk about this and see if there is any common ground where we can reach some agreement even a small scale agreement.

Rather than following the traditional decision-making routine, Sweetland had a reason to delay making the decision and at the same time provide an opportunity for additional public input.

On the second day, the meeting site was changed from the rented hall in Ignacio to the forest supervisor's office in the Federal Building in Durango. Only the smaller group of participants selected the previous afternoon met.

By two o'clock that afternoon, they intended to have a series of recommendations to place before the larger group.

As the second day of meetings began, the mediators were concerned about the arrival of the Evergreen Lumber Company representative. A momentum toward small timber sales and low impact recreation had begun to build the first day that seemed counter to the lumber company's interests. On one hand, it was the lumber company representative's problem as he was the one who had not shown up the first day, but it would be the mediators' problem if his presence caused the mediation effort to blow up.

Upon his arrival, the mediators took the lumber company representative aside and explained to him what had happened the first day. From their initial meeting with the president of the company, the mediators knew that the company's primary concern was the wilderness designation question. They informed him that the wilderness designation question was not being discussed and identified the issues that were. They also told him that if he entered the meeting and began to make numerous demands, he would cause the meeting and its efforts to move toward consensus to fall apart. If he wanted to have a significant say in the direction of the discussions, then he should have come on the first day.

The lumber company representative listened to the information provided. At the beginning of the meeting, he sat outside the table and listened to the discussion. As he began to feel more comfortable, he joined the group sitting around the table.

The meeting began with Danielson and his clients presenting their proposal. It was not well received by the other participants. The other interests turned the logic used by the Vallecito group on end and asked why the Vallecito group's interests could not be moved elsewhere within the national forest instead.

Rather than locking into those positions, the group as a whole discussed the problems with the proposal. Realizing its problems, the participants then moved on to other ideas for addressing the stated needs. The mediators did not have to intervene; the participants were able to address the issues raised and move beyond them.

According to Tice and Patton, the participants were more comfortable with the mediation process on the second day. They would tap someone they wanted to talk with and go off and caucus. As a result, the mediators played less of a role during the small group meeting.

In searching for a solution, the perceived impasse of the previous day dissolved when it was suggested that the area be divided into two parts, each representing a viewshed. Each section would then be dealt with separately in the mediation process. That division was acceptable to everyone; the area was divided into west (visible from Vallecito Lake) and east viewsheds. It was acceptable because most of those involved were primarily concerned with the west side of the ridge that was visible from Vallecito Lake.

With that separation, the participants began to find common ground between their positions. As they began to talk, it became clear that the groups were not separated by big differences. It also became obvious to them that the battle was not the Vallecito Coalition against the Forest Service. Although the Vallecito Coalition had been willing to confront the Forest Service, they were less willing to confront their neighbors. If they had a choice, they would try to find a way to accommodate them. In the small group meeting, as they confronted the stated needs of their neighbors, they began to realize they had to consider these other needs.

With the awareness from the first day that the cattlemen did not want roads, the discussion turned toward defining what the other interests meant by access. At one point in the following discussion, one of the mediators asked Gary Wilkinson, "What do you mean when you say you need access? Why do you need it and where?" Wilkinson responded that one of the preferred snowmobiling areas in the Durango area was currently only accessible from Pagosa Springs, the east side. He, and he assumed others, would like access from the west side, as it would reduce travel time. Wilkinson suggested that a motorized vehicle trail would suffice. The other interests considered the idea. They had concerns about the size of the trail, but knew that it could be negotiated. They decided that a motorized recreation trail would not hurt them, could provide some winter tourist business, and would satisfy Wilkinson.

As a part of that discussion about the area's west side, the participants agreed that timber should not be cut north of the proposed trail because it would be visible from the lake. This idea was acceptable to the timber company because the timber from the west side was not economical for them to cut. It would mean transporting timber to a mill more than one hundred miles away. The transportation costs would exceed any revenues generated by the sale of the resulting timber. They preferred access to timber on the ridge's east side, since it was closer to their mill. They would also prefer sales near the existing roads, as that would reduce the capital costs they would incur for road construction.

With general agreement on the west side of the ridge, the discussion's focus shifted to the east section of the planning area. Everyone was willing to allow timbering on that side. However, they were concerned about problems associated with the presence of large timber companies. The major problem was the tendency to bring in transient labor, which then creates problems for the local government and local economy. It was also claimed that the presence of large timber companies, with their transient labor workforces, tended to increase the amount of poaching. The local small timber operators stated they could do a more ecologically sound job of cutting the timber while not placing additional burdens on the economy. As the Forest Service had originally structured the size of the proposed sales, the small operators could not bid on them. They did not have the mill capacity to handle the timber, nor did they have the capital to build the many miles of road required.

The participants decided to support cutting timber on the east side of the ridge, but only if it was done from existing roads and the sales were structured so that small timber operators could handle them. The Evergreen Lumber Company representative was willing to accept this solution, since it allowed the cutting of timber. Their greatest fear had been wilderness designation, which would have totally eliminated access for timber. Although the sales would be structured in small sizes, bidding on them was still an option for the company. Since the Vallecito Lake viewshed had been protected from logging and roading, the Vallecito Coalition was willing to allow some logging, even though their original position had opposed logging.

During the above discussions, the Forest Service, represented by Paul Sweetland and others, listened and provided information if asked. The presence of the forest supervisor throughout these meetings is one expression of the seriousness with which he watched the effort. As they had done throughout the two days of meetings, the Forest Service participated only as an information resource, not as an active participant.

Having made significant movement toward a consensus, the small meeting participants reported their conclusions to the larger group as scheduled. Initially, their recommendations were met with some resistance. The mediators saw it primarily as a problem of needing to bring the other participants up to the same level of understanding about the reasoning behind the recommendations.

As the group as a whole moved toward a consensus, it became evident to several participants that in order to protect the area's values, they would need to establish an advisory group to work with the Forest Service and monitor its activities. The idea was adopted and written into the recommendations.

After some discussion, the entire group agreed to adopt the consensus recommendations, which were given to Sweetland at the end of the meeting. Since he had been there through the discussion, he responded immediately: "I have no problems with 80 percent of what was recommended. And I need to mull over the 20 percent carefully before making a final decision" (Jackson 1983f).

As a part of his consideration of the remaining 20 percent, Sweetland invited the participants to ride the areas still in question (Slide Mountain and Trout Creek) with him to attain a better understanding of the issues. They would then hold a second set of meetings to work on the remaining 20 percent.

The recommendations from the first set of meetings were divided into two groups. One group addressed the area east of the ridge and the other west of the ridge. For acreage west of the ridge, their recommendations considered the Lion Creek motorized recreation trail, the establishment of an advisory group, and the exclusion of timber sales and roads north of the stock driveway that follows the ridge. The second group of recommendations focused on where logging should be done, the use of small-size sales, and the protection of wildlife values.

Additionally, the two days of meetings produced a seventh alternative for the transportation network. It reflected their concerns for small timber sales and encouraged low-impact recreation.

The results of the two-day meeting were published in an article in the *Durango Herald*: "Shaky Wilderness Compromise Reached." The story repeated the specifics of the consensus recommendations, Sweetland's response to them, and observations by various participants. One assessment of the recommendations was:

> It attempts to satisfy the economic and ecological concerns of both tourist-oriented businesses and lumber and cattle businesses in La Plata County. (Jackson 1983f)

Danielson was pleased with the outcome. "Everyone gave a little, and everybody got a little."

> We preserved what was most important to us. We got what we really needed—preserving wildlife migration, room for non-motorized recreation—but we had to give some, too. (Jackson 1983f)

He warned the Forest Service that it would "have to carefully consider what it removes from the plan." If the Forest Service did not treat all interests equally, Danielson said, the agreement had the potential to unravel:

> These compromises aren't like items on a Chinese restaurant menu—where you can go down and pick out what you want. Sweetland's going to have to be very careful, or the compromise could be destroyed. (Jackson 1983f)

The Interim Period

As attention shifted to the trail ride and the next set of meetings, Danielson and the Vallecito Coalition put forth in the newspaper and radio interviews the message that they had made all of the concessions they were going to make. They warned Sweetland that he should keep that in mind as he considered the remaining 20 percent. If he was not careful, the entire compromise could be lost.

Steve Pargin, a cattleman, led the trail ride. Most of the local participants in the mediation went along; those who did came away from the experience with a better understanding of the geological instability around Slide Mountain as well as its wildlife sensitivity. They also came away with an increased resistance to timber cuts in that area. The Forest Service had claimed the timber was high risk and needed to be harvested because it was susceptible to insect infestations. Upon seeing the stands of trees, the participants disagreed.

During the interim period, it became public knowledge that Sweetland was being transferred to the Angeles National Forest in California for reasons unrelated to this dispute. This information added an element of uncertainty and urgency to the mediation process. The interests had no idea who would replace Sweetland and the idea of trying to resolve this conflict with someone new did not appeal to the participants. As much as the local people did not like Sweetland's ideas, they knew where he stood. They now had an additional incentive to complete the process at the next set of meetings. This incentive became more potent when it became known that the district ranger and timber specialist were also being transferred.

The October Meetings

As the various groups approached the second set of meetings, the conflict dynamic had changed: now all of the multiple-use interests opposed the Forest Service, and the Forest Service came to this round of meetings as an active participant. Sweetland felt sure that there was enough consensus among the multiple-use interests for the Forest Service to now come to the table.

The October 5 meeting began with Sweetland telling the group his problems with their recommendations from the first set of meetings. According to Wilkinson, it seemed as if they were back at square one except that the interests were unified as a group. Sweetland still wanted to timber the west side of the ridge and thought the question was merely one of how to do it.

Rather than walking out, the architects of the consensus recommendations explained why they had reached those conclusions. In that meeting, they were able to narrow the consensus gap by fine-tuning the recommendations from 20 percent to 5 percent difference. There were still two areas of disagreement, however. One involved the Lion Creek recreation trail; the other concerned timbering and road-building in the Slide Mountain–Trout Creek area. The participants decided that additional time was needed to gather information and to determine a position. The meeting adjourned with another scheduled for October 10.

In the interim, the dialogue between the multiple-use interests and the Forest Service continued. Danielson proposed new ideas to Sweetland to obtain his reaction to the proposal. By the time October 10 arrived, it was fairly easy to reach a consensus on the two remaining areas of concern. The bulk of the meeting was spent trying to determine wording that would be acceptable to everyone.

The two additional consensus recommendations consisted of increased detail on the proposed Lion Creek motorized recreation trail and the establishment of a three-person geotechnical team to study the Slide Mountain and Trout Creek areas as to the suitability for logging and roading. They also solidified the role of the advisory group in future forest management decisions by identifying specific tasks that would require group involvement. One hundred percent agreement did not exist at the end of the meeting, and Sweetland did not feel he had the time to hammer out the exact wording with the multiple-use interests' agreement. He had to issue the decision notice within two days. Sweetland drafted the decision notice and sent a copy to Luke Danielson on October 11.

Over the next two days, Danielson continued to talk with Sweetland about the wording of the decision notice. According to Sweetland, the dialogue between him and Danielson was primarily "wordsmithing." Finally, because of time pressure, Sweetland called an end to the discussion. According to Patton, he said, "This is how I'm going to write it, and if you have to sue me, sue me."

On October 12, Sweetland held a press conference to announce his final decision. Pontius, Harper, and Carrington were also at the press conference and made statements. The final decision incorporated the two recommendations arising from the October meetings. To summarize, the first recommendation addressed the Lion Creek recreational trail for two- and three-wheeled motorized vehicles. Timber sales were banned in the northern part of the area. The advisory group would be included in management decisions concerning the southern portion, which would be logged. During the discussions, the Forest Service had stated that it did not have any funds to construct the recreational and stock trail. In response, the local people stated they would attempt to raise "funds or in kind services."

The second recommendation addressed the need for further study in the Slide Mountain–Trout Creek area. It laid out the conditions for the selection of a three-member geotechnical team to study the area. Additionally, it deferred until after 1993 four proposed timber sales. It was decided that the road system to serve the still-planned timber sales would be "local intermittent roads, single lane, out-sloped with native materials and ten miles per hour" (Sweetland 1983b). The roads would be closed to the public except for firewood gathering during the summer months. These decisions gave the "green light" to the Forest Service to work on the West Prong sale, which was scheduled to be cut in 1985.

In the final decision notice, the amount of timber cut was decreased by 40 percent, accompanied by a significantly reduced road system. It also established an ongoing role for the citizen advisory group. According to Sweetland:

> I'm pleased with the decision we've reached. And I'm pleased about the continuing role of the Vallecito Advisory Group. They are in a strategically sensitive area and will be involved in other issues in the San Juan National Forest. (Jackson 1983g)

In the press conference, Sweetland also commended the process used to achieve the agreement:

> I've found the compromise process we used an excellent process. We've come a long, long way from those heated arguments at that first meeting on June 2. It's taken a lot of time on the public's part to get out and make these decisions. (Jackson 1983g)

No one representing the Vallecito Coalition and the multiple-use interests ever formally agreed to the final decision notice. After the October 10 meeting, they met to consider their options. Appealing the decision notice was still a viable option for the Vallecito Coalition since the issue of future appeals had not been part of the negotiation process. However, they decided it was not worth contesting the entire decision notice for the 2 percent difference that still remained. They decided it would be more effective to work with the Forest Service through the Advisory Group as a means to address their needs. According to Margaret Harper of the Homeowners Association:

> The plan will give us an opportunity to solve the remaining problems without the impression that the whole area is going to be invaded. (Jackson 1983g)

At the press conference, Danielson concurred and warned the local people and the Forest Service that the process needed to be ongoing:

> I think that the Forest Service has shown a great deal of sensitivity to the public's concern in this matter. But the process has got to be ongoing. The strides we've made are only as good as continuing what got us this far in the first place. (Jackson 1983g)

The ongoing monitoring of the decision's implementation has additional importance, given that both Sweetland and the district ranger, Cartwright, were transferred shortly after the decision notice was issued. (The transfer of personnel every few years is common practice in the Forest Service.) As a result, the decision notice would be implemented by people who did not share the common experience and understanding that had evolved from the mediation process.

Pine River Advisory Council (PRAC)

The advisory group essentially consisted of local individuals, representing each multiple-use interest, who were involved in the second set of meetings. When it was established, it had the following membership:

Wendall Bartholomew	Timbering
Gene Bassett	Former warden, Fish and Game
Carl Brown	Rancher and timbering

Donna Carrington	Former president of Chamber of Commerce and operator of Pine River Lodge
Peg Harper	Vallecito Homeowners Association
Steve Pargin	Rancher
Bob Pontius	Vallecito Valley Property Owners Association
Gene Roberts	Wilderness Trails
Carl Weston	Durango Audubon Society
Gary Wilkinson	Recreation vehicles

The nonlocal individuals, such as Bloemeke, now contend that they, too, are supposed to be members of PRAC. The local members and the Forest Service insist that it is only supposed to be the locals.

The confusion over this point arose over who should receive a copy of the draft EA for the West Prong timber sale. In response to the confusion, the new district ranger, Bert Kulesza, decided to send copies to everyone, including Bloemeke and Danielson, rather than continue to debate about who should receive the EA.

Due to forest supervisor Sweetland's departure and his replacement by John Kirkpatrick, along with a similar change at the district level, the Forest Service's activities on the planning area were slowed while the new personnel became acquainted with their responsibilities and surroundings. PRAC used the time to get itself organized.

One of the first tasks the advisory group faced was the establishment of its bylaws, which included how it should operate, organizational structure, and dues. Danielson served as a consultant to the advisory group during this process, which they determined should have ten to fifteen members who reflected the balance of interests represented at the mediation. They would have co-chairmen, with one individual from the consumptive-use perspective and one from the nonconsumptive perspective sharing the leadership role. The co-chairmen would alternate in chairing the council's meetings. No formal dues were established, though individual members contributed various amounts up to $20. Voluntary donations would be accepted from organizations in the area. The dues and other monies were to be used for reproduction of minutes, postage, telephone bills, and so forth. The council's assets were not to exceed $500. Within the decision notice, the entity had been called an "advisory group." As part of their organizational efforts, the group took the name Pine River Advisory Council (PRAC) to reflect its concerns for the entire area, not just Vallecito Lake.

In its initial meetings with the Forest Service, PRAC and the new Forest Service personnel determined that they would use the decision notice as written as the basis for their interactions.

In speaking with several members of PRAC, it is clear that they did not want to be perceived as an "environmental spokespiece." They wanted to be independent from the environmentalists and the Forest Service and saw their role as "contributing to solutions to all of the problems of the valley."

According to Pontius, they now "realize that nothing stays static, there will be changes." Their goal is to find what is the best balance to serve all interests. He characterized PRAC as "the balance wheel between the interest groups and the Forest Service." PRAC sees its involvement with the Forest Service decisions as an ongoing process.

The new district ranger, Bert Kulesza, sees PRAC as one portion of the public. He is willing to work with them and involve them in forest management decisions but does not see them as representing the *entire* public. He has found them to be very cooperative and willing to learn because they want to be involved. Compared with his previous experiences, PRAC is unique—as a group they represent multiple interests instead of a single interest.

Analysis

Participants in the San Juan National Forest case were able to resolve their differences in a manner that satisfied each group. The success of this case is, to a large extent, due to the foundation laid by three key characteristics of this process: the strong ties maintained between participants and their respective constituents; the efforts taken to bring expertise to bear in settling differences and in building a common understanding of the issues at stake; and, finally, in the attention given to implementation of the final agreement.

Constituent Response

Although the mediation participants had not achieved 100 percent acceptance by the Forest Service of their recommendations, they were relatively satisfied with the decision notice. Since most of them were involved as representatives of various interests, the next level to consider was whether their constituents were satisfied with the agreement. In general, the constituents *were* satisfied with the decision notice. Donna Carrington presented it to the Chamber of Commerce board. Although initially she received a few complaints about the logging, after her explanation of why that had been included, everyone seemed satisfied. She did not receive any angry phone calls from the public at large. Others, such as Margaret Harper, representative of the Homeowners Association, and Carl Weston, the Audubon Society representative, called meetings to inform their membership of the results. Their efforts were essentially met with apathy. Out of 125 in the Homeowners Association, only 20 people attended the meeting. The Audubon Society membership was glad that Carl Weston had taken part in the mediation and was going to participate in PRAC, but they only wanted to be informed if something important was happening.

Danielson, as the attorney representing the Chamber of Commerce and the Pine River ranchers, felt that the usual problems of bringing one's constituents along was not so great here compared with other situations in which he had been involved. He attributed the lack of problems to the selection of people who first had support from their own interest groups and also were respected within the community. He said that he had few problems with his clients, as the Chamber of Commerce president and Keith Graham, Jr., accompanied him to the mediation table.

Use of Expertise

Luke Danielson realized early in the conflict that they would need expert assistance to strengthen their case. At the first public meeting, they had an expert, Richard Guadagino, speak on their behalf. He was a metallurgist by profession, but was a self-taught hydrologist.

Subsequently, the Vallecito group hired Robert Curry, a geotechnical expert, to work with Danielson. Curry testified at the July public meeting called by Kogovsek. He also accompanied Danielson to Sweetland's office to discuss the possibility of resolving the conflict locally rather than through the appeals and legal process. Curry also participated in the mediation process and was present as the Vallecito group's expert. Curry brought up some of the concerns voiced on the Slide Mountain area; concerns about the feasibility of roading and logging in an area with a history of instability. He also raised questions about soil stability, sedimentation, and erosion for the entire planning area.

Curry was hired because the clients were concerned about what they called the "fog show" presented by the Forest Service. They wanted an expert on their side to point out when they were being given what they referred to as the Forest Service "party line" for roading and timbering and also to indicate what was good data that they could use to make decisions. Curry has continued to be a resource to PRAC as they have continued to work with the Forest Service. He was selected by PRAC to be their expert on the three-person geotechnical expert study team identified in the settlement to look at the Slide Mountain area. PRAC approved—with Curry's advice—the selection of the second member of the team, an expert who had to be acceptable to both parties. The person selected was a Forest Service geotechnical expert from California. The third member of the team was the local Forest Service geotechnical expert.

None of the individuals interviewed expressed any concern about Curry's presence at the mediation. They seem to have developed a trust in his ability to show them the "truth."

Implementation

Implementation of the decision notice has been occurring slowly in the year and a half since the notice was issued. The primary reason for the slow pace is the transfer of the Forest Service personnel involved in the mediation.

The draft EA for the West Prong timber sale was restarted by the new district ranger. Given the events that had preceded it, Kulesza felt it was prudent to redo the EA to ensure that it considered all of the key concerns for the area. The draft EA was finally sent out to PRAC for review in August 1984. In general, PRAC and the others who received the draft EA were satisfied. The final EA was issued in the fall of 1984 and bids were taken for the sales.

In July 1984, the three-person geotechnical team visited and evaluated the Slide Mountain area. Curry has submitted his report, but the Forest Service and PRAC are still waiting for the others to submit theirs. Once that information is in, the Forest Service will begin to consider how it will manage the area and whether and how it will road and log the area. As stated in the decision notice, the Forest Service will consult with PRAC during the decision-making process.

In August 1984, the Forest Service took a trail ride with PRAC members to look at the proposed Lion Creek motorized recreation trail. PRAC members were quite upset with what they observed. The new trail, which had been flagged with surveyor's stakes, appeared to be identical to the proposed logging road that the Forest Service had flagged the previous summer. From PRAC's perspective, the Forest Service had not put in a trail. The new proposed trail was too steep for snowmobiles and the construction costs to meet the proposed specifications seemed prohibitively expensive. The Forest Service could pay for the trail construction out of its roading budget if the trail was used for logging. Inherent in the trail proposal shown to PRAC in August was the exclusion of the use of volunteer labor, called for in the decision notice, in the trail's construction.

In light of all these problems with the proposed trail, PRAC expressed its displeasure to the Forest Service. As of January 1985, due to the response received, the Forest Service decided to postpone any actions on the motorized recreation trail.

Interviews

Wendall Bartholomew, Logger	January 17, 1985
Gene Bassett, Retired, Department of Wildlife	January 11, 1985
Steve Bloemeke, Colorado Wildlife Federation	June 18, 1984
Carl Brown, Rancher/snowmobiler	January 10, 1985
Donna Carrington, Chamber of Commerce	
president	July 20, 1984
Luke Danielson, Attorney	June 27, 1984
	October 26, 1984
	September 15, 1985
Keith Graham, Jr., Large ranch owner	July 18, 1984

Margeret Harper, Homeowners Association   July 20, 1984
Bert Kulesza, District ranger   July 18, 1984
Guenivere Marrs, Resort owner   July 18, 1984
Dennis Neil, PIO San Juan National Forest   July 17, 1984
Steve Pargin, Grazer/rancher   January 15, 1985
Leah Patton, Mediator   November 13, 1984
Mark Pearson, COSC   August 3, 1984
Bob Pontius, Property Owners Association   July 20, 1984
Gene Roberts, Resort owner   January 15, 1985
Chris Sanborn, The Wilderness Society   July 3, 1984
Paul Sweetland, Forest supervisor   June 20, 1984
                                               August 20, 1985
Orville Tice, Mediator   November 13, 1984
                                               June 21, 1984
Carl Weston, Durango Audubon Society   October 24, 1984
Gary Wilkinson, ORV shop   October 25, 1984

References

Danielson, Luke J. Letter to Paul Sweetland. May 17, 1983a.

Danielson, Luke J. Letter to Paul Sweetland. May 19, 1983b.

Jackson, Deborah. "Residents: Leave Primitive Area Alone." *Durango Herald*. May 18, 1983a.

Jackson, Deborah. "Open Space Council Says Area Suitable as Readless Corridor." *Durango Herald*. June 20, 1983b.

Jackson, Deborah. "No Compromise in Sight on Timbering Proposal." *Durango Herald*. July 31, 1983c.

Jackson, Deborah. "Disputing Interests Agree to Mediation." *Durango Herald*. September 7, 1983d.

Jackson, Deborah. "Negotiators Move Timber Talks to Durango." *Durango Herald*. September 8, 1983e.

Jackson, Deborah. "Shaky Wilderness Compromise Reached." *Durango Herald*. September 9, 1983f.

Jackson, Deborah. "Scaled-Back Timber Sales Plan Approved." *Durango Herald*. October 12, 1983g.

McGaugh, Scott. "Vallecito Residents Fight Timber, Roads Proposition." *Today Newspaper*. June 1, 1983.

Marrs, Guenivere. Carbon copy of letter to Forest Department. February 1982.

Sweetland, Paul. "Guest Editorial: Factual Comments Needed." *Durango Herald*. June 1, 1983a.

Sweetland, Paul. *Decision Notice and Finding of No Significant Impact for East Creek–Beaver Meadow–Mosca Creek Transportation Area Analysis*.

U.S.D.A. Forest Service, San Juan National Forest, Durango, Colorado. October 12, 1983b.

Tice, Orville, and Leah Patton. "Dispute Settlement: The San Juan National
Forest Vallecito Case History." (Draft) The Mediation Institute, Seattle,
WA. October 1983.

U.S.D.A. Forest Service, San Juan National Forest. *Environmental Assessment
East Creek–Beaver Meadow–Mosca Creek Transportation Planning Area
Analysis.* Durango, Colorado. January 1983.

Watson, John L., and Luke J. Danielson. "Environmental Mediation." *Natural Resource Lawyer* 15, no. 4 (1982): 687–723.

Wiggans, Tamara. "Forest Users Edge Towards Consensus." *High Country
News.* November 14, 1983.

"Ours—Vallecito Compromise." Editorial. *Durango Herald.* September 12,
1983.

CASE STUDY 2:
Fitchburg Water Supply Mediation

Sharon L. Edgar

This case study illustrates a citizen-encouraged mediation over replacement of an outdated and contaminated neighborhood water supply system in the city of Fitchburg, Wisconsin. It was only through the persistence of a neighborhood group that the process was begun and the citizens' concerns addressed. After exhausting the traditional avenues for obtaining action on the problem, the citizens pushed for the state and the developer to sit down together in hopes of devising a more rapid solution. What evolved from their efforts was a joint problem-solving process formally facilitated by a professional mediator. While not a party to the formal mediation, representatives of the neighborhood group were present during all deliberations, thereby keeping pressure on the city government and state Department of Natural Resources. The process avoided a protracted lawsuit and allowed a fine-tuned solution to be developed, one that included an addition to a neighborhood park. It also gave all parties an opportunity to realize what in fact the problem and available solutions were, thereby clearing up misconceptions about what the state was demanding and what citizens needed. The process had ongoing benefits to the citizen representatives, increasing their involvement and influence in city affairs. This case study sketches the structure and progress of this EDS process. Moreover, it illustrates the key role that citizens can play in encouraging official decision-makers to adopt a more direct and collaborative process in order to deal effectively with issues of immediate concern to the citizens. Unless otherwise noted, information and quotes in this case are from the author's personal interviews with participants.

The Situation

Fitchburg, Wisconsin, with a population of approximately thirteen thousand, is a suburb of Madison. Within Fitchburg, there is a central urban service center that is serviced by a municipal water utility. Outside the central urban area are pockets of residential development, each built by a different developer. For the most part, these residential neighborhoods do not have municipal water or sewers. Private wells built by the subdivision developer and septic tanks provide water and sanitary services. There is very little publicly supplied water in Fitchburg.

One residential area, the Greenfield neighborhood, is serviced by three private systems. Part of the neighborhood was built by Jim Gold and is serviced by the Gold well system. Another part of the neighborhood was built by Frank Kowing and his company, South Side Development. Until recently, this latter area was serviced by the original well system that Kowing built. A number of other homes in the area are serviced by separate, individual wells. The Kowing and the Gold systems, both built in the 1940s and 1950s, were meant to be temporary systems that would last for a limited number of years in the hope that a municipal water system would eventually service the neighborhood.

In the late 1970s, the Gold system needed repair, but developer Jim Gold did not respond to the problem. A group of Gold system residents came together to form the Greenfield Neighborhood Association. The group convinced other Gold residents to withhold payment, pressuring Jim Gold to repair the system. The group also pressured the Wisconsin Department of Natural Resources (DNR) to in turn pressure Gold. Jim Gold responded and corrected the problem. Tom Ruda, town board member and Gold system resident, led this fight. Ruda was the first president of the association.

Although the active residents in the Gold system dispute were also the originators of the Neighborhood Asssociation, the association was not formed as an "activist" group. Instead, the association was formed as an informational group, and it provided an organizational framework for the active residents. The association helped disseminate information and bring people together. After the Gold system dispute was resolved, the Neighborhood Association expanded so that it represented the entire Greenfield area, including both Gold and Kowing homes. Functionally, however, the two developments did not operate as a unified neighborhood. The association was the main link between the two.

The Problem

In 1978, some of the Kowing wells began to show signs of trouble. Kowing homeowners were experiencing water pressure problems and were concerned about contamination from nearby septic systems (*Wisconsin State Journal*, January 15, 1981). Concerned residents contacted the Kowing heirs, requesting that they inspect the problem, but the Kowings did not respond to their satisfaction. Finally, they went to the Bureau of Water Supply within DNR. The DNR had regulatory authority over municipal water quality and it was the agency's responsibility to ensure safe drinking water supplies for Wisconsin residents. Initially, the DNR did not respond to the complaints, but the number of complaints grew until the DNR was stimulated to take action.

In the summer of 1978, DNR Water Supply staff began routine monitoring of the six Kowing wells. The number–one well registered a seriously high bacteria count, making the water unsafe for human consumption. The shallow, temporary wells were being polluted by the neighborhood's septic systems. After continued evidence of polluted wells and increased occurrence of neighborhood complaints of poor water quality and low water pressure, the DNR decided the system was insufficient to service the area, and, therefore, the system would either have to be repaired or replaced.

The DNR had two regulatory options. The first option, their traditional response, was to petition the developer, South Side Development Company, to repair or replace the system. After evaluating the situation, the DNR decided that this option was too uncertain. It was not clear to the DNR that the developer's heirs, Donald and Lowen Kowing, would be legally responsible for replacing the system. In each homeowner's deed, Kowing contracted for a ten–year service period under the assumption that by that time, municipal water would be extended out to service the area. Since most of these ten–year contracts had expired, the DNR assumed that upon reasonable notice the Kowings could abandon the system entirely, leaving the residents with no water (Friedman 1981). The agency was not certain that the Kowings had any obligation for the system and did not want to risk the possibility of the Kowings abandoning it. The DNR felt that the Kowing family was anxious to terminate their responsibility to the development and would, therefore, not be willing to replace it. As a result, the DNR decided not to take action against the Kowings.

Instead, the DNR went to the town board. Since a small municipal system already existed, the DNR felt it was reasonable to ask the town to expand the system to service the Greenfield area. Thus, on September 5, 1978, the DNR issued an order to the town government to replace the Kowing system with a public municipal system (DNR staff had determined that repairing the existing system was unfeasible) (Friedman 1981). In the same month, the town board and the town attorney, Jack Koeppl, decided to challenge the DNR order and, if need be, go to court. The town resisted the order for several reasons:

• There was initial debate over the seriousness of the water quality problem. Although the DNR had decided there was a problem, some town board members and the town attorney were not convinced the system needed to be replaced. Testing done by the town did not indicate as serious a problem as the DNR claimed.

• The town board did not want to disrupt the land use plan by opening up new areas to unorderly development as a result of extending the municipal water system.

- The town board did not want to finance expansion of a public system. The policy was "pay as you go," meaning that water was usually supplied by private developers and paid for directly by homeowners.

- The town wanted action taken against the Kowings. Tensions existed between the town government and the Kowing family. Frank Kowing was known to have been a bad developer. The Kowing water system was poorly designed and constructed. In the past when Kowing requested permits to expand the system, the board would deny the permits because the system was poorly designed. (Kowing put the original system in before there was a strong town government to watchdog his actions.) Kowing resented the board's attitude. As a result, there was some animosity between the town government and Kowing. Town officials felt that the DNR should have taken action against Kowing and even considered taking legal action against the developer themselves (*Fitchburg Star*, November 8, 1979).

Within the neighborhood, feelings about the problem were mixed. Most solutions being proposed were neighborhood-wide, meaning that replacement costs would fall upon *all* Greenfield residents and not just Kowing homeowners. Everyone was concerned about the financial burden that replacement would impose. Some residents believed that sewers would solve the water problem, and therefore, that a new water system was not the answer (*Fitchburg Star*, November 8, 1979). Even Kowing residents experiencing water problems felt threatened by the town's claims that residents would be assessed full replacement costs. These fears kept some Kowing residents from strongly advocating that action be taken.

Yet, many Kowing residents were becoming very vocal. Some formed a separate water committee that became the vocal subgroup of the association. Association member and Kowing resident Jeanie Sieling was one of the primary representatives. Concerned residents sent angry letters to town board members and used the local paper to present their points of view. They also attended town board meetings to air their concerns. Sieling was editor of the association newsletter at the time and often included personal editorials presenting the concerns of active Kowing residents.

The association as a whole tried to remain relatively neutral, since the organization represented the entire Greenfield area. Although the association's position was that replacement of the system should occur if necessary, it did not take the strong "anti–town board" position of the active Kowing residents. With new president Bruce Braun, the association helped the vocal residents by providing information about the status of the dispute in the agency and when public hearings were being held. The newsletter kept all residents abreast of the situation and the association sponsored informational meetings. But the association did not speak out against the town board as the active Kowing residents did.

Both the active residents and the Neighborhood Association were somewhat aligned with the DNR. DNR staff had attended some of the early neighborhood meetings, trying to help residents solve the problem on their own, before the DNR decided to take actions themselves. Sieling felt that the residents were developing a strong working relationship with the DNR. Association president Bruce Braun was also a DNR employee.

Moving Toward Resolution

By the time the DNR condemned the Kowing system in August 1979, it was clear to all parties that there was indeed a water quality problem and that the current system would somehow have to be replaced. The next step was deciding how.

Informal negotiations began in July 1979 between the town board, the Kowings, the DNR, and the Public Service Commission (PSC) (Krinsky n.d.). The PSC had regulatory authority (rates and construction) over the existing municipal utility serving the central urban area of Fitchburg. The DNR asked the PSC to join the battle in hopes that the additional political clout would encourage the town board to replace the system.

A tentative agreement was reached that would establish a sanitary district (Friedman 1981). Three district commissioners would be appointed from the town and they in turn would decide on a replacement strategy. The sanitary district would be eligible for federal funding. The PSC initially agreed to the tentative stipulation, then pulled out due to some legal uncertainties about their role. When the uncertainties were resolved, the PSC changed positions again, and agreed to sign. In the meantime, however, the town board had discovered through public hearings that neighborhood and town residents did not support a sanitary district. Citizens were worried that federal funding would not be available, thus the financial burden would fall on the town. As a result, the town pulled out and the agreement dissolved.

The ball was back in the DNR's court. Concern for the water supply was building in the neighborhood. Active residents continued to communicate their concerns to the DNR, supporting the agency's efforts. They wanted a new water system with as little financial burden as was practical and saw the DNR as representing their point of view. The DNR considered going back to the original order that the town had contested, but the agency did not want to subject the residents to the delay a court case would cause. The town also threatened to assess full costs to Greenfield residents if they were to replace the system, a resolution neither the DNR nor the Neighborhood Association wanted.

The DNR had successfully used environmental mediation before, in a solid waste dispute, and the Kowing situation seemed another likely candidate for mediation. The Water Supply staff thought that a mediation process might get the town and the developer to work together toward a solution. The DNR suggested mediation and the Neighborhood Association (including the active individuals) heartily agreed. In November 1979, the DNR contacted the Wisconsin Center for Public Policy, a private, nonprofit organization located in Madison (Friedman 1981). Mediator Ed Krinsky was assigned to the case.

The DNR and the Neighborhood Association entered the mediation more or less as one party. Both had the same interests—proper and orderly replacement of the system at reasonable cost to the homeowners.

The town entered mediation because the DNR had temporarily rescinded their order in hopes of resolving the issue in mediation. The town board also accepted mediation as a way of satisfying the angry Kowing residents. The Kowings entered mediation out of desperation. The family no longer wanted any responsibility for the water system and hoped to turn over that burden to the town.

Mediation

Ed Krinsky mediated four sessions over a period of one year. The DNR (an attorney and Water Supply staff); the town attorney and town board members (including Tom Ruda); South Side Development (an attorney and the Kowings); two representatives from the Greenfield Neighborhood Association (Bruce Braun and Jeanie Sieling); and the attorney for the Public Service Commission all attended the first session on January 16, 1980. Resolution seemed uncertain (Krinsky n.d.). Whereas everyone, including the town and the developer, agreed that a new system was needed and some design criteria were discussed, the town would not accept financial responsibility. In addition, all parties agreed that more information was needed about possible new well sites.

There was considerable delay before the second meeting, partially as a result of political tension between the town and the PSC. Since the PSC was not a necessary party to the mediation, they consulted with the DNR and agreed to drop out to ease the tension. Before the second meeting, the DNR explored possible new well sites, using information provided by the development company and came back to mediation with a priority list of acceptable well sites.

The second session was held on May 13, 1980. The parties began to talk about specifics. Design and location of the new system were discussed using the DNR list. Krinsky maintained order at the meeting, preventing the town from dominating or not listening. Through discussing the DNR well site information, the town realized that they did not have to pipe municipal water out to the neighborhood. Instead, they had the option to drill wells that would service only the immediate area. The town had assumed originally that the DNR order required that the neighborhood be serviced by the municipal utility system. This realization alleviated their concern that new areas would be opened to development. Slowly, the town began to accept responsibility for replacing the system, and by the end of the second meeting, the possibility of a sponsored solution seemed likely.

South Side, anxious to see a town-sponsored system, offered the town financial assistance, but the town turned down this initial offer as inadequate. The town and the developer agreed to meet separately with Krinsky to discuss the possibility of a financial settlement further (Krinsky n.d.). At the close of the second meeting, the Neighborhood Association and the DNR were well on their way toward achieving their primary goal—getting the town to replace the system.

In the remaining two meetings, July 8 and January 13, the town attorney and the attorney for the developer continued to negotiate a financial settlement (Friedman 1981). Krinsky served an active role by pointing out where compromises were being made. As the town and the developer chiseled out an agreement, the DNR watched over the negotiations to ensure that the new system would be installed correctly and in a reasonable amount of time.

A final agreement was signed February 11, 1981. In the agreement, signed by the town, the developer, and the DNR and supported by the Neighborhood Association, the town agreed to replace the system. South Side would operate their current system while the town constructed a new one. The financial settlement included $10,000 (twice the Kowing's initial offer of $5,000) and land. Because the Kowings claimed to be "cash poor," they offered land toward the settlement. The town not only requested land for well sites, it also requested land to add on to the existing Greenfield Park. The agreement included three parcels of land, two for wells and one for the park. The DNR agreed not to force any upgrade of the existing system during the replacement period. The Neighborhood Association did not sign the agreement because they were not legally giving anything, but the association was mentioned in the signed document as supporting the agreement. The agreement has since been implemented.

Everyone involved in the negotiation was satisfied with the result to a certain degree. The DNR did not have to sue. The town board was able to push a segment of the financial burden onto the developer, although the town would have liked a larger financial settlement. And South Side was able to wash its hands entirely of the system, although at a substantial cost. Above all, the neighborhood residents got a new, safe water system.

Conclusion

The Neighborhood Association and the subgroup of active citizens were most influential as the dispute evolved. Both the association and the active residents were instrumental in keeping the problem "alive" in the eyes of the DNR and the town board.

Kowing residents introduced the problem to the DNR. Through consistent complaints and pressure, the residents motivated the state agency into "owning" the problem. Without this vocal constituency, it would seem unlikely that the DNR would have initiated routine monitoring of the wells, let alone become such a strong advocate of the neighborhood concerns. Sieling, one of the most active Kowing residents, felt that the neighborhood residents had developed a productive working relationship with the DNR prior to mediation. In addition, association president Bruce Braun was a DNR employee, which no doubt helped the association gain legitimacy in the agency's eyes. By the time the dispute reached mediation, the DNR was voicing the same concerns as the association and the active residents.

Active Kowing residents were also instrumental in getting the town board to the mediation table. Although the board and town attorney felt they could win in court and were still questioning the seriousness of the problem while going into mediation, resident pressure made a legal battle a politically unpopular option for the town. When the DNR suggested mediation, the association and the neighborhood residents supported the notion—drawing the town to the mediation table.

Within mediation, the association played more of a symbolic role than anything else. According to Tom Ruda, the association's presence spoke to the town and the DNR, telling them to work toward a resolution. The association did not need much actual power in mediation, since the DNR was working toward the same ends. Braun and Sieling represented the association in mediation. Neither was very vocal, although they participated occasionally—pushing toward resolution. Braun worked behind the scenes, using whatever political power he had to pressure participants into coming to a resolution. Sieling maintained communications with fellow Kowing residents to inform them of progress being made in mediation. Therefore, the pressure that residents put on the town board to get them to the bargaining table no doubt kept them there—the association's presence in mediation was a reminder of that pressure.

Sieling was very impressed with mediation. She appreciated being in a situation that the town could not dominate, unlike town meetings. According to Sieling, Krinsky played an active role by keeping the town board members "in line" and forcing them to listen to other perspectives. Sieling called mediation that "great equalizer." Lack of technical and legal expertise was not considered a problem because of DNR support of the citizen concerns.

Moving On

The signed agreement was implemented. Tom Ruda, first president of the association, Gold system resident and town board member during the initial stages of the dispute, lost his board seat as a result of the dispute. Many neighborhood residents felt Ruda should have responded directly to their concerns. He has since regained his position. For Jeanie Sieling, third association president, this was her first political battle. Her experience was instrumental in gaining her a position on what is now the City Council. The Neighborhood Association still exists in name but is not active.

Interviews

Bob Baumeister, Wisconsin Department of
  Natural Resources   March 15, 1984
Bruce Braun, Greenfield Neighborhood
  Association   March 8, 1984
Jack Koeppl, Attorney, City of Fitchburg   April 6, 1984
                                                         April 23, 1984
Edward Krinsky, Wisconsin Center for Public
  Policy
Marsha Penner, Attorney, Wisconsin
  Department of Natural Resources   March 14, 1984
Tom Ruda, Past President, Greenfield
  Neighborhood Association, City Council
  Member   April 4, 1984
Jeanie Sieling, Greenfield Neighborhood
  Association   March 8, 1984
J. Leroy Thilly, Attorney, South Side
  Development Corporation

References

Friedman, Jan. "Fitchburg Water Supply Case," Oberlin College, August 1981.
Krinsky, Edward. "Fitchburg Water Supply Case, Summary Notes," Wisconsin Center for Public Policy, n.d.
Final Agreement, Fitchburg mediation.
Fitchburg Star, October 19, 1978.
Fitchburg Star, November 8, 1979.
Fitchburg Star, January 1, 1981.
Wisconsin State Journal, September 21, 1978.
Wisconsin State Journal, November 30, 1978.
Wisconsin State Journal, January 17, 1980.
Wisconsin State Journal, January 8, 1981.
Wisconsin State Journal, January 15, 1981.

3 Structuring an Effective Environmental Dispute Settlement Process

Nancy J. Manring, Kristen C. Nelson, and Julia M. Wondolleck

Although two environmental dispute settlement (EDS) processes seldom look exactly alike, there is nonetheless a set of core characteristics that provides a common backbone to these processes. Susskind and Cruikshank (1987) have outlined the elements of three key phases of what they refer to as the "consensus-building process" (see table 3.1). The first phase consists of those steps necessary to set the stage for effective negotiations. Susskind and Cruikshank call this phase a "prenegotiation." Contrary to the common image portrayed in movies and late television news broadcasts in which the unshaven bargainers emerge with their settlement in hand after a grueling thirty-six hours of negotiations, steps significant to the structure and effective progress of negotiation occur even before the parties sit down together and begin formal bargaining.

Because the structure of the environmental dispute settlement process—how the agenda and ground rules are set up, how information necessary to decision-making is acquired, and who participates in this and later negotiation phases—is so critical to the actual progress of the negotiations themselves, a large portion of our case analyses has been devoted to increasing citizen effectiveness in this initial phase of any negotiation. Particular attention has been given to procedural questions that determine the makeup of a given EDS process and the ground rules governing this process as well as to the issue of representation—how to ensure that all key stakeholders are appropriately represented.

Strategies within the negotiation phase itself—inventing options for mutual gain, packaging agreements, producing a written agreement, and binding the parties to their commitments—are given less attention in this chapter because effective strategies in this phase have been thoroughly addressed in this literature in both general terms (see Fisher and Ury [1981], and Lewicki [1985]) and specifically related to environmental and other public disputes (see Carpenter and Kennedy [1988], Moore [1986], and Susskind and Cruikshank [1987]).

Susskind and Cruikshank's final phase—the postnegotiation phase—involves the implementation and monitoring of the negotiated agreement.

TABLE 3.1
The Consensus-Building Process

Prenegotiation Phase
Getting started
Representation
Drafting protocols and setting the agenda
Joint fact-finding

Negotiation Phase
Inventing options for mutual gain
Packaging agreements
Producing a written agreement
Binding the parties to their commitments
Ratification

Implementation or Postnegotiation Phase
Linking informal agreements to formal decision-making
Monitoring
Creating a context for renegotiation

Source: Lawrence Susskind and Jeffrey Cruikshank, *Breaking the Impasse: Consensual Approaches to Resolving Public Disputes* (New York: Basic Books, 1987).

Citizen groups can have a very critical and ongoing impact during this phase, and we have devoted special attention in our analysis to these issues as well.

There are a number of factors that a citizen group must strategically deal with in preparing for and participating in a negotiation process and then following through with the negotiated agreement. This chapter describes the experiences and recommendations of those citizen groups involved in the cases presented in this book, as well as the reflections of other citizen representatives in similar processes, in developing strategies for the following six stages of involvement:

1. Dealing with your interests

2. Dealing with the EDS process

3. Dealing with the issues

4. Understanding the facilitation style

5. Reaching final agreement

6. Implementing and monitoring agreements

Dealing with Your Interests

There is no surer way to fail in a negotiation than by not preparing. Hence, the first step for a citizen group to strategically think about regarding an

EDS process occurs long before he or she sits down at "the table" with the other parties. Questions to be addressed include: What are your organization's concerns and objectives with the issues to be discussed in the EDS process? What, specifically, do you hope to accomplish in this process? How will you incorporate checks and balances in communicating with your organization to ensure that the momentum of the process does not cause you to lose sight of your interests? Who are you and who are you *not* representing? How will you maintain communication with your constituency? What are your alternatives and how might you be improving these alternatives in order to strengthen your position within the EDS process?

Several individuals who have participated in EDS processes commented that the momentum established by the drive toward consensus can be disarming at times and this is particularly so if the citizen group has not done its homework and maintained effective communication with the larger organization and its constituents. David Doniger, a Natural Resources Defense Council (NRDC) attorney, represented the NRDC in the U.S. Environmental Protection Agency's negotiated rule-making process over wood stove emissions. At the Conservation Foundation's 1988 National Conference on Environmental Dispute Resolution, he emphasized that citizen groups always need to keep an eye on their objectives and priorities in order to avoid being co-opted: "You grow to like these people [and] don't want to reach an impasse." He cautions that through the EDS process, citizen group participants learn that the other parties at the table are reasonable people, individuals not too different from themselves, and, thus, in that desire to reach agreement, citizens can't let the congeniality and momentum of the process let them lose sight of why they are there to begin with. Preparation will ensure that the agreement be truly what is best for a citizen organization and that elements of the process do not cause a group to be swayed from its objectives.

Susskind and Cruikshank have written that the primary concern of citizen groups in the prenegotiation phase should be building coalitions:

> Try to organize the largest possible number of groups and individuals with shared interests. Next, figure out the smallest number of representatives you need to send to the table. Work hard on the representation issue, clarifying your BATNA and aspirations, because a united front will give you additional bargaining power. (1987, 208)

If citizens are participating as part of a coalition, it is critical to build a mutual understanding of the objectives and issues to be pursued and their relative importance. Another surefire way to undermine a group's effectiveness is to have conflicting messages coming from different members of the same coalition.

Michael Wheeler, an MIT professor affiliated with the Harvard Program on Negotiation, has studied disputes that persist despite the concerted efforts of all parties to find solutions to them. He has found that disputes often are not solved when "the coalition is built on what they oppose, not what they want" (1987). Until an organization or coalition reaches a common agreement on its goal and objectives for an EDS process, it is very difficult for a citizen group to productively participate in the process and capitalize on the opportunities presented in it.

Your organization's structure, goals and objectives, available resources, and other ongoing activities are some of the key factors to consider in determining your best strategy in an EDS process and whether or not participation even makes sense for your group. How to ensure that your organization's interests are addressed in the process, how to manage communication effectively within your group, and whether or not coalition-building makes sense for you are all issues that you must grapple with before entering, or choosing not to enter, an EDS process. These and other issues related more broadly to the citizen organization are discussed in detail in chapter 4, "Maximizing Organizational Effectiveness."

Understanding the EDS Process

EDS processes are not set in stone; seldom do two of these processes look alike. Hence, it is important for citizen participants in these processes to understand that they have some control over the structure of the process and can mold it to ensure that it fits their needs.

Clarifying Procedures and Process

One key opportunity to shape the process occurs at the outset, when ground rules governing the process are established. Citizen representatives in the cases analyzed in this book felt that a clear presentation of the preliminary rules gave them a good foundation from which to participate in the dispute settlement process. In the case studies in which no attempt was made to establish clearly all ground rules and procedures, citizen representatives floundered, and were not as effective during the negotiations because the procedures were not well structured or understood.

The early and purposeful establishment of ground rules paved the way for a successful EDS process involving the Wilderness Society, Sierra Club, Arizona Wildlife Federation, National Parks and Conservation Association, and Energy Fuels Corporation over wilderness designation, uranium mining, and protection of areas of the Arizona Strip along the northern boundary of Grand Canyon National Park (Marston 1984).

Michael Scott of the Wilderness Society commented: "It was reasonably uncomfortable—sitting across from mortal enemies. I was thinking: Why should I show our concerns with the Arizona Strip?"

Energy Fuels Corporation was undoubtedly facing the same dilemma. So, they established ground rules at the outset to ensure good-faith bargaining and to build trustworthiness. These ground rules included:

1. No talking to the press.

2. Wilderness Study Areas would be negotiated one by one. But agreements on individual areas were not final. Everything depended upon a final review of the total package.

3. If final agreement was reached, it would be supported by everyone and communication would continue through the legislative process.

All parties involved in this EDS process attributed this early discussion and agreement on the ground rules governing the process to have fostered the effective dialogue. The success in this case led to negotiations with timber companies over yet another Wilderness Study Area.

In some situations, the participants determine all of the rules; in a more formal process, a third party intervenor may lead the participants in a special effort to reach unanimous agreement on procedures to be followed by all the parties. If little attention is given to these ground rules, citizen representatives should recommend that time be set aside to clarify and gain explicit agreement on the procedures to be used in the EDS process. Citizen representatives may decide that some rules need modification, or that the timeline or some other feature of the process needs to be altered. Citizen representatives in the case studies analyzed in this book wanted the flexibility to change the process rules whenever the participants saw fit. In several cases, participant control over the process was reported to be the most important factor influencing the decision to continue despite the long-drawn-out meetings. Representatives that did not like serving on government-sponsored committees attended every meeting in the EDS process. One representative commented that "we weren't there to meet someone else's agenda."

Goal-setting. One of the first items participants should discuss are the goals of the EDS process. Goals are heavily influenced by the specific conflict situation. In some cases, reaching an agreement on a single issue will be the goal; in other cases, a specific goal cannot be determined until the participants talk for a while. Whether the goals are set in the first meeting or in later meetings, they serve as a focus that will guide the remainder of the EDS process.

Procedures for Reaching Agreement. What procedure will be used to reach a final decision should be clarified before the group begins to discuss the substance of the issues. In the Wisconsin groundwater case, the participants developed the agreement through a "consensus" process, but made the final decision by majority vote. In this case, the process occurred within a legislative committee in which voting is the accepted means of decision-making. In other case studies, the participants used consensus decision-making; everyone had to agree to the document before it was considered final. In three of these cases, there was a full consensus. In two other cases,

Sand Lakes and San Juan, the government agency with legal authority over the issue took control over a set of partly finalized recommendations before a complete consensus had been reached. In both cases, the citizen participants decided that 90 percent consensus on the issues was acceptable and switched to a lobbying strategy to influence the agency's decision on the remaining points.

Establishing Timelines.   A timeline or schedule helps groups in an EDS process to pace the workload. It also serves as a contract that deters a party from prematurely deciding enough work has been done. One reason the agencies in the Sand Lakes and San Juan cases were able to decide that "enough agreement had been achieved" was that the participants had not committed themselves to a process timeline. Setting a timeline gives the participants a framework in which to prepare and plan and is particularly important for citizen groups with limited resources. All participants should have a clear understanding of the timeline, including when the group plans to meet and the tasks for each meeting. In some instances, the projected length of the process and number of meetings may be difficult to determine. The groups may be participating in several exploratory meetings or strategizing for an evolving negotiation process. If the process has no predetermined end time, the participants can establish "blocks" of agreed interaction; at the end of each such block of activity the parties can reassess their interests and establish the next "block," or abandon the process. An EDS process can range anywhere from one month to two years, and entail a few full group meetings or require numerous subcommittee meetings combined with full group meetings (see table 3.2).

Dealing with the Media.   Participants also should decide how to deal with media representatives. When the participants need privacy to comfortably explore sensitive issues, it may be undesirable to allow reporters in the meetings. In the San Juan case, the group worked out an acceptable procedure with the local press that satisfied everyone. The meetings were closed to the press, but the reporters could interview the participants after each session. In the Common Ground process, the participants decided that the staff members to the EDS process would make all of the press statements between the confidential meetings. When the final agreements were reached, all participating parties accepted interviews to publicize the agreement.

Using Committees and Working Groups.   To negotiate several issues with numerous parties requires use of multiple small group arrangements. In our cases, subcommittees and working groups effectively produced the first draft of negotiating documents. These subgroups did the background work, initial authoring, and wordsmithing that is too tedious and cumbersome for a full committee. Subgroups should be a microcosm of the large process with balanced representation from the different parties.

TABLE 3.2

Case Study	Process Length (from initial meeting to the final document)	Number and Type of Meetings
Site Specific		
Fitchburg mediation	One year	Four full group meetings: (two to three hours).
Pig's Eye attempted mediation	One month	Four full group meetings: (two and a half hours).
San Juan mediation	Eight weeks	Four full group meetings: (two full-day sessions and two half-day sessions).
Sand Lakes negotiations	Two years	Several full group discussions. Many small group negotiations.
Policy Level		
Wisconsin groundwater legislative committee	Fourteen months	Nine full group meetings. Thirty-two subgroup meetings.
Negotiated investment strategy	One year	Six to eight full group meetings: numerous subgroup meetings.
Common Ground collaborative problem-solving	Two years	Twelve full group meetings (all day): numerous subcommittee meetings.

In the Common Ground case, the whole task force identified issues and worked on a definition of the problem; when negotiations became unwieldy, the facilitator suggested working groups. In the first year, the task force chose to work as a whole because trust levels were low among the parties and everyone wanted to be part of the writing process. During the second year, however, they used subgroups to work on the remaining two issues: wetlands conservation and farmland preservation. The subgroups met between meetings to produce draft agreements to be considered by the whole task force. The participants were positive about this approach but found that because the subgroups represented the same diversity of interests as the larger task force, there was still substantial conflict. The subgroups merely reduced the number of people debating, not the number of differences. In the larger task force, the facilitator guided the dialogue and kept participants focused on the issues; in the subgroups, there were no facilitators. One subgroup had a significant increase in conflict—to the point of nearly abandoning work on their issue. Thus, citizens using subgroups for negotiations may wish to start with a facilitator, or call one in if the conflicting parties develop an adversarial relationship that is counterproductive to producing a draft agreement.

The NIS process used working groups from the outset. A three-member committee, with representation from the government, business, and the citizen teams, was selected for each issue. Graduate students working under the mediator were assigned to facilitate each of the working group sessions and to assist the representatives in forming a draft agreement. Lawrence Susskind, the mediator in this case, recommends this format for its efficiency, and its contribution to a strong agreement that is an integrated piece rather than a collage of loosely tied amendments.

The San Juan case also involved subgrouping. Near the end of the second day of negotiations, the full group realized that more work needed to be done if they were going to reach agreement. To make the process more manageable, they selected a group half the size of the original to continue the process. Every representative felt comfortable delegating the remaining negotiations to the smaller group.

It is important to make a clear distinction between the first draft document produced by subcommittees and an acceptable final agreement. In every case where a subgroup wrote a draft or negotiated an agreement, the whole group had the final word, revising the agreement until it was acceptable to all representatives. It appears that citizen representatives can best serve constituent interests by participating in the most appropriate working group. However, the rules of the EDS process need to clearly state that every representative has the right and responsibility to disagree with a document if it does not acceptably represent their constituents' interests.

In some instances, citizen representatives felt tremendous pressure to go along with the draft document because a subgroup had put so much work into producing it. In the Wisconsin groundwater legislative committee, a citizen representative who had not participated in the major working group felt "blackmailed" into accepting the document. The advocates of the document emphasized the long hours of negotiation and the delicate balance of interests contained in it. They admonished other participants not to upset the "finely balanced" agreement by calling for changes when the full group was in session. As any EDS process progresses, there will be pressure to go along with an agreement, but there should also be room to say, "No— we need some changes." Citizen group participants must ensure that this latitude exists and feel confident using it. After all, no negotiation is successful if *your* interests are not addressed.

Representatives' Roles. In a joint problem-solving process, the representatives often are individuals speaking for an interest area (environmental, business, government) through particular formal organizations. This type of representation can be difficult when the lines of communication from "representatives" to constituents are nonexistent or vague, or where the assumption is that the EDS "consensus" will be transferred to a larger community. In the NIS case, the citizen team members were very unclear as to whose interests they should represent and how they would link up with other community members.

In a policy dialogue, the conventional wisdom emphasizes that the representatives are not speaking directly for a particular organization but are present as "influential members of organized interests." For example, Common Ground representatives worked on policy-level issues for two years. From the beginning, it was made clear that all agreements would be signed by individuals speaking in an organization's interest but not as official representatives of those organizations.

Finally, it is assumed that the representatives in an EDS process are accountable to their sponsoring groups. As a formal signer for an organization, the representative is expected to check all agreements with the leadership and membership of his or her organization because the agreement binds that organization. In the Pig's Eye case, the representatives spoke for an organized constituency and their position encompassed the group's interests.

Not all of the cases fit comfortably into these categories. For example, in the Fitchburg mediation, the citizens were not a formal party in the process. The negotiation was held between those parties responsible for replacing the new water system, not those parties affected by the water quality problems. In this instance, the citizen interests were represented by the state Department of Natural Resources (DNR). The citizens had no control over the DNR's decision-making, but they observed the negotiation sessions in a "watchdog fashion." Most likely, future EDS processes also will have a variety of representation patterns.

Once representation is clear, the participants need to understand the different forms and limits of each representative's decision-making authority. Some representatives will be free to speak openly for their organizations, whereas others may have to check with the organization first. Often a group's decision-making process influences the representatives' freedom to act with delegated authority. For example, the Common Ground process had fourteen representatives with different decision-making authority. One representative was the organization's president. He felt confident speaking to 70 percent of the issues and checked with his board of directors for the remainder. Another representative was given full authority to decide any issue. The organizational decision-making process for two other representatives required a full review of every agreement by the staff in one group and the membership in the other group. Identifying these variances in decision-making authority allowed the Common Ground process to develop realistic timelines and expectations, and allowed its representatives to understand each other's organizational constraints, which in turn affected the EDS process.

The Need for All Stakeholders.   For an EDS process to be effective, all major stakeholders must be represented. If a major interest is absent from the process, it is possible that they will block or demand changes in any agreement reached. Hence, should parties to a dispute decide to pursue an EDS process, they must decide who should be invited to participate. If other parties have already made these decisions, the invited citizen groups may want to review the list of participants and suggest the inclusion of any missing parties.

In one of the cases analyzed in this book, the Sand Lakes citizens and the involved state agency did not do a thorough assessment of all the possible stakeholders; one county with authority over land contained in the negotiated settlement was not involved in the EDS process. During implementation of the agreement, this county was unwilling to abide by the negotiated agreement's interpretation of regulations limiting motorized boats. It took six months of separate negotiations with this county (and the involved state agency still had to override local authority) to implement parts of the agreement. In retrospect, the citizens believed the difference of interpretation could have been dealt with in the EDS process, thereby preventing the secondary negotiations that slowed down implementation and increased animosity between the local officials and the state agency.

Stakeholders May Decline.   Not all parties may be willing to participate in an EDS process. When one or more stakeholders decline participation, the participating parties must decide if the process can continue without the particular group present. In the Common Ground case, two agricultural groups chose not to participate for the first year, primarily because of overcommitted calendars. The convenors decided there was sufficient representation of these interests (seven agricultural groups) and began the process. During the two-year process, the Common Ground Task Force convenors were able to keep the two absent groups informed of the EDS issues and progress, thereby preventing any unnecessary surprises for the potential allies.

In negotiations over a site-specific dispute, it seems to be more critical that all stakeholders participate, but there can be creative responses to a refused invitation. In the Sand Lakes case, the industry representative declined an invitation from the citizens to discuss their differences. He preferred to let the agency resolve the dispute through traditional decision-making channels. The citizen organizers decided that negotiating with the agency alone was an acceptable second best. An agency staff member effectively bridged the gap by working informally with the industry representative while interacting directly with the citizen representatives through the EDS process.

In summary, if a key representative is not going to participate, citizen strategists can (1) ensure that the nonparticipant's interests will be represented by other participants, (2) develop an acceptable alternative to face-to-face negotiations, or (3) discontinue the EDS process and pursue other options. Another possibility is to develop strategies to bring the absent party to "the table."

Persuading Reluctant Participants.   Willing participation is essential for an effective EDS process but often representatives must be informed, cajoled, or pressured before choosing to participate. In the Common Ground case, the convenors wanted the leadership of several organizations to participate in the joint problem-solving process. They appealed to the leaders' egos by emphasizing the need for their involvement in important policy formation that would change the state agenda. The convenors also used their own network to gain full participation from other groups. One organizer described it as an exchange: "If they participate in our program, we will participate in theirs at some future date."

In highly adversarial situations, incentives or sanctions may develop to create a political context suitable for mediation. Many strategies can be used to encourage participation in an EDS process. If negotiations cannot occur without a certain party (for example, the agency with authority over a controversial decision), political incentives can be brought to bear on that party's decision. In the San Juan mediation, local citizens disagreed vehemently with the U.S.D.A. Forest Service plan. They stirred up substantial public controversy on the local, state, and regional levels; bad publicity, intergovernmental strife, and a threatened lawsuit were all present. There also were other incentives for the agency personnel to appear open to this level of public participation. Congressional representatives had sent letters of inquiry, suggesting a dialogue between the conflicting interests. The political context was created for negotiations; the agency agreed to participate, first as an observer, and later as a full participant.

Selecting and Bounding the Issues

In an EDS process, participants need to recognize the complex nature of environmental issues, and make the process as manageable as possible by selecting and bounding the issues to be discussed. If the conflict is site-specific, there may be multiple problems and particular issues will have to be selected. If it is a policy-level negotiation, the group may have to select issues from a broad public policy debate.

In the Common Ground policy dialogue, the participants worked on both agricultural and environmental issues. The representatives developed a list of issue possibilities by "brainstorming" numerous options. Everyone freely suggested ideas; the group consolidated similar ideas and eliminated those that went beyond the scope of an Illinois issue. In the NIS case, each team separately developed a list of important topics that, when combined, produced four areas of primary concern: (1) community development; (2) education; (3) crime, safety, policy; and (4) pride, image, beauty. A fifth issue, human services, later emerged as a combination of several concerns.

After selecting issues, most groups attempted to define the boundaries of the issue or the limitations placed on the negotiable subjects. Many formats are possible for bounding the issues. The parties appeared to be most effective when they bounded the issues according to (1) the parties' authority over the outcome, (2) what the parties considered to be negotiable, and (3) what problem-solving was possible given available time and information.

Many participants found that it was useful to clarify what governmental authority had responsibility for the potential issues to be worked on in the EDS process. Identifying the existing decision-making authority can help reveal issues that go beyond the feasible realm of an EDS process. The appropriate scope of issues for a particular EDS process is evaluated differently, depending upon whether or not the decision-making authority is engaged in the process and what the involved parties believe they can collectively persuade the established decision-making authority to do as a result of the EDS effort. For example, the San Juan mediators stated from the outset that "wilderness" status for the area in dispute was nonnegotiable because only Congress could determine wilderness status. Issues in the Pig's Eye mediation were limited to those falling within the St. Paul city boundaries.

The issue may also be bounded by the parties themselves. If there is any topic that is absolutely nonnegotiable, it needs to be identified at the outset. The facilitator may choose not to push parties to decide what is nonnegotiable during the first session in order to avoid hardened positions. In preparing for the process, however, interviews with each party may reveal some nonnegotiable issues that all parties agree should not be on the agenda.

The final consideration in bounding the issue may be a projection as to what is "doable" given limited time and information. The Common Ground participants decided to start with one issue the first year, but felt confident working on two issues the second year. Since the parties were all Illinois interest groups, they bounded the issues by addressing only Illinois state-level concerns that needed agricultural and environmental cooperation.

Prioritizing Issues. The place an issue has on the agenda can be very important to citizen organizations. Citizen organizers commented that it is wise to place critical issues at the beginning of the agenda. No matter how well planned, the time ran out in every process; the final agenda items were rushed or in some cases dropped due to lack of time. Citizen participants whose principal concerns were tied up in the last issues to be discussed were unhappy with the final agreements, and questioned using the process for future conflicts. Strategically, these participants had very few options in the last moments of the process. Unless the remaining issue was critical to their acceptance of the rest of the agreement, representatives found themselves pressured to accept what had been done and pursue action on their other issues of concern in some other forum. In most cases, this did not critically compromise the citizens' interests, but it did mean that they spent long hours working on other issues while some of their principal concerns were not being addressed in the EDS process.

Understanding the Facilitation Style

The citizen representatives in our case studies found the facilitator's role and performance pivotal to the success of the EDS process. Most participants interviewed during the research felt that the facilitator provided a central source of leadership and resources for the process, educating those who were unfamiliar with the procedures and easing the dispute settlement process in an acceptable manner.

In order to fulfill these tasks, the facilitator must be trusted by all of the representatives. Citizens used words such as "competent," "unbiased and skilled," or "excellent at holding people together" to describe their high confidence in those individuals facilitating the EDS processes studied. This level of confidence is established as the representatives evaluate the facilitator's process style and personal judgments and find them acceptable or unacceptable, given the values and norms of the citizen organizations. Each citizen leader involved in EDS processes must decide on the particular values most important to his or her respective group and use them to assess potential facilitators of a specific EDS process.

Facilitation can be done by an outside third party or, in some instances, by a participant in the EDS process. A third party intervenor is often asked by the representatives to assist them in using an EDS process to reach a mutually acceptable agreement. The labels "mediator" and "facilitator" are used interchangeably here and in the literature to describe an individual who employs group process skills to assist in collaborative problem-solving among disputants.

Another option for facilitation is to use a participant facilitator—someone from within one of the parties. A participant functioned as facilitator in the Sand Lakes and Wisconsin groundwater cases. However, the data indicate that participant facilitators were helped in ways they valued when they had the assistance of an outside third party during the process. In the cases with participant facilitators, third party consultants were not direct participants in the process, but rather served as process or strategy consultants for the facilitator or citizens. A brief description of each facilitation style with examples from the cases follows.

Mediators do not dictate solutions, but they may suggest solutions or use their facilitation role to move the parties toward a specific solution. The mediator's role in settling environmental disputes, which originated in collective bargaining practices, varies depending on the individual's values and professional norms; some mediators actively participate in forming the agreement, whereas others prefer to place more stress on process facilitation, leaving all substantive negotiation to the participants. In the Fitchburg case, Dr. Edward Krinsky, of the Wisconsin Center for Public Policy, served as mediator. He worked on both the issue substance and process with all the parties.

The NIS case documents the work of a mediation staff, led by the principal mediator, Dr. Lawrence Susskind, then executive director of the Harvard Program on Negotiation. As an active mediator, Susskind used a form of interest-based negotiation from the beginning. He and his mediation staff assisted the participants on both process and substantive issues in arriving at a negotiated policy strategy for guiding future planning and investment decisions in the city of Malden, Massachusetts.

The San Juan case was mediated by Orville Tice and Leah Patton of the Mediation Institute in Seattle, Washington. Tice and Patton worked as active mediators during the first day of negotiation, but left the substantive issues to the participants on the second day once the group was comfortable with the process. In the final suggestions, they merely noted technical omissions or made process suggestions when the group requested their assistance.

In the Common Ground case, a third party facilitator, Philip Marcus, introduced and helped the involved parties use group problem-solving techniques. This intervention formalized a process of working together that previously had been informally functioning for some of these groups and was nonexistent for others.

As mentioned, some third party intervenors do not make a distinction between mediators and facilitators, using the terms interchangeably. Instead, they identify differences between *content* and *process* intervenors; between individuals who actively influence the substance of the discussion and those who guide only the process, not the content of interaction. However, the distinction between mediators and facilitators becomes important when participant facilitation is being considered. Participants would never assume the mediator role, which by definition is a nonpartisan individual who assists in disputes.

The benefit of participant facilitation is that it ensures that the parties control the process design and implementation. It also can empower participants by increasing their facilitation skills. The drawbacks of participant facilitation center on the possible difficulties with stakeholders' trust in the facilitator and the potential lack of facilitator experience and skill. If the facilitator is not competent in leading a group through an EDS process, conflict could escalate or the process break down. The stakeholders also may question the degree of detachment and fairness by a facilitator who has a stake in the outcome. If such questioning exists, it could lower the participants' trust and willingness to participate.

In the Wisconsin groundwater and the Pig's Eye cases, problems arose that involved the participant facilitators. Representative Mary Lou Munts chaired the Wisconsin groundwater legislative committee during the entire process. As a Wisconsin state representative, Munts had a constituency to represent and legislative allies with whom she was comfortable working. The environmental representative in this process was not confident that Representative Munts could impartially facilitate the groundwater protection dispute; a third party intervenor would have been more acceptable to him.

In the Pig's Eye attempted mediation, another government official facilitated the process with advice from an outside consultant. The facilitation was complicated by the fact that the adviser had a dual role. While she advised on the process dynamics and occasionally ran the meetings, she also participated in substantive discussions of the issues. As an employee of the mayor's office, her comments were perceived as official statements, despite the fact that she did not participate as the mayor's representative. This dual role was confusing for all the representatives and became problematic as the mediation came to a stalemate. The business representatives did not trust the facilitator or the intent of the EDS process, and the citizen representatives became disillusioned with the adviser's role.

A successful case of participant facilitation occurred in the Sand Lakes issue-based negotiations with Peta Williams, who facilitated the citizen alliance meetings and jointly facilitated the negotiation sessions between the citizens and the Department of Natural Resources (DNR). The DNR personnel and citizen representatives commented that they trusted Peta Williams to do a conscientious facilitating job. Some representatives mentioned that there could be problems with participant facilitators if they did not recognize the difference between their own interests and the group's interests. However, the participants commended Williams for stating her opinions and still ensuring that everyone's point of view be heard. Some representatives credited Williams for holding the different citizen and environmental groups together in one alliance.

Process consultants serve as advisers to participant facilitators by assisting them in the process design and critique during problem-solving negotiations. The consultant is often an experienced mediator/facilitator who serves in a limited advisory capacity and leaves control of the process to the participants. The Sand Lakes facilitator, Peta Williams, was advised by Dr. Patricia Bidol, adjunct professor in the School of Natural Resources at the University of Michigan. Through phone calls and periodic meetings with Peta Williams, Dr. Bidol reviewed the evolving negotiation process and assisted in troubleshooting any problems that arose.

The strategy consultant is the final third party role exemplified in the case study data. The strategy consultant serves as a behind-the-scenes coach for the citizen leaders in an EDS process. The consultant observes the citizen leaders during the process and works to empower the citizens with effective "strategies and techniques of team development and dispute management."

The citizens maintain control over decision-making and should be able to accept or reject the strategist's advice.

An example of the strategy consultant's role is Bonnie Anderson's work with the Sand Lakes citizen alliance. Anderson, a University of Michigan School of Natural Resources graduate student working with Dr. Bidol, assisted the citizen alliance during the final months of the negotiation process. By attending all of the organizational meetings and the negotiation sessions, she was able to provide the citizen leaders with feedback and advice about options available for the next meetings.

Reaching Final Agreement

Eventually, the EDS process reaches a point at which the participants either decide to abandon the process or find themselves coming close to an agreement. Citizen participants may consider leaving the process if the agreement does not protect their interests. Depending on the circumstances, this choice can have substantial costs in reduced public support and lost political legitimacy with the other stakeholders; regardless, it may be a necessary action to protect the integrity of the group's interests. Another option is to agree to the parts of an agreement that are acceptable and publicly reject the sections that are not. One environmental representative in the Wisconsin groundwater case voted against the proposed groundwater bill because he felt it was "too weak to support." He publicly identified the sections that needed improvement and lobbied for changes during the legislative sessions in which the results of the EDS process were acted upon. It appears that when this approach is done openly, with a minimum of personal slander, the citizen organization can maintain its political legitimacy and still work for the best interests of its constituents. Without question, there are risks to this strategy as well. It could potentially tarnish the future efforts of the citizen group to participate in collaborative problem-solving efforts or cause those aspects of the agreement that the citizen group strongly supported to come under attack also by others.

A final agreement in an EDS process can take many forms, depending on who is signing the agreement, how it is linked back to an established decision-making process, and whether there is majority or unanimous support for the agreement. Though these factors varied among the cases studied, all groups felt a final written text of the agreement was essential to prevent misunderstandings, and to ensure accountability and commitment by all the stakeholders. Having a written text minimized differences in interpretation that could result after complex negotiations, and also provided a document for future reference to assist all parties in remembering and abiding by the agreement.

Who signs the agreement and the agreement's format often depend on its anticipated use and the political context. The written document may be a legal contract between official organizations, as in the Fitchburg case, when the town, the developer, and the Wisconsin Department of Natural Resources signed the agreement. The citizen group did not sign the final agreement because they had no legal or financial responsibilities for replacing the neighborhood water system.

The document may be a recommendation signed by individuals speaking on behalf of several organizations' interests, as the Common Ground and Sand Lakes case studies illustrate. These representatives decided the political and bureaucratic difficulties of having each organization ratify the agreement outweighed the advantages of official organizational signatures.

The last type of final agreement exemplified in the case studies were documents with individual signers who spoke for a specific interest area (farmers, citizens, government agencies, tourist businesses, lumber companies). In the San Juan, NIS, and Wisconsin groundwater cases, the signers committed themselves to supporting the specific recommendations incorporated in the document by lobbying other individuals, organizations, and government bodies in support of the recommendations.

It appears that the format of the final document is strongly influenced by whether the conflict is site-specific or policy-level, and by how the recommendations will be communicated to and included in already established decision-making processes. The final agreements in the seven case studies included a proposed legislative bill, a recommended text for a management plan, recommendations to a specific decision-maker, and policy recommendations to the appropriate agencies. The agreements were different because each was designed to connect back into the pertinent established decision-making process. For example, the Sand Lakes citizen alliance commented on the DNR draft management plan by writing their own version. Negotiations in this case became a process of combining the two proposed plans into one recommended text that went to the Michigan Natural Resource Commission for approval. In the NIS process, the participants agreed on six issue statements that included 150 recommendations for improving life in Malden. These recommendations were sent to the appropriate city agencies for their action.

The last consideration for citizen strategists is whether the final agreement will have unanimous or majority support by the participants. Some agreements are only signed if there is total agreement among the participants. In the NIS and Common Ground cases, all decisions were made by group consensus; disagreement over a statement meant that it was either revised or dropped from the final document. However, full consensus decision-making was only one of the mechanisms used in the case studies. Representatives may work in a "consensus" process and then use a majority vote to determine the final document. In the Wisconsin groundwater case, the proposed legislation that had been developed through a consensus process subsequently was voted on by the full legislature. Voting implies that there can be a dissenting voice that does not find the agreement acceptable. If one

EDS goal is to reach a mutually acceptable agreement, the participants are not advised to make decisions by voting; to leave some interests dissatisfied with the process results could undermine the original intent of the process and return the dispute to the same point at which it began. It could also prove detrimental to citizen interests when their voice in the process is outweighed by other conflicting voices.

In addition to voting or consensus, there is still another scenario for settling the dispute. In the final meetings of some negotiations, the group did not necessarily reach 100 percent agreement. In several cases, where the disputed issues involved regulations or management plans, the agency with authority decided that sufficient agreement was reached. Taking the EDS process discussion as substantial advice, agency personnel developed a so-lution for the remaining problems in which representatives could not come to agreement. Citizen leaders and representatives can respond to this situ-ation in several ways. They may decide that the citizens have had most of their issues and interests adequately addressed, and change their strategy to informal lobbying for the remaining issues. For example, when the Michigan DNR said, "Enough, we're going to recommend this revision [of the ne-gotiated management plan] to the Natural Resources Commission," the Sand Lakes citizens alliance had to make a strategic decision: whether to support or attempt to block the plan. After several heated alliance meetings they decided to support the proposed plan at the NRC public hearings. The alliance used the remaining month before the NRC hearing to informally lobby for the further changes. In the hall before the NRC hearing, Peta Williams was still suggesting language changes that the DNR representative incorporated in the final document.

Citizen strategists also may decide that an agency took unilateral control of the recommendations from the EDS process before important citizen concerns were addressed. In this situation, the involved citizen organizations may want to use a public relations campaign—press, powerful allies, etc.— to bring the agency back to the EDS process. In the San Juan case, the citizens felt that after a period of successful problem-solving and negotiation, escalating the conflict was not appropriate; they did manage, however, to pressure the agency personnel into another meeting. At this meeting, they narrowed the area of disagreement by fine-tuning the recommendations from a 20 percent to a 5 percent area of disagreement.

Implementing and Monitoring Agreements

Data from the seven case studies indicate that monitoring was often neglected by citizen organizations in a rush to end the process, or because the citizens' resources were overtaxed and representatives felt "burned out." To avoid these problems, it is suggested that representatives plan for implementation of the agreement, including the possibility of their monitoring it, before the last few meetings, and possibly include implementation and monitoring stipulations in the final text of the agreement. Citizen monitoring can increase the likelihood that implementation will reflect the spirit of the final agreement as well as keep the citizen group involved with the issues.

To determine the most appropriate monitoring strategy, citizen leaders and representatives need first to analyze the implementation plans: the who, how, and when of implementation (assuming the final agreement addressed the what and why). Who is implementing the recommendations is critical for several reasons. By knowing which agency or other organization has legal authority over the recommendations, citizen organizations can assess the implementing organization's potential resistance to the recommendations and other difficulties and assess their level of confidence in the organization and its commitment and ability to implement the agreement. To reduce resistance, citizens may choose to keep key personnel informed throughout the process or include the implementing organization as one of the participants in the EDS process. Including the "implementers" in the evolution of reasoning behind each recommendation can provide clarity in the often confusing transitions from recommendations, to decisions, and, finally, to implementation. If there is no resistance and there are high levels of confidence in implementation capabilities, the need for monitoring may be minimal. For example, Fitchburg citizens trusted the state DNR, given their positive collaborative relationship, to ensure implementation of the new water supply system; they did not develop a formal monitoring plan.

Implementation can be complicated by a change in agency personnel. New agency staff may be unfamiliar with the intricate trade-offs that contributed to a mutually acceptable agreement, or may choose to alter implementation to meet their interests. Citizen monitoring can help preclude agency changes in implementation as citizens educate new personnel about the agreement's intent. In the San Juan case, the forest supervisor and the district ranger were both transferred shortly after the San Juan decision notice was issued. As a result, the citizen monitoring plan became very important for effective implementation.

How the agreement is carried out is another concern: how might thorough and timely implementation be ensured? In the Common Ground case, citizen representatives determined which agency to lobby. They kept these agency personnel abreast of all developments in the EDS process and, once an agreement was reached, lobbied them to accept the recommendations. In this situation, informal communication, followed by lobbying, was the major implementation strategy because government officials were not included in the EDS process itself.

When the recommendation will be carried out also is an important concern for citizen organizations, particularly if the problems involved ongoing environmental degradation or some immediate crisis. Our cases suggest that implementation usually takes longer than initially anticipated. Most participants attributed these delays to slow bureaucratic processes, but felt that monitoring prevented implementation from bogging down entirely.

Once citizens understand the who, how, and when of implementation, they can better design effective monitoring plans. There are a variety of methods for monitoring agreements. Serving as the "watchdog" can be by formal or informal means: observing and lobbying, delegating oversight to a legal authority, hiring a third party to monitor, or establishing a citizen task force for monitoring. If the citizen organization has limited resources, their active constituency is small, or the leadership needs to focus on another project, informal lobbying may be the best strategy.

For example, the citizen organizations participating in the Sand Lakes negotiations did not possess the resources to keep their coalition together for the long term; they also had no intention of continuing beyond the EDS process. Thus, Peta Williams did not negotiate for a formal monitoring process. Some participants felt this failure to incorporate monitoring could have been problematic. However, most of the participants lived near the Quiet Area and occasionally spent time in the Area. They felt that their close proximity along with their direct observation of implementation resulted in an adequate though informal monitoring of the negotiated management plan. In addition, Jerry Theide of the Michigan Department of Natural Resources was concerned that the citizens remain informed about the ongoing implementation; he sent at least one progress report to Peta Williams for distribution to the alliance members. In retrospect, the citizen organizers felt this strategy worked well for Sand Lakes monitoring because the group trusted Theide with the oversight responsibilities, and representatives could informally observe the progress of the DNR's implementation. However, this arrangement gave them no formal recourse should the results deviate from the final agreement.

Informal monitoring by citizens combined with formalized agency monitoring is another option. For example, the Fitchburg citizens were well aware of the progress of the installation of the water supply system, but the legal contract delegated oversight responsibility to the Wisconsin Department of Natural Resources. The neighborhood committee was pleased to have the DNR legally monitoring the developer's financial contribution and the city's installation of the water system. Though the EDS process improved communication between all parties, the citizens felt informal monitoring was a prudent strategy.

There are several ways in which citizen groups might formalize the monitoring process. Two possibilities illustrated in our case studies are (1) using an implementation and monitoring plan designed by outside consultants, or (2) using a citizen task force in an evolving monitoring process.

At the end of the NIS process, the participants asked the NIS staff to prepare an implementation and monitoring plan with specific action proposals and implementation timelines for each recommendation. Although it was not part of the final agreement, Dr. Susskind felt this plan, combined with citizen lobbying, would pressure "public officials and others responsible for implementation to live up to their commitments." At the six-month review meeting, Susskind agreed to hire staff to evaluate the progress of implementation. Susskind's persistent review and lobbying kept the final recommendations on the "public agenda." He also went to great efforts to meet with the various governing bodies to ensure the program's long-run success under newly elected officials. The NIS staff implementation plan was probably the best option for the Malden citizens. As individual representatives with no organizational resources and little power, carrying out an effective monitoring strategy would have been quite difficult.

If citizen groups want to build their organization, however, abdicating monitoring responsibility to an outside consultant may be counterproductive. In this situation, a citizen task force may be a better option for evaluating implementation and opening a new path for participation in environmental decision-making. For example, citizens in the San Juan case created the Pine River Advisory Council (PRAC), a multiple-use interest group, to monitor Forest Service implementation of the agreed-upon recommendations. PRAC was established as a formal organization with bylaws, shared leadership, membership from the EDS representatives, and a budget supported by membership dues. The new district ranger was willing to work with PRAC as a unique group representing multiple interests; however, he does not view the group as the only spokesperson for the public. PRAC plans to continue its advisory role in future Forest Service decisions. Citizen strategists may not need to create a new organization, as the San Juan citizens did, but instead could use existing organizations to support a monitoring task force. A citizen-controlled task force could continue citizen involvement in environmental decision-making and build a power base for future projects.

Conclusion

Regardless of the negotiating sophistication of an individual or group, a citizen representative can have a significant impact if he or she pays attention to the critical components comprising an environmental dispute settlement process—representation, agenda-setting, ground rules, process structure, data gathering, and how final agreements will be reached—and ensures that these are satisfactory at the outset, before formal bargaining even occurs. Similarly, citizens can increase their influence and abilities in formal negotiations if they strategically prepare, prepare, and prepare some more before the negotiations begin.

It is important to clarify a group's interests and goals and objectives for the negotiation and the relative priority of each *before* sitting down at the table. It is critical to always be aware of the group's alternatives both at the table as well as away from the table and, moreover, to be developing these alternatives in order to increase power and influence within the negotiations.

Along the same lines, it is important during preparation to give consideration to the needs and the incentives facing the other parties at the table. How might your own needs mesh, complement, or conflict with theirs? How might you develop and then present an option in a way that highlights the benefits to the other participants, not only to your own group? What might some fallback strategies and options be? How are you going to maintain communication with those you represent? These are all issues that must be thought out in detail *before* the negotiations even begin.

While citizen groups should be encouraged to build their portfolio of negotiation strategies, to a large extent this comes from "learning by doing," and the experience of numerous negotiation sessions. And, as seen in our analysis, citizens were usually able to develop these skills as they went along. In the same light, regardless of their level of negotiating sophistication, by keeping a keen eye on the implementation structure and being directly involved in the ongoing monitoring of the agreement, citizen groups can have an important influence on how a dispute is settled.

Before moving on to chapter 4 and a discussion of the key organizational issues and dilemmas posed by citizen group participation in an EDS process, two case studies from our research are presented. Both cases illustrate some of the strategic dimensions involved in structuring, running, and participating in a dispute settlement process. The Common Ground Consensus Project case describes a two-year effort to reach agreement on joint issues of concern between agricultural and environmental groups in Illinois. The Malden negotiated investment strategy case represents an effort by different sectors of the community in grappling with immediate issues of concern as well as in charting a course for the city's future. Considerable attention was given throughout both processes to the procedural tasks involved in accommodating problem-solving on multiple issues and among many groups and individuals.

References

Carpenter, Susan, and W. J. D. Kennedy. *Managing Public Disputes: A Practical Guide to Handling Conflict and Reaching Agreements.* San Francisco: Jossey-Bass, 1988.

Fisher, Roger, and William Ury. *Getting to Yes: Negotiating Agreement Without Giving In.* Boston: Houghton Mifflin, 1981.

Lewicki, Roy J., and Joseph A. Litterer. *Negotiation.* Homewood, IL: Irwin, 1985.

Marston, Ed. "Industry and Government Charge Environmentalists with Bad Faith Negotiating." *High Country News* (April 7, 1984): 12–13.

Moore, Christopher W. *The Mediation Process: Practical Strategies for Managing Conflict.* San Francisco: Jossey-Bass, 1986.

Susskind, Lawrence, and Jeffrey Cruikshank. *Breaking the Impasse: Consensual Approaches to Resolving Public Disputes.* New York: Basic Books, 1987.

Wheeler, Michael. "The Need for Prospective Hindsight." *Negotiation Journal* (January 1987): 7–10.

CASE STUDY 3:
Common Ground Consensus Project
Kristen C. Nelson

The Common Ground Consensus Project was a policy dialogue designed at the outset to proactively and collaboratively develop viable policies and legislation regarding environmental and agricultural issues. It was a two-year collaborative problem-solving process on issues that frequently had divided the agricultural and environmental communities in the state of Illinois. The project was foundation-funded and was therefore able to employ a professional facilitator and staff. As a result, the participants could keep their focus on substantive issues, leaving the process and meeting logistics to the facilitator and staff.

Because of the variety of organizational structures in the many groups involved, the process needed to incorporate significant flexibility. Some representatives were able to speak for their groups while others needed to have organizational approval before agreements could be reached. Communicating with constituencies proved a time-consuming and, at times, difficult task. It was not always easy for the groups to convey the intricacies of the trade-offs underlying specific agreements. While the process did not involve groups other than those in the agricultural and environmental communities, they did keep close contact with state agency representatives and legislators. As a result, some of their proposals have since been legislatively enacted.

A selection of the key procedural concerns that this case illustrates includes:

- Choosing participants and then selecting representatives within the participating groups.
- Hiring a facilitator and defining what specific role they might play.
- Deciding on the goals and objectives for the process at the outset and then establishing ground rules and an agenda.
- Accommodating diverse organizational hierarchies and decision-making abilities in a process involving multiple parties.
- Dealing with the media.
- The role that sub–working groups and committees can play in fostering joint problem-solving.

- Procedural steps that can help in overcoming historical animosities and poor relationships and build trust and communication between participants.
- Different group process techniques that might be used under different circumstances.
- Linking the process to established decision-making authorities.

Unless otherwise noted, information and quotes in this case are from the author's personal interviews with the participants.

The Political Background

For years, Illinois's agricultural and environmental interests have battled on the legislative front. Legislation repeatedly has been defeated for lack of agreement between these two groups. While natural areas designation and scenic rivers bills were hotly contested issues between farmers and environmentalists, these groups managed to work together on the Illinois "bottle bill." The bottle bill demonstrated the possibilities for collaboration when the Sierra Club and the Farmers Union both testified in its favor. On the other hand, the Scenic Rivers Bill debate illustrates the potential for miscommunication between the two interests. One farm lobbyist describes his opposition to the bill:

> We were constantly being confronted with controversial legislation. Environmentalists are often trying to get something at the expense of the landowner. Take the Scenic Rivers Bill, . . . when it first came up they were going to turn our farms into a recreation area with no carrot, no incentive for the landowners. We gathered our forces and fought it—ended up defeating it. It wasn't because of values or that we didn't see some good in the ideas. The river bill is just one example of the environmental interest at the displeasure of the agricultural interest.

In contrast, some environmentalists felt the farmers were dragging their feet on urgent environmental reform. They perceived a conservative approach that thwarted any attempt to protect the natural environment. Both groups' concerns and issues overlapped, but the level of cooperation between the two was minimal.

The Common Ground Consensus Project

In light of the relationships between the two groups, the Illinois Environmental Council (IEC) felt there had to be a better way to realize common interests and push for joint policy. "IEC was established in 1975 to provide a permanent environmental interest group in the state capital for concerned citizens and organizations throughout Illinois" (*IEC Illinois Environment*

1982). It continues as an umbrella organization for many Illinois environmental groups and seeks to build a strong organizational network around
educational programs and legislative lobbying. In 1982, Jerry Paulson, an
IEC board member, proposed the Common Ground Consensus Project.
They wanted to "bring farmers and environmentalists together in a consensus project—an effort to educate, to understand, to appreciate unfamiliar
facts and viewpoints, to iron out differences in an atmosphere of trust, and
eventually to reach agreement on some points" (*IEC Illinois Environment*
1982).

For several months, Paulson and the IEC staff explored the consensus
project idea with government agencies and interest groups. They talked
with Jim Frank, of the Natural Resources Division of the Illinois Department
of Agriculture. Frank had worked with both environmentalists and farmers
on a variety of issues. He suggested several farm groups whose participation
would be important for a program of this type. Virginia Scott, IEC assistant
director and Common Ground Consensus Project grant manager, discussed
the idea with the environmental groups that were IEC members. As people
talked, support for the idea began to grow. Jerry Paulson recognized that
it would take time for a true understanding to develop between the groups,
but he saw a forum as a start. From his recent experience as a member of
the Illinois Environmental Consensus Forum (IECF) (*Galva News* 1983), he
recognized the possibilities for a similar dialogue between agricultural groups
and environmental groups.

Funding was necessary to initiate the Common Ground Consensus Project. IEC's organizational resources were already overcommitted to education, lobbying, and other membership actions. The staff began searching
for support funding for "the development of an agricultural/environmental
consensus in Illinois." In August 1982, the Common Ground Consensus
Project (CGCP) received a one-year, $30,000 grant from the Joyce Foun-
dation, whose strong interest in environmental issues and citizen organizations focuses on the Great Lakes region. Similar funding was given for
the second year of Common Ground. The grant provided for issue identification, research, and education regarding combined farming and environmental issues. The budget covered the equivalent of one and a half staff
salaries, office supplies, phone bills, and miscellaneous meeting costs. IEC
sponsored the Common Ground Consensus Project by offering administrative services and an office for the staff. Written into the grant was a
cooperative agreement between IECF and IEC that supported the Common
Ground process and provided a facilitator for group meetings.

Common Ground Task Force Start-up

To achieve its objectives, CGCP organized a task force whose representatives
were from agricultural and environmental organizations in Illinois. This

task force was to be responsible for identifying issues that could be supported by environmentalists and farmers. Hopefully, a consensus agreement would result in common information, understanding, and joint action on these issues. The key component to the project was combining issue identification with action plans. Throughout the process, IEC staff were able to research background papers and provide support services for the task force.

Virginia Scott invited a wide range of organizations, hoping to cast the broadest net among conservation, agricultural, environmental quality, and land use groups. To meet the project objectives, IEC developed the following criteria for group selection:

1. Total group should number about 14.

2. The group should fill out the philosophical spectrum.

3. Some common ground should already exist between the invited organizations so there is a possibility of collaboration between organizations.

4. Organizations should be active in political process.

5. Organizations should be non-governmental.

6. Organizations should have possibility of communicating to a larger constituency. (Common Ground Task Force meeting minutes)

Using these criteria, Virginia Scott began inviting environmental organizations along with those farm groups suggested by Jim Frank, of the Illinois Department of Agriculture. After a month of phone calls and informational sessions discussing the philosophy of Common Ground, fourteen organizations agreed to send a representative to the task force meetings. Later, an additional organization agreed to attend, bringing total membership to fifteen.

Common Ground Participant List

Convenor

Illinois Environmental Council — (Ken Mitchell) is a statewide coalition of environmentalists which includes 60 organizations. The council works on a consensus basis toward legislative action. It also publishes a newsletter.

1. *American Agricultural Movement in Illinois* — (Charles Guthrie) is an activist farm organization interested in farm economics, soil and water conservation and supporting the family farm.

2. *American Planning Association* (Illinois Divison) — (Herman Dirks) is an organization of planners in local government. The Illinois Chapter of APA lobbies for better planning and works with other organizations on common objectives.

3. *Association of Illinois Soil and Water Conservation Districts* — (Joan Bradford) is a special unit of government which promotes soil and water

conservation through districts. It has been assigned the responsibility of helping the state meet non-point source pollution standards, and it provides technical assistance to landowners.

4. *Audubon Council of Illinois*—(Jerry Paulson) is one of two Audubon organizations in Illinois. Initially it was concerned with wildlife issues only, but its concerns have expanded to include other environmental issues.

5. *Illinois Farmers Union*—(Harold Dodd) is an affiliate of a national group which is concerned about passing effective legislation for rural people and for farmers.

6. *Illinois Livestock Association*—(John Killam) is primarily interested in cattle although livestock and grain operation usually go together. It is concerned with soil and water conservation and the preservation of natural resources.

7. *Illinois State Grange*—(Russell Stauffer) was organized after the Civil War. It is a legislative body concerned about the conservation of agricultural land for agriculture and about soil erosion. It is unique in that it is also a farm family fraternity.

8. *Illinois Society of Professional Farm Managers and Rural Appraisers*—(Jerry Savill) represents 350 farm managers and appraisers in Illinois who work through banks and private institutions to manage 15–20% of Illinois farm land. They are the direct contact between farm owners and farm operators.

9. *Illinois Wildlife Federation*—(Frank Bender) works on legislation which affects wildlife and land. It also sees land as a source of livelihood for many people.

10. *League of Women Voters of Illinois*—(Judy Beck) is a non-partisan political organization that is concerned about issues of long-term economic growth and conservation issues.

11. *Illinois Women in Agriculture*—(Helen Henert), affiliated with the Farm Bureau, is comprised of farm women who are interested in agriculture.

12. *Izaak Walton League of America, Illinois Division*—(Leo Windish) focus is conservation including soil conservation and the effect of waste. The league trains young people in the ethic and technique of conservation.

13. *National Farmers Organization*—(Dale Nass) is an affiliate of a national organization which emphasizes the need for collective bargaining for its constituents. It is also concerned about the survival of the family farm.

14. *Sierra Club; Great Lakes Chapter*—(Jack Norman) is concerned about conservation matters. It plans outings and is therefore concerned that there be places for these outings to occur. (Common Ground Task Force meeting minutes)

Scott did not invite the Illinois Corn Producers or the Illinois Pork Producers. Both groups were considered and not included because they did not work on any natural resource issues. These groups were primarily concerned with lobbying over issues affecting the price of their agricultural commodity.

The invited organizations felt hopeful about the potential gains from increased communication and joint action. Most representatives had been involved in legislative lobbying at the state capital, where factionalism had often wasted resources and produced unnecessary antagonism. One legislative lobbyist summed up his decision to join by saying:

> Well, in the negotiating process of each piece of legislation you get some compromising. Even then it is a fight and somebody wins, or loses. Most battles should be done at the board table before going over there to the Legislature. I don't know of any other option like this one [Common Ground]. In my eleven years I have not seen anything of this sort. I think any time you can get rid of conflict it is good.

IEC was pleased so many organizations were willing to participate. The agricultural response was positive and some environmental links were new. Scott comments, "We were pleased to have the Illinois Wildlife people with us. That was a real bridge . . . they are usually the hunting and fishing people and not always willing to work with environmentalists."

The Farm Bureau and the Illinois South Project were invited but were the only organizations to decline participation. Illinois South Project (ISP) chose not to participate in the first year of the Common Ground Task Force for several reasons. Rodney Walter, ISP staff, explained:

> We were not involved because soil erosion was not one of our issues. In addition, we already played the Common Ground role. We were already talking to most of the groups there—our strategy is built on networking and coalition building. Since we are a small group . . . we have very limited resources and decided not to stretch them by duplicating what we were already doing.

ISP is an environmental/farm organization participating in the Farm Land Coalition. ISP felt the Farm Land Coalition filled the same needs for southern Illinois as Common Ground wanted to do for all of Illinois. The Farm Land Coalition worked on environmental and farm land issues by combining organizational resources and strategies. Limited resources, lack of issue fit, and duplication of efforts were ISP's primary reasons for not participating in 1982.

The Farm Bureau wanted to keep abreast of the situation, but declined direct involvement due to its size, decision-making structure, and organizational history. With 309,309 members, the bureau is significantly larger than any other organization on the Common Ground Task Force. It also has a very complex decision-making hierarchy. Participating in a consensus process outside the organization would have been extremely difficult because the Farm Bureau would not delegate authority to one representative to speak for the group and make decisions. Finally, over the years, the Farm Bureau has often found itself in conflict with many other farm organizations. As a result, the Farm Bureau did not believe it could join other Illinois farm groups and focus on the agricultural/environmental interface.

CGTF: The First Year

As the first meeting approached, concern surfaced about how to conduct a discussion between such disparate groups. The Illinois Department of Agriculture provided meeting space in their facilities near the Capitol. This meeting location was chosen to increase comfort and familiarity for the farm participants. Virginia Scott knew that, in addition to location, a strong facilitator would be key to increased comfort and communication. Phil Marcus, executive director of the Illinois Environmental Consensus Forum at the University of Illinois, was contracted as a facilitator experienced in environmental mediation around natural resource issues. Illinois Environmental Council staff believed Marcus would provide "an important element of neutrality as well as outstanding skills in dynamics." Marcus defined his role as a facilitator that "does not participate in the substantive deliberations, but suggests problem solving tools which the group can use, maintains the agenda, avoids dominance by one individual or group, and helps the group be aware of their problem solving process" (Marcus 1984). Marcus would also debrief with the IEC staff by reviewing the meeting minutes and identifying consensus agreements and points that needed further discussion.

CGTF Operating Procedures

In the first meeting, September 23, 1982, the Common Ground Task Force (CGTF) established ground rules, reviewed representation, and identified issues for collaboration. Phil Marcus encouraged the task force to agree on an acceptable group process that would facilitate decision-making and task completion. The CGTF focused at first on participant roles, representation, objectives, members, and meeting process (Common Ground Task Force meeting minutes). By defining each participant's role, task force members were able to clarify their expectations for each other. The IEC staff provided the task force research and secretarial needs. The Common Ground Task Force members' roles ranged from providing leadership to learning to trust one another. This brief role description attempted to set specific tasks and provide for an attitude of cooperation. From role definition, they moved on to representation. The group recognized that some members could speak independently for their organizations whereas other members had to pass all statements by their board and needed time for this exchange.

The task force defined their own goals and objectives as: 1) to reach agreement on three important issues, 2) to communicate task force results to their own organizations and to government agencies, and 3) to exchange information which could enhance their own effectiveness. (Marcus 1984)

Membership criteria went beyond role definition to setting the context of the group. The task force agreed to limit participation to agricultural and environmental groups. It was also loosely stated that representation would be one person per organization. Representatives were encouraged to remain with the process for the sake of group continuity, but everyone understood that this would not be possible in all cases. Observers and press were not allowed at meetings as the task force viewed press presence as a discussion inhibitor. Outside of general comments by representatives, all press inquiries would be referred to Virginia Scott, IEC assistant director. The task force would review any specific progress reports before they were given to the press.

The task force also chose not to include any government officials or industry representatives. The director of the Illinois Department of Conservation was particularly interested in attending. Virginia Scott had to decline very diplomatically his willingness to participate by emphasizing the grass roots organization priorities of the task force. Common Ground goals called for consensus and cooperation between agricultural and environmental organizations. The CGTF felt any additional parties would increase the areas of disagreement. Common Ground was designed with limited but potentially realizable goals partly due to this selective participation. Finally, the task force reviewed all of the organizations present and proposed additional members that should be invited to join the CGTF. After discussing the original membership criteria, two groups were invited to participate: the Illinois Society of Professional Farm Managers and Rural Appraisers and the Illinois Women for Agriculture. Both groups accepted.

CGTF Process: Consensus-Based Problem-Solving

Phil Marcus facilitated the meeting using a collaborative group problem-solving methodology. As he explains it, "This technique emphasizes joint, cooperative work among interests who first agree upon the nature or definition of the problem and then work to develop solutions which respect the fundamental interests of the cooperating groups" (Marcus 1984). Marcus guided the task force through brainstorming, interest identification, issue clarification, and discussion. According to Dodd, "We'd all throw out our ideas about what we thought the group should focus on. He'd write them on all these pieces of paper—all over the walls. Then we'd go through a process of elimination, combining the ideas that were similar, you know some ideas are the same, each person just states it in a different way." Marcus worked for consensus. All items on the wall charts, minutes, and reports came from the group as a whole. Nothing was reported as an individual's idea, and any disagreement was reported as a group disagreement.

From September 1982 to September 1983, the Common Ground Task Force met six times, usually for a full day. An extensive series of group process techniques guided all meetings. During the first meeting, a brainstormed list of thirty-six issues was generated. The staff then organized these issues into six main topics: pollution control, soil erosion, protection and preservation of natural areas, protection and preservation of farmland, property rights, and integrity of farming operations. The second meeting focused on problem definition and issue selection. For each issue area, the participants defined existing conflicts, possible actions, and potential impacts of a Common Ground agreement. After considering staff time and an action timeline set for the 1983–84 legislative session, the task force decided to start with one issue and "do it well." In choosing an issue, the group agreed to:

1. Choose an area where we can have greatest impact.
2. Pick areas where there is something to talk about; where something needs to be done.
3. Pick areas where the Task Force believed they could reach agreement. (Common Ground Task Force meeting minutes)

CGTF's Goals

As the second meeting progressed, there was a great deal of confusion about which topic should be chosen for discussion. The hazy definitions of wetlands and natural areas made it difficult to agree on either topic. Several members had worked previously on the EPA Clean Water Act's Section 208 non–point source pollution regulations, which included a planning process for soil erosion prevention. As a result, there was some issue familiarity with soil erosion. Virginia Wood, of the IEC staff, described the issue decision: "Phil said, why don't we take soil erosion and we all said 'Yah, let's do it.' Maybe it was because there is less conflict in soil erosion. We'd get a success in the beginning and that is often important to a group."

The first problem selected was soil erosion and maintenance of soil productivity. The members also "agreed to complete a questionnaire on their problems, interests, and concerns about natural areas protection. This was to give them a headstart on the topic which would be considered in greater detail at the end of the year" (Marcus 1984). The task force spent the rest of the time defining the problem, why it existed, and identifying the key issues. One participant commented that "it was really true that you can't agree on a solution until you agree on the problem." No one in the Common Ground Task Force promoted soil erosion. The differences came out in contemplating solutions to the problem. The environmental opinion could be broken down into three different groupings. The first group wanted mandatory regulations. The League of Women Voters and Audubon Council had been involved with the EPA Section 208 water-planning process. In these meetings, they often demanded tough mandatory regulations of soil erosion as a political move to counterbalance the Farm Bureau, which demanded full voluntary recommendations for soil erosion control. The second grouping had not been involved with the 208 process. They did not know the specifics of the soil erosion issue, but they leaned toward mandatory regulations. The third grouping of environmentalists had very little experience with soil erosion policy questions. Due to their conservative constituency, they supported nonregulation.

The farm groups were uniformly behind voluntary measures. They felt the economic situation of the farm community and the federal agricultural policy were important external factors that affected soil erosion. Mandatory regulations for the farmer would not address these problems. The Soil and Water Conservation Districts often straddled the fence on this issue. They represented many farmland concerns and also felt the urgency of the erosion problem.

Both the farmers and the environmentalists were just beginning to talk. Soil erosion was a relatively clear issue, but still there was much discussion. One participant described the beginning stages:

> Early on, it was evident that there was ignorance and misconception of what people thought was important. In the beginning, the environmentalists were stating what they thought the farmers' view was and the farmers were stating what the environmentalist view was. . . . At the second meeting there was more free speaking and good listening; confidence, which is essential for compromise, was being built.

In evaluating the first two meetings, there were positive feelings about the open exchange and accomplishing the meeting objectives. It was suggested that they not spend "so much time getting through issues to real problems and to make sure there's hotter coffee." Several members observed the variety of styles each representative brought to the discussion. Some people wanted to explore general issues; others wanted to get down to specifics, to stop the emphasis on process and get down to the "nuts and bolts."

The group dynamics evolved as the participants learned what topics needed total group discussion and what items could be delegated to a volunteer subgroup for detailed work. The staff was asked to prepare a summary statement of soil erosion causes, concerns, and remedial measures. From this summary of the soil erosion problem in Illinois, the CGTF could have a common understanding of the problem "before moving to fashion solutions" (Common Ground Task Force meeting minutes).

After the second meeting, John Marlin of the Central States Resource Center, which had been working on joint agricultural and environmental issues for several years, asked to participate in future CGTF discussions.

CGTF members believed it was appropriate to include Marlin in the task force and invited him to the next meeting.

In December, the third meeting began with a suggestion from one representative that each organization prepare a soil erosion position statement and back-up paper. The task force chose to stay with the consensual process and interest-based discussions, rather than moving toward a positioning process. They agreed to reconsider this process at the meeting's end. One group requested that natural areas preservation be discussed; the task force agreed to do so if time permitted (Common Ground Task Force meeting minutes).

Clarifying CGTF's Task Goals

As the task force considered the soil erosion summary statements prepared by the staff, they identified areas of agreement and disagreement. If there was a major objection, the statement was set aside for discussion. Marcus used this "negative vote" technique because he believed there was substantial agreement. He explained, "It gives a group confidence that it can reach agreement. Also, by phrasing the question in the negative, it will usually elicit non-trivial objections, rather than insignificant problems" (Marcus 1984). Of the twelve summary statements put together by the staff, four were agreed upon, four were agreed upon after revision, one was dropped, and three were sent to a subcommittee for clarification (Common Ground Task Force meeting minutes).

Summary Statements Agreed Upon Without Discussion

1. Farmers lack a price for their commodities which would enable them to make the long-range investment in soil erosion control.
2. Farmers lack the capital for investment in soil erosion control.
3. Increased production of row crops, especially soybeans, has increased soil erosion.
4. Soil erosion programs must compete with other interests for funds on both the state and national level.

Summary Statements Agreed Upon After Revision

1. A variety of government policies and economic conditions have encouraged farmers to plow and plant as much land as possible.
2. Farmers lack incentives to prudently manage erosive lands. (The text should state erosive lands include other lands than croplands such as forest lands.)
3. Some farmers and landowners lack knowledge of soil conservation techniques and economics.

4. The lack of consensus on allocation of erosion control costs impedes the reduction of soil erosion.

Summary Statement Dropped

1. Voluntary guidelines may be insufficient. (The present program calls for an evaluation of voluntary guidelines in five years. Talking about voluntary or mandatory regulations without the context of incentives is misleading.)

Summary Statements Needing Clarification

1. Farmers who receive loans and assistance from the government are not required to use conservation practices.
2. There is an inadequate data base.
3. There has been inadequate targeting of SWCD and SCS resources.

A volunteer committee was set up to draft new versions and explanations of the statements needing clarification (committee members were Jerry Paulson, Harry Hendrickson, and the IEC staff). The committee was also charged with listing which statements were "doable." The group considered "doable" those suggestions that addressed a legislative or administrative issue, raised the awareness of constituencies, and/or helped decide critical needs (Common Ground Task Force meeting minutes).

Even though soil erosion was the major discussion topic, old concerns still had to be addressed. The earlier conflicts over the Illinois Natural Heritage Rivers Bill and natural areas preservation were discussed at the end of the meeting. Throughout the first few meetings, this bill was brought up repeatedly for comment. There was still mistrust and poor communication between the groups concerning natural areas preservation. Gradually, the task force dealt with the misconceptions and increased understanding of issues around the Scenic Rivers Bill. The unresolved trust and communication problems had to be dealt with before new common ground could be found. The task force wanted more technical information and organizational priorities on types of natural areas and assigned the staff to clarify natural areas definitions and to write a background paper.

Developing Action Plans for the Soil Erosion Agreements

The fourth meeting, January 4, 1983, focused on the soil erosion statements that had been accepted. The task force broke into small groups to develop possible actions for each statement and brought back recommendations to the larger group. The participants found it difficult to develop joint action plans after agreeing on the problem statements. The staff planned to summarize and disseminate these draft action plans and the task force members agreed to show the recommendations to their constituencies for feedback.

In addition to small-group work, the CGTF heard a speech by the director of the Illinois Department of Agriculture (DOA). By the fifth meeting, in March, the group had shifted its focus from problem definition to action and were able to identify acceptable joint actions. Phil Marcus described the meeting:

> We had divided into small groups to deal with the parts of the problem. At this point I think we got stuck on action. . . . What to do about the problem. But Judy Beck, a marvelous lady from the League of Women Voters, put a set of actions out to the group. She must have done it on the fly. The group picked them up in a minute. We had been tossing around for things to do but not hitting it on the head. Part of it was due to the political situation in the state at the time. We couldn't propose any new programs during a budget-cut year. She was savvy in what Springfield could do and what the group could support. She really contributed leadership when we needed it. The staff put it together on the spot with a press release . . . it was great. We had something agreed on and coming from the group in one day.

The recommendations were:

1. In order to receive commodity price supports, farmers must have a conservation plan.
2. Support the Conservation Tillage Risk Share Bill.
3. Support DOA request for funding to handle complaints and correct violations of the sediment and erosion program.
4. Support the Natural Resource Lands Incentives Bill. (Common Ground Task Force meeting minutes)

The Common Ground Task Force agreed on three priorities: (1) to encourage state funding of the cost-share complaint program, (2) to get state funding for fifty-eight (minimum thirty) additional county conservationists, and (3) to fund the soil survey on the original schedule—not the state-proposed slower schedule (Common Ground Task Force meeting minutes). Task force members directed the staff to send a copy of the CGTF agreements and the CGTF support statement for soil erosion funding to the governor, to send out press releases, and to notify each legislator.

According to Marcus, "The agreement met the task force's criteria for consensus, with 14 of the 15 organizations accepting it. The remaining organization 'stood aside' and did not oppose the agreement" (Marcus 1984). In general, the agreements supported the original concerns of the farm groups, recommending voluntary controls and encouraging conservation measures. The environmental representatives agreed on the need for considerable education about soil erosion with their own constituency as well as the farm community. Informally, some farm representatives agreed to consider minimal regulation if the evaluation of the five-year voluntary guidelines produced major concerns.

The sixth meeting, on June 3, served as a summary for the first year and a planning session for Common Ground's second year. Final corrections were made on the soil erosion report and the legislative/gubernatorial lobbying plans were reviewed. The legislature eventually passed the first two proposals:

- $50,000 was appropriated for the complaint program.
- $250,000 was appropriated for increased numbers of district aids.
- The soil survey still needed to be amended to HB 2315 for $122,000.

Harold Dodd, Illinois Farmers Union president, felt the third proposal would pass in the next legislative session and concluded, "We did get what we wanted . . . it works." The Common Ground soil erosion proposals were included in the Department of Agriculture budget. This first issue was a reasonably safe issue to support. Virginia Scott commented that "soil conservation in Illinois comes from a parimutuel fund. Our efforts mainly focused on keeping it from being cut . . . we supported it and kept it from being vulnerable." Other agricultural interests in Illinois, such as the Farm Bureau, were also supporting soil erosion measures but did not lobby with Common Ground.

Year Two: Natural Areas and Farmland Protection

In September 1983, the Common Ground Task Force reconvened in a two-day workshop at the Allenton House Conference Center in Monticello, Illinois. In this workshop, the CGTF discussed "land resource management": problem identification for farmland protection, managing forest resources, wildlife habitat and natural areas, and water and wetlands resources. According to Marcus, "Experts and specialists from state government and the University provided their perspective on [these] problems" (Marcus 1984). The CGTF used this briefing to gain background information and a mutual understanding of these complex issues. Participants were guided by the question "How can natural areas and farmlands be managed in a way that the needs and rights of landowners and environmentalists are considered?" After the presentations, the CGTF used the nominal group technique to rank and categorize issues; thirteen topics evolved. After a great deal of discussion, the CGTF grouped these topics into three categories of prioritized land management issues:

1. How can natural resource management be made attractive to landowners (includes forestry, grasslands, wetlands, streams, natural areas, prime farmland)?

2. How can decisions which affect agricultural lands and natural areas be more effectively made (tools/mechanisms/trade-offs, criteria, values)?

3. What is the appropriate governmental role in managing streams and wetlands? (Common Ground Task Force meeting minutes)

At the meeting, it was decided that the Farm Bureau and the Illinois South Project (ISP) would be invited to join Year Two of Common Ground. The task force wanted to have representation from all of the environmental and farm groups. With one successful year behind them and with these new issues, they thought the other groups might consider joining. Rodney Walter explains ISP's decision to participate:

> It made better sense for us to participate—farmland protection was one of our major issues. If this was one of the areas that farmland protection was being addressed in Illinois, then we had to seriously consider using our resources to participate. The second reason was that I was a new staff member . . . it offered a good opportunity for me to personally meet these people from the various groups.

The Farm Bureau again declined the invitation to participate for the same reasons expressed in 1982.

The second meeting allowed time for each representative to share his or her organization's interests on land resource management. Completing the discussion, the task force decided to work on wetlands and farmland protection. One participant described the issue choices as an exchange process. The first year had concentrated primarily on an agricultural issue, so the second year was going to focus on an environmental issue. The task force changed the question to "How can agricultural and other lands be protected from destructive conversion?" (Marcus 1984).

Reflecting on the first-year experiences, the CGTF members recognized it would be advantageous to work in subcommittees for the problem definition and initial strategy recommendations. The task force decided much of the technical wording and report development could be delegated to small groups. Subcommittee work would provide for more efficient use of the total group's time together. Marcus explained, "If the sub-groups are balanced they can be a sounding board and be very productive. I don't like [participants] to do the 'wordsmithing' in the large groups. This is a good place for that." The subcommittees would do the groundwork, but everything had to be discussed and agreed to by the entire task force.

Phil Marcus asked for volunteers to do the subcommittee work. If one committee was predominantly environmentalists, he suggested a farm representative volunteer to maintain a balance of interests. The Wetlands Subcommittee included Joan Bradford, Jerry Paulson, Herman Dirks, and Harold Dodd. The Farmland Protection Subcommittee included Rodney Walter, Joan Bradford, Harold Dodd, and Jack Norman. These committees spent time outside of the task force meetings gathering background information, defining problems, and writing recommendations for the task force's consideration.

Wetlands Protection Subcommittee Experiences

The Wetlands Subcommittee took considerable time defining the problem. As one person stated, "People started all over the place. It's like the legal definition of pornography, everyone has a different meaning." The environmental groups initially felt that any wetland was important and should be protected, but when they began to define a "wetland" and "regulation," they found they had differing opinions. There was also some underlying feeling that the farmers were just land hungry and not conservation-minded.

The farm groups all opposed regulations but varied in their appreciation for wetlands. Comments during those first meetings included: "It's a downright shame someone doesn't make it productive"; or "Those environmentalists want to fence off every wet spot in the field." The farm community was in general agreement on its basic concerns: regulation, trespassing, and liability. As one participant observed, "First we had to get the concerns on private property on the table." Farmers did not want any regulation that would damage the "rights of landowners to sell or manage privately-owned land" (Marcus 1984). They were also very concerned that wetlands designation could bring trespassing problems and a greater risk of liability in case of accident. The environmentalists had to consider seriously the farmers' interest in the legal rights of private property.

Recommendations of the Wetlands Subcommittee

As the differences were expressed in the larger group, some resentments surfaced, but they were directed at an idea or past actions rather than at individuals. The group built trust in the first year and began the wetlands discussion on much better footing than the initial work on soil erosion. They focused on a fundamental policy problem: "how sensitive or valuable lands could be managed in a way that balanced and respected public and private values" (Marcus 1984). In three meetings, held from January through March 1984, the task force intensively analyzed the Wetlands Subcommittee recommendations. As they began discussion, Marcus advised the representatives to consider: (1) if the recommendation was consistent with the interests of their group and (2) what would be needed to make it consistent with those interests.

The primary issues became defining wetlands, developing a wetlands inventory, regulation, and compensation. Jerry Paulson described the discussion: "At first we had to agree on a definition. That took a long time. My research indicates that the definition of wetlands is the key to discussion in any state. We finally came to agreement from the environmental standpoint which was monumental." The Common Ground Task Force members agreed that a wetland is land that must have the following characteristics:

1. The wetland is at least five acres in size.

2. The area is saturated with water often enough that it now supports vegetation especially adapted to wetland conditions.

3. The soils are typical of wetland conditions—whether that land be wet floodplain forest, marsh, bog, wet prairie, seep, spring, pond, or lake margin.

4. The area has significant value for wildlife habitat, flood management, water quality maintenance, aquifer recharge, or appropriate recreation. (Agreements of the Common Ground Task Force 1983–84)

This frame of reference made it easier to consider the other issues. Immediately, the group realized it had no idea as to the quality or quantity of Illinois wetlands. Harold Dodd stated: "We felt necessary information was important on wetlands. At first it was our effort to document, pinpoint, describe what a wetlands was . . . it was very important to do this for the farm interests. We have to say—this is it, this is its purpose, this is why it needs to be saved."

The CGTF identified potential wetlands management strategies by brainstorming and prioritizing management tools that would be acceptable to the representatives. These lists were given to the Wetlands Subcommittee as background for developing a consensual document.

Criteria for regulating wetlands and compensation to landowners became central issues at this point. Joan Bradford explained, "Basically we agreed to disagree on many aspects, such as the conditions under which there would be regulations. When we got down to the agreement we defined it very narrowly. An agreement on regulation at all was an accomplishment." The farm groups agreed that regulations to control wetlands were appropriate in three cases: for flood management, for pollution control, and for groundwater protection. Many of the conservation groups and hunting groups supported the above points but also argued strongly for wildlife protection as one criteria because of constituent interest in protecting wetland fowl. The agricultural groups could not support these concerns. Jerry Paulson described the final decision: "On the issue of protecting wildlife we agreed to disagree. The farm groups rejected wetlands protection to protect wildlife values which Audubon supports. They felt if hunters want to save wildlife they should pay for it."

Compensation for regulated wetlands is still a major issue, with protection of private property rights as the central concern. As understanding increases, the environmental groups recognize that the farmers have the legal right to drain wetlands. If that right is taken away, the farmers ought to be compensated, but how to compensate the individual farmer remains an extremely muddled topic. To simplify the issue, the Wetlands Subcommittee recommended a wetlands protection program based on the current Minnesota program. According to Jerry Paulson, "It was the program that most closely reflected the Common Ground criteria. We are not ready to write legislation . . . an inventory of the wetlands needs to be done. Our agreement was really a commitment to the inventory process and to deal with other issues that would come along. We share assumptions on where we are going." The staff was instructed to communicate with the governor's office about the CGTF agreements on wetlands programs and appropriations.

The Farmland Protection Subcommittee

The Farmland Protection Subcommittee had a different experience from that of the Wetlands Subcommittee. Here, problem legitimacy was not an issue, but rather problem definition and appropriate action. Everyone on the task force agreed that farmland protection was an important issue in the agricultural state of Illinois. Environmentalists and farmers found it to be a "motherhood and apple pie issue." For the Farmland Protection Subcommittee, both defining the problem and the subcommittee group process became highly contested.

Because of the debate over problem definition, potential solutions fluctuated between a comprehensive protection plan and a plan that focused on mining reclamation and zoning laws. Rodney Walter was very interested in addressing the issue of reclaiming strip-mined land to its original farmland state. His constituents felt poor reclamation was a monumental problem in southern Illinois. Another member of the subcommittee was concerned with urbanization and industrial zoning as it affected farmland.

In addition to these differences, interactive styles within the group led to continued disagreement. The task force spent a great deal of time on background information and wording of the problem, not on solutions. Some participants interpreted the slow progress as a stalling tactic. In contrast, other members perceived participants' actions as pushy and extremely confrontational, not consensual. These differences in problem-solving approaches made discussion difficult. Joan Bradford commented, "We went through the consensual process without a facilitator, which was very tough, but we came back to the large group with recommendations." The subcommittees represented the variety of opinions in the larger group, although they were attempting to reach consensus without a facilitator.

Farmland protection also encountered problems in the larger group. The wetlands issue had agency priority, and the task force literally ran out of time to discuss farm protection. The last meeting was the only major agenda space given to the issue. Despite limited discussion, a few general directions came out of the task force. It was agreed that more information was needed to assess the status of farmland in Illinois. In the past, farmland protection had received very little attention due to a lack of leadership in state government and to ambiguous organization support. Jack Norman noted, "Just the fact that we were looking at this issue was an important statement."

At the task force's request, IEC staff agreed to set up a meeting with the governor's planning staff in order to push for a review of the state's zoning enabling legislation that affects farmland. Jerry Paulson stated, "Our role is to say to the Governor that this is an important issue and that something needs to be done." Though resolving the farmland protection issue is beyond the Common Ground Task Force timeline, this initial work is a beginning for ongoing dialogue among the CGTF organization.

Final Conference of the Common Ground Task Force

In January 1984, the Illinois Environmental Council staff realized there needed to be something to cap off the Common Ground Consensus Project. The Common Ground Task Force representatives wanted to share the excitement and the accomplishments they had experienced over the past two years. The task force decided to plan a Common Ground discussion, involving key decision-makers of Common Ground organizations, representatives from appropriate agencies, and interested legislators. Their objective was to give the attendees a taste of what the task force had done. Marcus explained, "We wanted them to experience problem-solving. We also wanted to bring up new ideas from the grass roots; also to bring agencies, etc., in to see it [CGTF]." The task force members wanted "to educate members of Common Ground organizations on the issues and agreements addressed by the task force."

The program centered around the three Common Ground agreements— soil erosion, wetlands, and farmland protection. In a micro-session, the sixty participants went through the steps of group problem-solving for each issue: information exchange, identification of concerns, goals to share, and ways to work together. The task force members facilitated these discussions in small groups and Phil Marcus summarized the statements. In addition to problem-solving, the directors of the Department of Agriculture and the Department of Conservation offered the state's response to the Common Ground issues in a brief address to the group. One highlight of the afternoon was a hand-delivered letter from the Illinois governor that described the recently established interagency wetlands committee. This favorable response to Common Ground concerns added a feeling of accomplishment to the overall experience of improved communication.

Implementation of Common Ground Agreements

Implementation of Common Ground initiatives was one measure of Common Ground success. Soil erosion implementation went smoothly. The CGTF was able to reach agreement in several areas and developed successful action strategies. Wetlands analysis and strategies have yet to be tested. One lobbyist commented, "If we're talking about implementation of the wetlands—I'd have to be naive if I said the wetlands will have the same success as the soil erosion. It is a greater conflict . . . not conflict, disagreement." He went on to explain that the agricultural segments do not even compare the two issues: "It's like a peanut and a pumpkin. Wetlands have always been viewed as a detriment to farmers. It's seen as a 'downright shame someone doesn't make it productive.'" The issue has come a long way in common understanding and agreement, but it was not easy to accomplish. One participant said, "We're trying to explain to our constituents just what a wetlands is and why it's important to save. Some people have moved from tilling the thing over—to willing to listen and consider something else. That's a long way."

Discussion on the farmland protection issue was only begun by the Common Ground Task Force; further actions will have to come from one or two groups who make it a priority issue for their organization. Commenting on implementation of Common Ground agreements, one participant said, "It's sort of like advertising, you never know . . . I believe we've accomplished a great deal. It will affect future work a lot."

In attempts to implement the Common Ground agreements, the task force focused their lobbying efforts on Department of Agriculture and Department of Conservation appropriations and the governor's office. Throughout the process, these two government units received letters, press releases, and informational phone calls from Virginia Scott. Both departments responded favorably to lobbying on the soil erosion issue. Implementation of the wetlands agreements has taken much more time and political savvy. After a visit with the governor's staff member on natural resources by several CGTF members, Virginia Scott began persistent lobbying for a response to Common Ground wetlands concerns. She comments:

> The big deal was the letter on wetlands that had to be worked through many agencies. It was asking for an interagency approach and an advisory committee. . . . It took a tremendous amount of pushing and shoving on my part because I wanted to get something in time for our Conference. We got a hand delivered response during the Conference which must have been some maneuvering to get out. . . . It had to go through the Department of Agriculture, the EPA, [the Department of Conservation] . . . that letter was a real achievement.
>
> Committees are set up for an interagency approach to the Wetlands Inventory. It is wonderful. Mr. Hubbell is the Wetlands Committee Chair with the Department of Conservation. He was recruited from the Department of Agriculture partly in response to our [CGTF] concern that the Chair know agricultural issues.

Hubbell heads a committee of interagency technical experts as well as the citizens' advisory committee. Interests represented on this advisory committee include environmental, farming, utilities, aggregate mining, and real estate. Six of the twenty participants are members of organizations that were part of the Common Ground Consensus Project. Of the six Common Ground organizations represented, four members participated in the CGTF for two years. They comment on how much better prepared they are for this type of work than any other advisory board members. For them, the CGTF process was an exemplary experience for future work.

The farmland protection lobbying efforts resulted in a meeting between two members of the governor's planning staff and a representative group from the CGTF—Bradford, Norman, and Beck. The governor's staff appeared receptive to reviewing Illinois's zoning and enabling regulations, some of which date back to the early 1900s. The governor's staff are willing to consider including farmland protection in appropriate areas but believe it would be a formidable task. Outside of the initial lobbying meeting, nothing else has been done to implement the farmland protection agreements. Many groups have let it go due to crowded lobbying agendas and the vagueness of the Common Ground agreement.

Other potential stakeholders affected by the Common Ground agreements are Illinois legislators and industry representatives. The Common Ground Consensus Project had very little interaction with the legislature or industry. And the Common Ground experience did not change any organizational relationships with the legislators other than to "strengthen the hands" of CGTF members by gaining expertise in the three issue areas. By the second year, many legislators knew Common Ground had been dealing with soil erosion, wetlands, and farmland protection. There also was not much industry response. One participant observed that soil erosion did not relate to many industries and that on wetlands, utilities and the real estate business held off until there was a piece of legislation to target. For these reasons, she believed industry interests ignored the Common Ground process.

Conclusion

Many participants feel a need for Common Ground to continue. Some believe they've only scratched the surface and think it should become a permanent process. Others think this phase of the process has come to an end but support an ongoing informal dialogue between agricultural interests and environmental interests.

Illinois South Project is not interested in continuing Common Ground. Its goal was to work on farmland protection, and it feels this goal was not achieved. For ISP, too much time was spent on discussion and not enough on action. The Illinois Audubon Council representative to the CGTF felt a great deal had been done but there is still more to do. An original objective had been to educate the environmental constituency about farm issues; this objective has not yet been fulfilled. On the other hand, he found that the time task force representatives spent talking together was probably necessary for trust-building. The Association of Soil and Water Conservation Districts' representative offered these insights: "Yes, we achieved the goals of participation. I went first to figure out where groups were coming from and why; second to let them know our position. This process opened up lines of communication. It also made groups aware of shared issues."

As the participants reflected back on the Common Ground experience, the observations are of interest. Unanimously, there is now a feeling of increased trust between the participants. This trust laid the foundation for enhancing communication and networking between organizations. Common Ground's strength was a forum for talking, listening, and understanding. These successes did not come easily; they took a great deal of time. Some participants said that there was too much time spent on process and not enough on substantive action. Others felt the amount of time was necessary for building understanding and trust. The final unanimous assessment was that sharing the Common Ground experience with constituents was very difficult.

In summary, participants felt that consensus-based problem-solving builds trust because people can question assumptions; it avoids dominance by one organization; and it results in collaborative work that produces more sophisticated solutions than the "hall lobbying" of the legislative process. Two disadvantages participants mentioned were the slowness of the process and the difficult transition from a collaborative process to a competitive political process. They discussed the difference in approaches between a collaborative process and the traditional competition in the state legislature and there was some concern that the Common Ground process did not produce action plans for the more adversarial legislature. The collaborative feelings shared by the Common Ground participants were not going to be shared by other stakeholders during the development of an agency budget or a legislative bill. One task force member would have preferred a recognition of these possible conflicts throughout the process. Someone else suggested that in the future, the group could recognize the competitive process and include "discussion of how to approach it."

Interviews

Rodney Walter	March 20, 1984
Harold Dodd	March 22, 1984
Virginia Wood	April 2, 1984
Virginia Scott	April 10, 1984
	January 25, 1985

Joan Bradford   May 24, 1984
Jack Norman   May 25, 1984
Jerry Paulson   May 29, 1984
Phil Marcus   June 26, 1984
                                           January 23, 1985
Susan Denzer   June 30, 1984

Draft Case Study Readers
Virginia Scott
Philip Marcus
Jerry Paulson

References

The Champaign-Urbana News-Gazette, "Farmers, Ecologist Join Common
    Ground Stresses Land's Wealth," February 27, 1983.
Common Ground Conference, "Join the Search for Common Ground,"
    June 18, 1984.
Common Ground Consensus Project, Agreements of the Common Ground
    Task Force on Soil Erosion Control, Wetlands Protection, Farmland
    Protection, 1983–84.
Common Ground Task Force Conference Bulletin: Common Ground agree-
    ments.
Common Ground Task Force Meeting Agendas.
Common Ground Task Force Meeting Minutes.
Common Ground Task Force Participant List. Common Ground Task
    Force, Summary Report: Year I, Soil Erosion, June 1983.
Galva News, "Ag, Outdoor Groups Join," Regional-Farm, December 7,
    1983.
IEC Bulletin. "An Update on Legislation and IEC Activities," March 1983.
IEC Illinois Environment, "Common Ground: A Special Issue on IEC's
    Agricultural/Environmental Consensus Project," November 1982.
IEC Illinois Environment, October 1983.
IEC Illinois Environment, December 1983.
Marcus, Philip. "Strategy and Process in Conflict Resolution: An Analysis
    of Two Environmental Negotiations in Illinois," July 12, 1984.
Scott, Virginia. Letter to Mr. Jim Reilly, Chief of Staff, Office of the
    Governor, May 22, 1984.
Thompson, Governor James R. Letter to Virginia Scott, Common Ground
    Consensus Project, June 25, 1984.

CASE STUDY 4:
Malden Negotiated Investment Strategy
Lisa V. Bardwell

The Malden, Massachusetts, negotiated investment strategy (NIS) case, like the Common Ground case just presented, was a proactive policy-making process. It did not evolve out of a site-specific dispute in the traditional forum. Instead, it was an attempt to bring together diverse groups within a community to discuss issues of mutual concern in order to jointly chart a course for the city's future. These groups had seldom collaborated in the past. In situations such as this one, keeping the process together is even more difficult because there is no common issue, crisis, or dispute to pull people together.

The Malden NIS tested, in a local context, innovations to the NIS process previously applied to the allocation of federal and state social service monies in major cities in Ohio, Minnesota, and Indiana. In Malden, it involved three teams representing local business, government, and citizenry to address mutually agreed-upon issues in a community coping with economic decline. The process had foundation funding and involved several individuals serving as mediators and facilitators. While it presented a tremendous commitment of time and energy for the individual citizens involved, the NIS established a citizen voice on many issues where one had not before existed. The process paid particular attention to implementation of the agreements reached and, as a result, is still a viable force in the community even though the process itself has come to a close.

Some key procedural issues that this case illustrates include:

- Mobilizing an organization and a constituency and then keeping it interested in a proactive process rather than a process reacting to an immediate crisis.

- Building effective representation among all participating groups, particularly among the citizenry.

- Use of a neutral organization to help convene and legitimize the process at the outset.

- Use of a formal mediator with a staff to provide assistance.

- Recognizing the responsibilities and options for both participants and facilitator in developing process skills and understanding for all individuals and organizations involved.

- Recognizing inevitable time constraints when developing an agenda at the outset.

- Managing the logistics of a process involving so many individuals and groups with their own schedules and activities to maintain.

- Use of smaller "tripartite committees" or working groups to generate working documents for the larger group.

- Use of "single negotiating texts" to foster decision-making and agreements between the groups.

- Importance of having one or two key spokespersons for each "team" or interest area.

- Symbolic and procedural ways for citizens to build power and influence in an EDS process, particularly in situations where they do not have an organized constituency giving them support and guidance.

- Acquiring and then managing information.

- Generating media coverage when desired.

- Taking advantage of the doors opened by the process (particularly to citizens) in order to maximize the effect of the process.

- Use of an implementation appendix and building opportunities for monitoring and renegotiation of the final agreement in order to foster compliance with the agreements reached.

Unless otherwise noted, information and quotes in this case are from the author's personal interviews with the participants.

Background

Malden, Massachusetts, seven miles north of Boston, is a "typical" northeastern, industrial city. Its declining population, now about fifty-three thousand, has become increasingly blue collar, older, and poorer. As a result, during the early 1980s, the city confronted reductions in its tax base and revenues. At a time when the city's infrastructure and housing needed almost constant maintenance and repair, and its aging residents were requesting more services, the city cut its expenditures per capita by 47 percent. Moreover, the city's already diminishing property taxes had been reduced by a statewide tax reform measure (Proposition $2^1/_2$) and it faced a loss of almost half its federal aid.

Passed throughout Massachusetts in November 1980, Proposition $2^1/_2$ stipulates that a city may collect no more than 2.5 percent tax on a property's assessed value. While city officials blamed the decline in the quality and number of city services on the belt-cinching caused by Proposition $2^1/_2$, there was citizen concern over the city's handling of the revenues and its choice of program cuts. Two reports, the most detailed one from Touche-Ross, a prominent accounting firm, commissioned by the mayor, the other prepared by the University of Massachusetts, and requested by the mediator in the negotiated investment strategy (NIS) process analyzed in this case study, had specifics about lack of services, incurred expenses, and overall waste.

This information, which was used in the NIS process, confirmed for some citizens their feeling that the government was insular and hard to access. They saw Mayor Thomas Fallon as one who liked to keep things in City Hall. As closed as City Hall may have seemed to the citizens, the public employees' unions exerted their influence there. Fred Ciavarro, an NIS participant, warned, "If someone doesn't discuss things with them [the unions], they will take off on their own tangents." Strong union support had helped elect Mayor Fallon to his first term in 1981. As one Malden resident remarked:

> There's a lot of apathy in Malden, you can win the election if you have strong organization. Two years ago, he [Fallon] had the teachers, firemen, police. No one else had the organization when the election rolled around. This time [1983 election], he lost much of that. At first, no one thought they had a chance, and then they didn't have enough time to organize a campaign.

As a result, even though his popularity had declined dramatically, Fallon won a close election soon after the Malden NIS began.

While those who participated in the NIS had a strong commitment to Malden, this overall political apathy can hardly be overexaggerated. The city has been described as having a "negative self-image" (Zimmerman 1984) and, as Barbara Tolstrup, another NIS participant, explained, "Malden doesn't support things." Her involvement in preserving the city's legacy began in 1974, when the city decided to replace the old City Hall: "If I could have gotten just 100 people to back me up, I think I could have saved it. . . . 100 out of 50,000 and I couldn't even get that."

Some of the longer-term residents shake their heads and say that this apathy persists because Malden is a working-class city with high transiency, and people just want to do their work and go home. Most read the Boston papers, missing local information in the Malden press. Many of those owning substantial businesses are not residents. There is a solid church-going public and some very tight ethnic (Jewish and Italian) neighborhoods, but they do not usually work together. They feel there is no longer a core of long-term residents. Finally, they suggest, Malden is conservative, and people are suspicious of anything new. They would rather wait and see what happens . . . or let someone else do it.

The Generic NIS

The Charles F. Kettering Foundation of Dayton, Ohio, first developed the negotiated investment strategy in 1978 as an innovative

> approach to improve the use of public and private resources in local communities. . . . A central feature of the approach is that the local jurisdiction, the state, and federal governments should each develop strategies for particular places, which reflect their respective sense of priority among competing objectives and program activities to achieve them. It is expected that there will be differences of opinion about these strategies within and across jurisdictions. The major new ingredient . . . is that these differences would be the subject of a series of negotiations between local, state and federal negotiating teams, facilitated by the independent negotiator, which would— if the process works—result in agreements and commitments of all the interested parties to well-defined courses of action. . . . The Negotiated Investment Strategy then, is built on a negotiating process, involving teams representing three potentially different sets of interests. . . . It would be the purpose of the negotiation and the job of the mediator to find as much common ground as possible among the positions of the three teams. (Garn 1980, 3)

The NIS has guided the planned and coordinated investment of public and private monies in St. Paul, Minnesota, Columbus, Ohio, and Gary, Indiana (Charles F. Kettering Foundation 1979). In addition, this process has structured negotiations over the distribution of federal block grants to social service programs in Connecticut (Watts 1983).

The key elements of the model for these first NISes were:

1. Three negotiating teams to represent the city (including the private sector), the state and the federal government;

2. An impartial mediator;

3. A series of formal negotiating sessions among participants;

4. Written agreements containing mutual commitments;

5. Public review and adoption of the agreements;

6. Monitoring of subsequent performance by each party. (Garn 1980, 1)

While the Minnesota, Ohio, and Indiana NISes involved local, state, and federal government officials, the Malden NIS was the first to incorporate citizens. The mediator, Dr. Lawrence Susskind, saw it as an experiment, an opportunity to collaboratively develop a "3–5 year action plan pinpointing public, private, and voluntary commitments aimed at resolving key problems facing the community" (Cook 1984). Susskind was then executive director of the Program on Negotiation, a Harvard-based interuniversity consortium of academics and practitioners whose objectives are to improve the theory and practice of conflict resolution through research, education

and training, public education, and improvement of dispute resolution procedures. A foremost theoretician and practitioner in the dispute resolution
field, Susskind had mediated the earlier Columbus, Ohio, NIS and saw
Malden as a testing ground for innovations of the NIS process in public
sector disputes. The "recipe" for this NIS was:

> Take a place where people are accustomed to but dissatisfied with a decision-
> making process based on conflict. Inject a new process of collaboration,
> guided by a neutral mediator, where interest groups negotiate the framing
> of problems and development of solutions. Let the solutions involve actions
> on the part of the stakeholders so that cooperation is maintained and the
> community members themselves become a part of the solution. (Glover
> 1983)

The Malden, Massachusetts, NIS

A loose string of events connected Malden with Lawrence Susskind and the
NIS process he was advocating. The situation in Malden made an attempt
at an NIS particularly appealing to the Program on Negotiation staff:

1. Its problems were readily apparent;

2. The city did not have the option of spending large amounts of money
   to make those problems go away;

3. Interest groups were in potential competition for scarce funds;

4. Malden was small enough to be "handleable";

5. It was close to Cambridge and the Program on Negotiation;

6. There seemed to be a strong sense of community;

7. The situation was not yet a crisis; there was still time for talk. (Glover
   1983, Cook 1984)

Mayor Fallon had first heard about the NIS when Susskind spoke at a
1982 new mayors' conference at Harvard's Kennedy School of Government.
He met with Susskind to discuss the possibility of using mediation to address
Malden's problems. While the mayor's commitment is one key to potential
success of such processes (Garn 1980, 20), Fallon's gains were many as well.
He was running for reelection, and supporting the NIS would show his
interest in helping Malden. Because Susskind had obtained $25,000 from
the Lincoln Institute of Land Policy for what he hoped would be a nine-
month project (April–December 1983), the NIS would cost the city nothing.
Furthermore, Governor Michael Dukakis's development policy supported
local agreement before the commitment of state funds (Glover 1983) and
the Office of State Planning was interested in seeing if this process could
help other cities reach consensus on resource allocation.

After sounding out the Chamber of Commerce, Rotary Club, and church groups that would have a stake in such a project, Susskind decided there was adequate interest to proceed. Susskind commented, "I sensed there was some drifting mechanism for mobilizing the citizens. I went one step at a time—that's what you always do." The mayor gave his official backing, and the prenegotiation work began.

Prenegotiation: Establishing Teams

The terms "prenegotiation," "negotiation," and "postnegotiation" are those used by Susskind and Madigan (1985) to characterize the stages of the NIS process. These terms will be used here to structure the presentation and analysis of the Malden NIS.

The mediation staff suggested a division of interests for this NIS into local government, business, and citizen teams.

City Government Team

For the city government team, the mayor selected officials (both elected and appointed) as representatives. The team leader was purposely not the mayor, but was instead strategically selected to help legitimize the NIS. Susskind recalled:

> Here, if the mayor didn't play, I knew it wouldn't go. If he didn't start it, I knew he wouldn't play. I suggested that he step out and appoint a re-placement. I was afraid if it looked like the city had too heavy a hand [i.e., with Fallon as team leader] that people would think it was just a ploy.

Fallon appointed Ed Tarallo, the city planner, team leader. Most of the chosen senior managers or department heads willingly participated, offering input, especially as their job or knowledge related to the anticipated issue areas. Although it was politically wise to serve, there were no penalties imposed on those who could not. Members from the Malden Redevelopment Authority, school board, and the school superintendent also either directly participated or attended some of the sessions. While City Council representation was sporadic, the NIS staff kept it informed of all proceedings.

City Government Team

Tom Fallon	Mayor
Ed Tarallo	Planning Department (team leader)
Salvatore Baglio	Wire Department
Captain Neil Buckley	Police Department
Tom Callaghan	Mayor's Office
Morris Cocco	Code Enforcement Department
Neicei Degan	Council on Aging

Arthur Green	Department of Public Health
William T. Green	Police Department
Jack Kelly	Department of Public Works
Ed Lucey	Malden City Council
Paul Phaneuf	Malden Public Schools
Charlie Toomajian	Malden School Committee
Stephen Wishoski	Malden Redevelopment Authority

Business Team

The Chamber of Commerce invited all of its members to a meeting to determine what interests would best constitute the business team. The business community in Malden is not cohesive—there are small, local merchants ("your mom-and-pop store"), bankers, developers, and large corporate offices. The group identified eight major interests (merchants from two shopping areas, real estate, legal, medical, banking, manufacturing, and utilities), each of which was to delegate a representative. The Chamber of Commerce also selected three at-large representatives, and two seats for self-delegated latecomers were left open.

Business Team

Bernie Rotondo	Data Printer, Inc. (team leader)
Joel Adler	Lester's Floor Covering
John D. Carney	Massachusetts Electric Company
Paul Carroll	Memory Lane Restaurant
Robert Chapman	Century Bank and Trust
Gerald Downen	Malden YMCA
Paul Duffy	Dentist
Judith Escott	JE Realty and Insurance
Donald Favorate	Nelson's Bakery
Richard Harold	Dentist
George Julian	Underground Hair Salon
Stanley Krygowski	Malden Hospital
Bruce Male	Traveling Nurse Corps
San Reinherz	Reinherz Realtors
Ted Riter	Malden Trust Company
Geraldine Rooney	M & M Supply
Ed Shapiro	Bank for Savings
Carol Sullivan	Malden Chamber of Commerce
Theodore von Kamecke	Von Kamecke Corporation

Citizen Team

At Susskind's request, the Malden Interfaith Clergy Association hosted the first meeting of interested citizens. He had chosen the association because:

> Malden is a town of churches and synagogues. To reach the community
> without going through city government, since there aren't neighborhood
> organizations in all areas, we went through the churches. They didn't smack
> of politics.

The association had active representation from all denominations and
contacts with a large proportion of the community. John Knight, president
of the association, expressed enthusiasm about the prospect: "I am sold on
the idea of 'people power.' I feel the people can be involved *and* get things
done." Press releases in the local newspapers, flyers sent home with all
public school children, notices in church bulletins, and invitations sent to
civic clubs and organizations announced the first public informational meeting.

Many of the forty who attended initially came out of curiosity. Fred
Ciavarro, who later became the citizen team leader, said, "I wanted to see
if this was just a title, an occupier of time, or would be a working thing.
It was worth a try—no guts, no blue chips (no risking, no winning)."
Others, like Barbara Tolstrup of the Historical Commission, came by invitation. Margaret Glover, the first citizen team mediator, recalled, "It was
a mixed bag. A rabbi had twisted the arms of six or eight to come with
him; there were people new in town; those with particular peeves they had
or were fighting out with the city; a group that was habitually involved,
and some with political aspirations."

After an introduction, Susskind led a general discussion identifying interests everyone felt should be represented on the citizen team. By general
consensus, the group decided to work for representation by the eight wards
in Malden and by including others who could speak for consumer interests.
The core of twelve who volunteered to serve on the citizen team was to
receive support, input, information, and when necessary reinforcements
from the larger reservoir of citizens. Theoretically, this "team-building"
framework would allow some participants to reduce their commitment
when necessary and would be able to incorporate latecomers smoothly into
the process.

According to Susskind and Madigan:

> Ongoing recruitment was especially important, because many key parties
> initially refrained from participating because they were skeptical of the
> process. . . . Ongoing team building efforts allowed the NIS process to
> continually absorb new important parties as the process gained credibility.
> In the end, negotiations were able to focus on team concerns (and not just
> on the concerns raised by individuals). (1985, 179–203)

Although the group was excited about the prospect, it was these original
twelve who continued with the process. Gail Jackson, one of the citizen
members, speculated that the creation of the core team made some others
feel their input was no longer important, and they dropped out. The core

team represented a diversity of interests, including the YWCA, Alcoholics Anonymous, Loyal Order of the Moose, B'nai Brith Girls, and the League of Women Voters.

Citizen Team

Fred Ciavarro	Ward 7 (Boy Scouts) (team leader)
Helen Brock	Ward 3
Celia Brown	Ward 7 (Malden Public Library)
Joe Churchill	Project Triangle
Gail Jackson	Ward 5 (Human Rights Commission)
Rita Hashem	Ward 2
Reverend John Knight	Ward 3 (Malden Clergy Association)
Ed Lemberg	Ward 7
Dorothy McNeil	Disabilities Issues Commission
Sarah Plummer	Tri-City Community Action Program
Steve Schnapp	Tri-City Community Action Program (TRICAP)
Joseph Shepard	Ward 7
Harold Sparrow	Ward 7
Barbara Tolstrup	Ward 8 (Historic Commission)
Deborah Wayne	Ward 6

Facilitation Staff/Mediators

Susskind brought with him several assistant mediators, most of them graduate students from the various universities associated with the Program on Negotiation. Because the NIS was a learning experience for all, the duration of these mediators' involvement was tied to the academic calendar. The first group (until December) included Mark Sarkady, an organizational development consultant, Brad Rendle, a Malden resident who had contact with the business community in Malden and some experience in group process, and Margaret Glover, a Harvard Business School graduate student interested in dispute resolution. Ann Cook, a graduate student in urban planning at MIT, joined the group in September. Each mediator was to oversee one of the larger teams (citizen, business, or government), as well as work with one or two of the committees that were addressing the chosen issues (see next section). Susskind chaired most of the full negotiating sessions when all the teams met together. The mediator staff turned over at the end of the school semester, November and December 1983. At this time, four new mediators, Sebastian Persico, Karita Zimmerman, Larry Dieringer, and Denise Madigan came onto the scene. Except for Madigan, who also served as administrative coordinator, all were graduate students at Harvard or MIT. Observers from the offices of Senator Paul Tsongas, Congressman Edward Markey, and the governor also monitored the experiment.

Negotiation: "Team Building"

The citizen, business, and government teams convened in their first full negotiating session on June 30, 1983. Susskind explained the fundamentals and experimental nature of the process. The NIS staff outlined two goals: (1) to engage in a process in which participants would shift from typical competitive/adversarial stances to a more collaborative, common-interest-based focus; and (2) to address Malden's problems. The teams would develop and detail policies, programs, and action projects to address these goals. Their commitment to these recommendations through ratification of the final agreement, while not legally binding, would be a powerful statement of intent. Susskind and Madigan wrote:

> The mayor, council, and key city departments might have to draft and vote on ordinances or alternate budgets; private investors would have to seek the financing necessary to proceed with expansion plans; neighborhood meetings would have to be held to market site specific development plans in particular areas of the city. (1985)

First, the group established basic ground rules about team membership, media access, keeping records of agreements and minutes, communication amongst teams, relationship of the NIS to other ongoing negotiations, role of the NIS facilitation staff, and the final agreements. Each team then submitted prepared Statements of Concern, prioritized lists of the issues they felt most important to address. There was substantial overlap in the issues presented: providing more human services for the elderly, enhancing Malden's self-image, increasing revenue, maintaining the population at fifty thousand (to qualify for certain federal aid programs), upgrading the city's aging infrastructure, improving education, dealing with Proposition $2^{1}/_{2}$, and reformulating the city's master plan. Four issue headings (Community Development; Education; Crime, Safety and Policy; and Pride, Image, and

Beautification) encompassed primary concerns of at least two of the teams. An addition of four more topics (Revenue and Finance, Youth, Business Commitment to City, and Housing) completed coverage of all teams' top five issues. Susskind led the group through a pulse-taking exercise (show of hands) to attach priorities to the issues. The group settled on five agenda items: Education, Community Development, Crime and Safety, Revenue and Finance, and Pride, Image, and Beautification. They hoped to negotiate these items in that order, through September and October, and then to study the remaining issues in the late fall. The first full negotiation was scheduled for September 19, 1983. A few months later, when it became apparent that the timetable had been too optimistic, the last three topics (Youth, Business Commitment to City, and Housing) were coalesced into a sixth, Human Services agenda issue.

Generating Documents: Tripartite Committees

With the above topics in mind, and using information about the expertise and interests of various members, team leaders worked with their mediator to choose tripartite committee members. These committees, made up of representatives from each of the three teams, were to do what mediator Persico called "the brainstorming" and come up with a "single negotiating text" for addressing their specific issue. Each committee articulated statements of concern, gathered information, identified problem areas within that concern, and developed recommendations for dealing with that problem area.

Generating single negotiating texts in committee was a departure from other NIS processes. Zimmerman explained their use: "Single-text negotiation simplifies multi-lateral decision-making by providing one set of solutions that can be agreed or disagreed upon—as opposed to negotiators generating all proposals at the negotiating table" (Zimmerman 1984).

The committees used information provided by the NIS facilitator staff, outside experts, and their own personal knowledge and networks to write the texts. These members were responsible for briefing their respective teams on the committee draft. The teams, after often extensive discussion, took a revised version to the full negotiation session. The drafts were also reviewed by outside boards, organizations, and interested people.

In the full negotiating session, all the teams together worked toward a revised text describing the issue and recommendations for addressing it. The public was welcome to attend and comment at the large negotiation sessions. (On the average, it took four to six tripartite meetings and two four-hour large negotiating sessions to reach a consensus on each issue.)

Although the other teams did not, the citizen team reconvened twice to discuss each issue so that the citizen member entered the tripartite process with a clear understanding of the team position. In July, the committees

Tripartite Committees

	Education	Community Development	Crime	Pride	Revenue/ Finance	Human Services
Citizen	Brown	Ciavarro	Jackson	Tolstrup	Ciavarro	Hashem Schnapp
Business Government	Rotondo Phaneuf Toomajian	Escott Wishoski	Shapiro Buckley Green	Julian Kelly	Krygowski Tarallo	Harold Degan

began drafting preliminary documents, and by October were prepared for the first full negotiating session.

The Turning Point

The first tripartite committee to finish was Education. The whole NIS had moved more slowly than expected. Problems coordinating meeting times, gathering and locating information, and just working with a concept and process about which many participants were still unclear had delayed by one month the first session of the full group. This meeting, however, marked a turning point as the group finally *saw* the process work.

A 52 percent cut in education monies from 1977 to 1982, and a feeling that the general quality of education had declined, most concerned the committee. Its recommendations included ways: to involve parents; to make the schools more responsive to community needs, and in turn to encourage community support and use of community resources for the schools; to motivate students to perform and act responsively; and to increase teacher awareness of students' needs.

The session ran into trouble when the school superintendent, Paul Phaneuf, who had exercised considerable power in that position for almost thirty years, as Glover put it, "tried to gum up the works." The superintendent corrected what he saw as misinformation in some of the recommendations, was negative about their implementation, and vehemently objected to the suggested inclusion of citizens in the budgeting process. His statement to the *Harvard Crimson* (the Harvard College student paper) later reechoed the substance of his earlier tirade. He cites as an example the NIS recommendation that:

> There should be greater publicity given to the ways in which the schools make financial decisions. Citizens should be encouraged to use this information and increase their understanding of the school's budget process.
>
> Phaneuf says all of the School Committee's budget meetings are open to the public and advertised in the local papers but that few citizens ever attend. "Hell, they just don't attend the budget meetings. The people who are saying this are the ones we never see." (*Harvard Crimson*, July 9, 1984)

His belligerence startled everyone. However, according to Fred Ciavarro, the group heard him out and continued negotiating: "I took the hands of the people [citizen team] to hold them back. We let him commit himself and then we lowered the boom [rebutted him]. Once someone's upset, they'll say things to hang themselves." Celia Brown recalled, "It was mainly Larry [Susskind] and Mr. Phaneuf. Larry was doing beautifully; he didn't need any intercession. It ended, the Superintendent retired, and that was that."

This challenge, a replay of the more typical adversarial confrontations, had the potential of destroying the infant process, especially because so many participants either did not yet believe in or could not envision the negotiations working. Instead, the experience solidified the group's understanding of how a mediator could handle conflict. The citizens, seeing that their suggestions did matter and carried some clout, also realized that they must be more cautious in their work.

The Final Document

With familiarity of the NIS mechanics in hand, the group produced, over the next nine months, six single-negotiating texts that included almost 150 recommendations for improving life in Malden. The local newspaper, the *Malden Evening News,* published the draft recommendations and announced four public hearings that would be held in late May and co-chaired by NIS team members. A total of thirty-five individuals attended the four meetings to offer feedback and suggest revisions to the recommendations. The response, according to Madigan, was "universally positive." Some of the changes emerging from these meetings touched on the use of abandoned public buildings, reinstituting summer school, and availability of specialized education possibilities for both special and average students. After reconvening to negotiate revisions based on these comments, the group ratified the document on June 15, 1984. A public service announcement released by the program highlighted some of the recommendations:

1. To override Proposition $2^{1}/_{2}$ for one year with specified uses for the money generated;

2. To offer tax incentives for early tax payment;

3. To add performance-based incentives to city salary guidelines;

4. To create a coalition of public and private service providers and consumer representatives to monitor the delivery of human services;

5. To begin biannual citywide cleanup with city equipment and volunteer labor;

6. To design a process allowing citizen and business groups to review, comment on, and reshape the city master plan.

Postnegotiation

At the teams' request, the NIS staff also prepared an Implementation Appendix outlining specific steps for carrying out each recommendation. The technical document offers "suggestions" and is not part of the ratified agreement, but the staff hoped it would help to "minimize claims that the recommendations coming out of a mediated negotiation are infeasible." Susskind hoped a monitoring plan with a "who would have to do what when" checklist will "promote an efficient division of labor . . . serve as a useful tool for monitoring implementation. With specific action proposals and timelines in print (including regular six month reviews of the implementation progress), the document adds to the pressure on public officials and others responsible for implementation to live up to their commitments" (Susskind and Madigan 1984). The third pressure the NIS staff hoped to institute was commitment from organizations with representatives on the teams to lobby for implementation of specific recommendations. "If every recommendation becomes the responsibility of at least one organization, the necessary pressure will be brought to bear on the key boards, agencies and groups that have to act" (Susskind and Madigan 1984).

Some of the identified problems were remedied even during the process: the synchronization and adjustment of traffic lights occurred soon after discussion in committee. In an effort to alleviate some of the tension between the mayor's office, union, and police force (with subsequent apathy and poor performance), the force has instituted in-house training. The Little Leagues and Boy Scouts are maintaining some of the parks; and citizens can participate in neighborhood cleanups with city trucks hauling the trash.

Officially, the NIS staff projected the NIS as an ongoing three- to five-year plan. Susskind knew that:

> there was no way that [implementation without continued input from the third party] could have worked. When we entered the process, we knew that the post-negotiation stage would be critical. The implementation has to be designed into the process and that includes continuing involvement of the third party. There is no way that can be self-executing. I am still in touch with cities I worked with ten to twelve years ago.

While the mediators' roles would be reduced and it was up to the community to follow through, the Program on Negotiation agreed in late September 1984 to help disseminate information and speak on the NIS, convene the group for the six-month review session, and, as a special effort, to help with the formation of the human services coalition.

Susskind and Madigan returned to Malden at the beginning of 1985 for the first organizational meeting of a human services task force that was to conduct feasibility studies on the NIS human services recommendations and then to establish its goals. Most of the citizen team and a number of the business and government team members attended. While emphasis of this group will center around representatives from human services organizations, Tolstrup noted, "each organization will have its own priorities to push and we [citizens] will keep them in line."

At the six-month follow-up meeting in 1985, Susskind discussed implementation with the team leaders and the mayor. He agreed to hire staff to work with the city, do a "box score" analysis on the progress of each of the recommendations, and see that the results were distributed to the participants and press. By May 1985, Sandra Lambert had completed "Malden's NIS: One Year Later." The report was based on interviews with thirty NIS team members and individuals who had been named in the original agreement as central to implementation of specific recommendations.

Lambert reported that thirteen of the recommendations had been implemented as stated. She wrote:

> Not surprisingly, fiscal constraints have been the most significant barriers to implementation. The lack of increased revenues and the anticipation of further cutbacks have restrained action on certain issues. What is notable, though, even in the face of such restraints, is the mobilization of resources through local partnerships. Moreover, the failure to form certain partnerships that were thought to be necessary has not, in fact, impeded implementation. The initiative taken by just one or two parties has been sufficient.
>
> Community commitment to the NIS Agreement remains strong. In most instances, the individuals named as lead actors responsible for implementation remain committed. Even where the leadership of an organization or agency has changed, the newly elected or appointed individuals seem to have been made aware of the NIS agreement and continue to work toward its implementation.

Susskind also met with various governing boards—the city council, school board, Malden Redevelopment Authority (MRA), and some informal groups. Because the city has elections every two years, Susskind sees an important link between the ongoing success of the NIS and whether those elected will embrace the NIS recommendations as their agenda.

Dynamics of the NIS: The Teams

Government Team

Ed Tarallo had served under four mayors and held the respect of almost everyone in City Hall. He interpreted his role as a team leader as working with the team, keeping it as cohesive as possible, accomplishing the agenda, and minimizing personal interaction problems. Initially, he was not very clear about what was happening, nor on the NIS goals, but after several meetings, he saw them as "trying to come out with something that could be implemented, that could be accomplished." Other city team members entered the process feeling shackled by the city's limited financial resources, skeptical about the process, the media coverage, and the prospect of inter-action with business and citizens. Some members of the other teams started by feeling the city government was not so much corrupt as inept. They assumed it also had the upper hand, and in the end would do whatever it wanted. Much to their surprise, the other teams found the government representatives "seemingly forthright and sincere"; their comments con-structive, and their knowledge of the city mechanics a great advantage.

Business Team

Bernie Rotondo, human relations manager for Data Printer, Inc., became leader because those present at the first business meeting felt the city's largest employer should head it. He tried to provide a logistic (physical meeting place) and symbolic focus for the group and saw his actions exemplifying Data Printer's support—he tried to show that he had no axes to grind. Personally, Rotondo was interested in seeing if the process could work. When he could not attend, Judith Escott, a prominent businesswoman and real estate agent, chaired the team meetings.

Rotondo tried to create a cohesiveness within the many business interests and also to overcome the hesitation many had about entering a process they (1) did not fully understand, and (2) that involved dealing with the gov-ernment. Over time, however, the issue shifted from "Who are these NIS people? What do they want to do? Can it be done?" to the real concern, Malden.

Rotondo felt his success was limited. Given the diversity, skepticism, and antipathy, he was left with only a small core, mostly those who had committed themselves to the process from the beginning. The stability of the team representation centered around these people, who were primarily small business owners and Malden residents.

Gradually, the business team became more dominant, recognizing its role as a supporter with money, training, and people. On issues such as involving parents in the schools, cleaning up the central business district, and the quality of city services, the citizens felt more allied with business than government. Business members proved helpful for citizen understand-ing of development and even for explaining the ever-baffling city finances. Regardless, citizens felt that few business (or government) representatives ever put on their "citizen hats," and that their monetary interests predom-inated. Persico felt the business team was the weakest, and that their "civic responsibility" was not as strong (Zimmerman 1984).

Citizen Team

The concern uniting the citizen team was Malden, which embodied not only financial and political concerns, but the quality of life in their neighborhoods. This sense of community persisted, in part, because many of the members (Tolstrup, Sparrow, Jackson, Hashem, and a "latecomer" of only twenty-three years, Ciavarro) were long-term residents and homeowners, who knew or were at least acquainted with one another and with some members of the business and government teams. Barbara Tolstrup, for example, brought to the process several women she felt would contribute; another citizen team member had been an old high school mate of Tolstrup's. The team was predominantly white (three were black), over thirty-five, and lower-middle class. They came to the process with what Margaret Glover characterized as a "healthy level of suspicion" that the city was corrupt or at least inept, and with an acceptance of the business team's financial focus. They adopted a we-versus-them attitude, expecting little from the process, because the government "always got what it wanted."

Glover noted that they were also astutely aware of potential power plays and strategized against them. She viewed the citizens' selection of Fred Ciavarro as team leader as a part of that strategy. A big man physically, he was fluent and unintimidated, "a good bulwark against the onslaughts." As a local contractor, Ciavarro could have served on the business team as well, but chose the citizen team instead. He felt the team needed the balance of strength he could bring to it. He did not want the business or government teams to think of citizens as "ranters and maniacs," the "lunatic fringe," who become too emotional to negotiate: "I would listen and absorb, then try and sort people and their personal grinds from gripes for the neighborhood." His view of the team was almost paternalistic—citizens have skills they don't use, and they must be taught to balance their abilities with their knowledge in order to gain credibility. Business/citizens, such as himself, could especially help offset the vision of the "public protagonist" as belligerent and ignorant. A number of participants echoed mediator Dieringer: "He made a critical difference. Without him, I can't imagine how the citizens would have fared."

The team rallied around Ciavarro, finding invaluable his intelligence, humor, and ability to pull out points of utility as a balance to his interests as businessman, citizen, homeowner, and parent. Initially hesitant, the team relaxed after the first two negotiation sessions. Ciavarro noted, "They began to see their strengths and abilities; that their people were equal to business and government. Distrust didn't matter anymore because no matter what, they knew they could hammer it out tongue, tooth, and nail. They weren't intimidated." In fact, as Glover observed, the citizen team became "pretty feisty."

The team's inner dynamics provided an opportunity for acquiring speaking and listening skills, and for working through disagreements. Ciavarro commented, "We had many [inner controversies], but the beauty of it was we could use ourselves as the three teams and see the diversity and differences so we could anticipate what might happen in the full session, and see that [even if] we all differ [we can come to some agreements]." In general, business and government representatives seconded the citizens' evaluation of themselves as sharp, committed, hardworking, and not afraid to speak out. Rotondo watched them pull together and come up with "some good stuff. . . . Their positivism was refreshing; their pride and concern helped me understand the city better."

NIS Staff/Mediators

The NIS staff worked with both the tripartite committees and the larger citizen, business, and government teams. Initially, the mediators' role involved educating the teams about the process itself, what Glover phrased, "getting everyone lined up and marching in the right direction." Faced with some skepticism, the mediators, according to Glover, "had to go on faith and intercede a lot to get people to listen." Once the tripartite process began, the staff duties concentrated more on helping the group focus on political realities, generating solutions, synthesizing the results of team meetings, and working toward consensus. While the mediators might guide, or refocus, discussion, they did not decide on content. Glover continued, "They can only frame the problems and only endorse the outcome." The bottom line was their responsibility to the process. They "seek to promote an agreement that will be viewed fair and efficient by the community at large" (Susskind and Madigan 1984).

The project coordinator was responsible for managing the flow of information, scheduling meetings, and compiling the overall documentation of the entire process and, in what little time she had left, also try to do public relations and marketing of the process. Assistant mediators received nominal payment or subsidy through university research assistantships, or class credit. Susskind was not paid.

Sponsorship by what citizens perceived as "Harvard" generated mixed reactions. Gail Jackson, a citizen team member, felt reassured: "We knew at least they'd be intelligent"; while Rotondo sensed that some of the business community was skeptical about the academic affiliation and "having to jump through hoops." Over time, reactions to the mediators differentiated between a recognition of their "role" and the evaluations of their actual performance. As information providers and administrators at the tripartite and team level, the NIS people were a "godsend." As mediators, citizen members recognized that they, like everyone else, were learning. Rotondo theorized that the NIS model of identifying concerns, problem-stating, diagnosing, and making recommendations works well if one has a skilled mediator and participants. Here, "it sometimes bogged down; thoughts were unclear and too generalized. Over time, though, we all got better at it."

By Barbara Tolstrup's account, the Pride, Image, and Beautification Committee could have profited from a stronger mediator. A little unhappy about her appointment to this committee, Tolstrup felt her historic preservation background made her vision of "pride and beauty" broader than those of the government member, the city engineer, and a business representative from the Mercantile Merchants Association who was most interested in cleanup: "Needless to say, it wasn't much of a meeting of the minds." The mediator seemed to "have dropped the ball," and the resulting statement was a "disaster." Although the citizen team, on her recommendation, dramatically revised the document so that it emphasized pride, Tolstrup felt the problem could have been avoided: "Our mediator, while good and sharp, wasn't interested, and seemed caught up in other things." (This mediator subsequently left the process.)

Different individuals resonated to different mediator styles as well. A response to Margaret Glover as "an iron fist in a velvet glove" contrasted with the perception that she didn't "seem to be all there all the time" and oversimplified too much. A gentle laugh at how much trouble Larry Dieringer had controlling the group's "rambunctiousness" countered a review of his excellent, sensitive performance. All the participants seemed willing to overlook the failings—irritation over information which didn't arrive on time, frustration that the mediator did not really understand what someone was trying to say—because most of the assistant mediators were "students" (and unpaid), who had their own schedules and lives. Madigan felt that few understood the mediators' motives for being involved. Perhaps it was because the citizens had such personal stakes in Malden and such a strong sense of what they wanted for it that they could absolve the staff and not be affected by the staff changeover in December.

The major factor that eased this transition was the continuity and leadership provided by Larry Susskind. He took on a slightly different role in the large negotiating sessions, one that the group acknowledged and did not expect of the other mediators. Steve Schnapp, another citizen representative, found him extremely knowledgeable, charismatic, and a great talker: "He could coalesce, synthesize, and make it palatable." In the sessions, Schnapp also observed, when the group fell into business and citizen accusing the city of not doing enough and the city rebutting it was doing all it could, Susskind's tactful manipulation and "sheer force of will," supported by some of the "level-headed" people, kept the meeting moving. Another citizen marveled, "You know, I don't know [how they kept the bickering out]. It's really strange. Everything was handled very well. There was conflict, but never the hollering!" Tarallo was a little more matter-of-fact: "Well, we didn't come to blows, or disband, and we got a lot done." From Susskind's example, the group recognized the imperative requirement for a strong professional mediator, who is respected and can "interject in an unbiased tone." They also realized that the mediator can only work at the level commensurate with the sophistication and dedication of those involved in the process.

Susskind perceived that while the team members were satisfied with his "activist" role, his persuasive personality made them a "little skittish." (No citizen interviewed made mention of this discomfort.) To set a limit on his activism, he suggested the group request substantive information and advice from other consultants (Susskind and Madigan 1984). Persico remarked on Susskind's approach: "He was very proactive. Sometimes being that way works, sometimes it doesn't; here it worked. In fact, I think they wanted Larry to be that way. They looked to him for help."

Power Dynamics

Ideally, the very structure of the NIS equalizes the power of the parties by using shared information and access to expertise, and a nonpartisan facilitator. The tiered team structure of the tripartite committee (members of different teams becoming a "team" on the tripartite level) also helps achieve parity. Participants, in addition to their own team identification, develop commitment to their tripartite agreement — one reached through cooperation with members of the "opposing" teams. The face-to-face, one-on-one interaction breaks down stereotypes, and, along with the presence of the mediator, can make domination by one "group" more difficult. Furthermore, the tiered representation set up a network of interrelations that stabilized the process and helped blur the citizen/business/government categories. Because so few core members dropped out, this web remained strong throughout the NIS.

Of course, each team played to its advantage when possible and some of the antagonisms persisted. The Malden Redevelopment Authority (MRA), for example, had representatives on the NIS; Ed Tarallo was their chief staff person. Some NIS participants continued to see its aims as inconsistent with theirs and those of the NIS. Virtually an autonomous entity, the MRA consists of citizens appointed by the mayor, some of whom have served for twenty years. One citizen member commented, "They come to you and tell you what's going to happen, and it doesn't work out that way." While it is slowly recognizing the possibilities of revitalization, the MRA's urban renewal to date has torn up much of the downtown area. Knight remarked, "They've left a lot of parking lots." The failure of previous efforts to affect the MRA and City Hall in general had left citizens feeling impotent and wary. Nevertheless, the citizens recognized over time that the government members were people, that they were elected, and that with the use of supportive media, and some organizing, citizens could make a difference.

Fred Ciavarro was especially attuned to power plays and worked with his team to diffuse them. The city government representative on Revenue and Finance, for example, blamed Proposition $2^{1}/_{2}$ for Malden's monetary problems. Ciavarro felt, "They were trying to brainwash us, work the NIS group to the point it would say $2^{1}/_{2}$ could be overriden." The citizen team asked for more information on the feasibility of an alternative solution in which the city would have to prove the need to override $2^1/2$ for each *specific* instance, thereby retaining the integrity of the proposition.

The interactions in the tripartite committees for the most part went very smoothly. They would meet three or four times with the required information, communication, and scheduling done by the NIS staff. As they worked together, the participants found that they all "wore many hats," which, if barriers were down, could be valuable sources of information. With improving Malden as their common goal, they could arrive at some agreements, and even develop sympathy and understanding for the other parties' roles and interests. Having one information base eliminated controversy over the "what" of the issues, and settling disagreements over the "how" became an exciting, though often frustrating, process.

The full negotiation sessions were dominated by the team leaders, all men. According to Persico:

> We had a lot of players and it's hard to be sensitive to all of them. The team leaders did most of the talking (they might get notes from others or a few would raise their hands), and just taking care of them was a job. Look at it this way: we were dealing with power disparities in that the government team had most of the information. They had the experts there on their team. The citizen team had knowledge in that they were the emotion, the soul of the process. Business had their quiet vested interest. Well, that was very hard to orchestrate. The citizens wouldn't understand or would be too emotional, but we still had to come up with a recommendation.

Conclusion

The NIS was a *proactive* policy-making proceeding, very different from most "dispute resolution" processes that are reactions to specific conflicts. Hence, it had its own set of problems and potentials. Keeping the process together can be more difficult when there is no common issue, crisis, or dispute to pull people together. Susskind had worked extensively in dispute resolution and collaborative problem-solving and policy-making (Susskind and Keefe 1980) and was acutely aware of the problems participants (especially citizens) might encounter in these processes. The major elements he considers necessary for successful negotiation are:

1. Team building and representation;
2. Mediation/facilitation;
3. Negotiation skills;
4. Access to information and joint fact-finding;
5. Adequate time for negotiations;
6. Perception of alternatives to a negotiated agreement. (Cook 1984)

Susskind designed this NIS to specifically address barriers to achieving these elements by incorporating six new "innovations":

1. Ongoing efforts at team-building (to deal with the representation problem).

2. Tripartite committees (to generate negotiating texts).

3. Public hearings on the draft agreement (to deal with the representation problem).

4. A detailed implementation appendix (to promote implementation).

5. The specification of monitoring/renegotiation/remediation roles for team leaders (to promote implementation).

6. Greater activism on the part of the mediation team (to deal with representation problems and to educate parties with limited substantive knowledge or negotiation skills).

The resulting process was an opportunity to participate in city government decision-making that few citizens in Malden had ever had.

Guided by the tight structure of the process and an "activist" mediator, and with moral support of the citizen team, citizens felt their input was important. Tolstrup explained, "The process needed resource information, and we provided the community knowledge. In this case, we didn't have all the power plays. For the first time, we were on equal ground and had some backup."

Over time, citizens had matured in their abilities to work together and to express themselves. Glover observed, "They realized they were formidable people, and this was an ongoing avenue that they could be good at." Others saw themselves as better listeners, more aware of compromising and looking at alternatives.

For Celia Brown, it was a political education, "like the League of Women Voters . . . something you need to learn *in* the process. We had the interest, had the facilities and the information gathering. We just needed the know-how and bravery to speak out." In her view, however, the increased power "we gained as a team, not as individuals per se." The team balanced out individual weaknesses.

In evaluating the process, Susskind remarked, "I never had high expectations. I never do. I hoped to get people together, have them explore their differences and see what we could learn. I feel we succeeded very well. The fact that we had agreement at all is a measure of success. I see success on three levels: (1) we had action on the content; (2) a consensus process people felt good about; (3) its success has generated interest in other cities."

Virtually every citizen member voiced Glover's sentiments: "If that [an experience in consensus and group process] is the only thing that happens, it's worthwhile." Other remarks in the same vein included: "It was a good

opportunity to meet government people and hear what they had to say."
. . . "Even if nothing comes to pass, I feel good about being able to talk
about the issues. It's working slowly, but it's [the mechanism] there." Tarallo
agreed: "As we got to know each other, suspicion diminished, the trust
factor built up. At least, I hope, we have security in that trust."

The Realities of Collaborative Policy-making

The Malden process was the first use of a community-level NIS, and proved
complicated and very demanding. While the NIS offers a potential *proactive*
mechanism by which citizens can participate in decision-making, the citizen
experience in this NIS highlights a number of issues for citizen groups to
be aware of in future, similar processes. The following section discusses
some of the issues encountered by citizen groups; how they were dealt with
in the NIS; and what other groups potentially involved in such processes
can learn from this experience.

Time Commitment

The success of the NIS hinged on the time and energy its participants were
willing to give to it. As a result, the NIS experience is both encouraging
and cautionary. Those involved knew that there would be a substantial
commitment of time and effort, but none expected it to be so much. While
they understood the exploratory nature of this particular NIS and the fact
that everyone was learning, they still felt time commitment should be decreased in subsequent NISes. Participants spent twenty to thirty hours over
a four- to six-week period drafting tripartite proposals, and then had citizen
team and biweekly large negotiation sessions to attend. In addition, there
were the unavoidable difficulties in scheduling meetings amongst so many
individuals. Although most government representatives allocated work
hours, many of the business and most of the citizen team members met
during their free time. The citizens, though, Jackson noted, "were used to
it." None of the citizens begrudged the time demand. As one of them
observed, "It was a worthwhile cause for myself and my community." What
did bother them, however, was that the time commitment may have discouraged the involvement of others, and thus potentially affected the adequacy of citizen representation.

Building Representation

Representation, especially of such nondefined groups as "citizenry," poses
a problem in most dispute resolution processes. Susskind has written:

> In a public resource allocation dispute, the mediator must do far more than
> simply "facilitate" discussion. . . . The mediator must constantly raise

questions about the adequacy of the groups' representation—if only to ensure the credibility of the entire process in the eyes of the public . . . the public sector mediator seeks to promote an agreement that will be viewed as fair and efficient by the community-at-large. Thus the public sector mediator must work hard to ensure community representation in the negotiation of the agreement. (Susskind and Ozawa 1980, 263–64)

The structure of this NIS with its team-building strategies that could incorporate latecomers, open meetings and public hearings for revisions, and the "activist" role of the mediator consciously attempted to ensure adequate representation. The NIS used networking in a two-step process. Susskind explains:

We had one network to get the people together and talking about what representation in their community meant—the criteria—and then relied on networks to fill in the gaps. We kept some open slots for those who felt they were unrepresented, but not one person ever approached us. . . . We were very careful about it. Representation here was not necessarily one of commitment [to having everyone represented], but one of sensitivity to needs. We got around the commitment by having them [the NIS teams] devise a draft which tried to represent citizen concerns, but which was also distributed for comment, with public hearings, etc. I saw it as an improvement on representative democracy.

While most participants echo Susskind's sentiment that the NIS was an improvement upon representative democracy, at least as traditionally exercised in Malden, the Malden setting proved a rigorous testing ground for Susskind's theories.

An issue that worried the citizen team (and concerned the NIS staff) throughout the NIS was overcoming the citizenry's apathy and having broad enough participation to ensure that the concerns and needs of all parties could be heard. The citizen team unilaterally felt as Jackson did, that while they had done as good a job as possible, and "even though it [the NIS] is a good idea, if no more citizens are involved, it can't be effective. They'll feel like they [the city] are putting something over on us again."

This concern emerged at the first meeting, when what enthusiasm there was (most were disappointed by the small turnout, albeit a turnout mirroring most such meetings in Malden) seemed to dissipate once the core team was chosen. The NIS staff tried to enlist participants through publicity and follow-up. Larry Dieringer, for example, spent hours calling those who had signed the attendance sheet at the first meeting. While some said they would like to participate, not one of them ever showed up. Most citizens saw themselves as individuals representing their "city" to the best of their abilities. Many of them belonged to and networked with their contacts in various social organizations. They did not feel obligated to speak for those constituencies, however, and signed the final agreements as individuals.

Some participants suggested that future NISes include two members from each team per tripartite committee and more researchers to back them up. Ciavarro thought that if the government and business teams had seen more of the community, they would have given more credence to citizen input. Furthermore, the citizen team would have felt more secure with the broader reserve of information and expertise.

While theoretically sound, in order to succeed, these suggestions must confront the reality of the process, which, in Malden at least, included an apathetic, uninvolved community and a burdensome time commitment on those citizens that did choose to participate. The NIS staff had tried on several occasions to enlist the participation of additional citizens without much success. In future processes, the citizens involved should realize that they are likely in a much better position of influence in the community to maximize participation and ensure representation than are the third party facilitators of the process. In order to allow broader involvement of citizens in future processes, as many citizens advocated, each team should also accept more responsibility for rounding out their teams and keeping their issues alive. If a citizen (or other group) feels it needs reinforcements to bolster its position or expertise, it is incumbent upon the group to see that it happens. This integral involvement is the essence of alternative processes.

Generating Media Coverage

Zimmerman's explanation of why processes such as the NIS may have so much difficulty getting people to participate touches on the tremendous impact good or bad media can have on a group's ability to drum up support and involvement:

> Unless the topic is viewed as controversial or relevant to their immediate lives, people are not always willing to devote the amount of attention a policy partnership requires. This realization does not invalidate the process . . . it simply requires proper planning of the structure and clear marketing of the process. Extensive publicity also serves as political leverage when implementing the agreement as well as restimulating interest in the proceedings. An informed public becomes the watchdog in a controversial negotiation. (Zimmerman 1984)

Garnering publicity and media coverage proved an uphill battle for the NIS staff. Although a smaller paper, *Prime Time*, once it heard about the NIS, reported on all the meetings, the larger local newspaper, the *Malden Evening News*, was not supportive. According to Madigan, the daily was never "very public spirited." It claimed to be financially strapped and could not afford to send reporters to meetings. It printed the short, "not very flashy" PSAs sent out by the NIS staff, but did not follow up with any human-interest stories nor more in-depth examination of the process. The crowning example of the media's antipathy was the *News*'s refusal to print the final agreement because it needed revenue and the request was too rushed. The paper offered to print highlights, but wanted to charge commercial advertising rates to print the document in full. Feeling the program had no choice (the daily had the largest readership in Malden), it paid what Madigan termed an "exorbitant" price and then the paper published only a reduced Xeroxed version of the mock-up.

A more general "media" difficulty involves what makes "news." A slow consensus process does not make catchy, exciting reading, and, in that sense, is not particularly "newsworthy." The more engaging human-interest slant was never adopted by the media. It would have been in the best interest of the process and *all* the participants to have pushed for more comprehensive and sympathetic coverage of their efforts. Recognizing the critical role of the media, future NIS participants should make an effort to tap into their contacts and influence with both the mayor's office and the local newspaper to promote news coverage and specific human-interest features on the process.

Developing Process Skills and Understanding

In undertaking a long-term policy-making process such as the NIS, the facilitator involved must make decisions about how best to convey an understanding of the process to the participants and help them to acquire the skills necessary for effective involvement. In so doing, the facilitator must juggle carefully the tasks of bringing people together in the process, educating them about it, keeping their interest and enthusiasm high, and making substantive progress. Time, budget, and staffing constraints, combined with the specifics of the issue history and context, clearly will influence how a facilitator chooses to proceed.

Susskind anticipated that the major difficulties with the NIS experiment itself would revolve around participants not understanding the *process*. He wanted that understanding to evolve, and chose to have the group learn by doing rather than with training workshops:

> My experience has been that they [pretraining workshops] don't take. What you need is on-line capacity, so that if there is need for information or training by the whole group, a team or individuals, you can work on it . . . like we did with the finance question [when they brought in experts to explain Proposition $2^{1}/_{2}$].

Susskind also "trained" in more informal ways, "in private conversations during caucuses, over a cup of coffee, or by setting an example."

Mediators worked through the team leaders to convey the process mechanics and group dynamic skills. Since the tripartite committees' job was to provide the full session with directed foci for negotiation, the process of generating the single negotiating texts called on not only the participants' abilities to negotiate and work toward an agreement, but also on skills in problem definition, fact-finding, and translating concerns into strategies. Although they did communicate with the leaders, the mediators wished they could have had more time to concentrate on training. Ciavarro readily assumed this role with the citizen team. When some of the citizens initially expressed uneasiness about their performance on tripartite committees, Ciavarro realized that they had not yet recognized their real strengths. In working with the citizen team, he focused on those individuals, showing by example how to talk and when to listen. He also assigned projects, made sure everyone participated, and tried to appoint members to the tripartite committee they requested.

Nevertheless, many would have liked more of an initiation. Rotondo remarked on the need for educating the business team. Both mediators and participants agreed with Dieringer: "I'm not sure of the mechanics given the real world [time and money constraints] but it [more structured training] would have helped. . . . The learning by doing probably made me learn more, but I think it hurt in terms of the process." Yet, while he could see potential advantages in earlier, more structured training, Dieringer acknowledged the enormous amount of time, energy, and logistics an ongoing training agenda would require. In the end, after the first go-round (Education), the process did become easier, more iterative, and, Glover observed, the quality of documents probably improved. In fact, when Dieringer joined the NIS staff, he found the citizen team well into the process, and "they got better and better."

Acquiring Information

Access to a shared information base is, theoretically, a way to equalize power in a negotiation setting. As is characteristic of any effort to comprehensively address complex issues — whether they be in the context of an alternative dispute resolution process or within the traditional administrative or planning setting — timely and complete information is hard to come by. This NIS process was no exception. With persistence, though, the NIS participants did receive all information requested.

The printed material conscientiously distributed to them was in Tolstrup's words "copious." The search for resource material occurred primarily at the tripartite committee level, as committees identified problems and formulated recommendations, be it requesting copies of city blueprints or asking state financial experts to explain the intricacies of Proposition $2\frac{1}{2}$. Members also found expertise within their own committees: the government representative could illuminate the ins-and-outs of City Hall, the citizen could verbalize the needs of a neighborhood. Madigan observed that often the person most knowledgeable about an issue would become less an advocate of a viewpoint and more a resource for the joint exploration of alternative solutions. How long this data-gathering took depended largely on the topic and type of information requested. The Revenue and Finance Committee, for example, had much more to digest than Pride, Image, and Beautification.

At times, the citizens did feel information was relinquished somewhat reluctantly and that they needed to approach different sources. Celia Brown saw the difficulty the Education group had in finding "cherry sheets" as partly a "cover-up." Cherry sheets are documents listing state funds given to the city annually, including its share of lottery revenues, obligations to pay for transportation, and so forth. They provide valuable budget information, and yet they "never seemed available" from the city and finally had to be sent by the state. Obtaining financial information for the Revenue and Finance Committee was especially difficult, but critical. The logistics of finance in Malden were such that as one citizen observed, "Everyone, even City Council, was confused." In the Crime and Safety Committee, changes in police representation left unanswered many questions brought up at prior meetings. Finally, the city assigned two permanent committee members. While the citizens knew the inconsistency was due in part to the inner turmoil between the union, police department, and city government, they also felt the erratic attendance of the police was a way to avoid providing information.

Participants' Recommendations

NIS participants and staff members had several recommendations for others entering a collaborative process like the NIS. In addition to those suggestions integrated into the case and analysis, other specific comments are listed below.

One of the strengths of the NIS was its marriage of a structured process and the "activist" mediator. As Zimmerman pointed out, though, this process is not appropriate for every situation. A conflict situation, for example, demands a process different from joint problem-solving. She also pointed out that in the brainstorming, noncrisis format of the NIS, consistent attendance by members at every joint session is less important if views are adequately represented by other team members. She stressed, "Consider your desired outcome before structuring the process" (Zimmerman 1984).

For groups wanting to initiate an NIS, Susskind made the following recommendations:

- Try to draft a statement of what you want to do. Check it out with the core of the other teams for any revisions they might have. Get a possible core team to work up a description of the process aims before you begin.

- Get yourselves a mediator/negotiator for the *prenegotiation* stage. Don't wait until you are in the process.

Others suggested:

- Limit the focus of the negotiating texts, not only to facilitate fact-finding, but also to keep the process from being so long that it exhausts the energy and commitment of those involved (Zimmerman).

- Work implementation and *monitoring* into the agreement. It must incorporate not just the content, but also the process possibilities for implementation (Dieringer).

- Always have a written agreement. "At least that way you have a fighting chance [to get something done]" (Schnapp).

- Formalize the exchange of information. Have documentation so that latecomers can catch up (Dieringer). (This was the role of the administrative assistant—it turned out to be a full-time job.)

Those interviewed had several suggestions for ways of encouraging participation in a process such as the NIS:

- Be aware and realistic about how difficult it is to enlist participation (Zimmerman).

- Have all the council members talk to their constituency and election commissions to draw people in (Ciavarro).

- At least *two months* before the process begins, before the establishment of business and government teams, pull out participants by having civic groups, tenant associations, PTAs, conduct meetings where they work out issues and help people understand how they can be involved (Schnapp).

- Emphasize action. Turn interest into active involvement (which would both engage people and make for some newsworthy events) (Sarkady).

- Involve the papers in doing human-interest stories (Madigan).

- Start early, in the high schools, teaching negotiation skills and discussing the process (Ciavarro).

- Involve students in the actual process (Sarkady).

- Obtain the support of those who must implement the potential agreements. Involve those directly interested, for the information they can share, if not their total participation (Dieringer).

In addition to wanting more substantive knowledge about city mechanics, finance, and the time to learn about them, citizens stressed the importance of knowing how to run meetings, to be an effective chair, and have good team and dialoguing skills. Some of the specific skills citizens wished or were glad they had during the process are mentioned below:

- "Keep good notes of your own. That way if the idea belongs in another place (e.g., Beautification instead of Development) it won't get lost in the crossover. Be aware and on top of the issues" (Jackson).

- "Cultivate negotiating skills—learning to listen, speak productively, to analyze and turn thoughts into proposals; how to work with a facilitator; how not to be quick triggered" (that is, how to vent emotions and move onto ideas).

These are skills needed not only by citizens but also by all participants. As Susskind commented, "Nobody's up to speed on negotiating, but everyone knows what they want. It's a process of educating everyone." In concluding, Persico suggested, "Little things could have improved our effectiveness—like having enough money to feed people. It was all volunteer, at night, and very time consuming. We'd all come straight from work for a 7:30 meeting, no food, and you start vegging out and can't concentrate."

Interviews

Citizen Team
Celia Brown	July 3, 1984 and January 10, 1985
Fred Ciavarro	July 4, 1984
Rita Hashem	July 10, 1984
Gail Jackson	July 6, 1984
John Knight	July 2, 1984
Dorothy McNeil	June 29, 1984
Steve Schnapp	July 6, 1984 and January 1985
Barbara Tolstrup	July 10, 1984 and January 1985

Business Team
Judith Escott	January 24, 1985
Bernie Rotondo	July 3, 1984

City Team
Ed Tarallo	July 10, 1984

Mediators/NIS Staff
Larry Dieringer	February 16, 1985
Margaret Glover	June 13, 1984
Denise Madigan	October 12, 1984
Sebastian Persico	February 1985
Mark Sarkady	September 12, 1984
Lawrence Susskind	March 21, 1985

Draft Case Study Readers
Denise Madigan
Lawrence Susskind

References

Cook, Anne. "Two Models for Citizen Participation: Copley Place, Boston and Negotiated Investment Strategy, Malden, Massachusetts." Unpublished paper, Program on Negotiation, Harvard Law School, 1984.

Garn, Harvey. "The Negotiated Investment Strategy: A Review of the Concept and Its Implications for Revitalizing Cities. Report for the Subcommittee on Revitalizing American Cities." November, 1980.

Glover, Margaret. "The Malden NIS: Part 1." Unpublished paper, Program on Negotiation, Harvard Law School, 1983.

Harvard Crimson, July 9, 1984, p. 3.

Charles F. Kettering Foundation. "Negotiating the City's Future: A Report on an Experimental Plan for Pooling Urban Investments and Bargaining to Coordinate Policy Goals," 1979.

Susskind, Lawrence, and Jeffrey Cruikshank. *Breaking the Impasse: Consensual Approaches to Resolving Public Disputes.* New York: Basic Books, 1987.

Susskind, Lawrence, and Frank Keefe. *Report of the Columbus, Ohio Negotiated Investment Strategy Project: Vol. 1,* 1980.

Susskind, Lawrence, and Denise Madigan. "Six Innovations in the Process of Public Sector Dispute Resolution." Draft document, Program on Negotiation, Harvard Law School, 1984.

Susskind, Lawrence, and Denise Madigan. "New Approaches to Resolving Disputes in the Public Sector." *Justice Systems Journal* 9, no. 2 (1985).

Susskind, Lawrence, and Connie Ozawa. "Mediated Negotiation in the Public Sector: Mediator Accountability and the Public Interest Problem." *American Behavioral Scientist* 27, no. 2 (1980): 255.

Watts, Sylvia. "Description and Analysis of the Connecticut Negotiated Investment Strategy Experiment." Master's thesis, Department of Urban Studies and Planning, MIT, 1983.

Zimmerman, Karita. "Negotiated Investment Strategies: A New Approach to Public-Private Partnership." Master's thesis in City Planning, MIT. Unpublished paper, Program on Negotiation, Harvard Law School, 1984.

4 Maximizing Organizational Effectiveness

Kristen C. Nelson, Nancy J. Manring,
James E. Crowfoot, and Julia M. Wondolleck

An environmental dispute settlement (EDS) process has the potential of affecting a citizen organization's ability to fulfill the three basic tasks of these organizations: to develop and maintain goals, obtain resources and create influence, and act to influence environmental decisions and actions so that they will fulfill the organization's goal. How each of these tasks is fulfilled determines whether or not an organization will survive and how effective it will be. This chapter focuses on the relationship of EDS processes to citizen organizations' capabilities and performances of these three basic tasks. Based on our research, this chapter will describe the impacts of EDS processes on the involved environmental and citizen organizations. It also will provide suggestions for what citizen organizations can do to protect and even enhance their capabilities for fulfilling the three basic tasks while being involved in EDS processes.

The cases providing the foundation for this book illustrate that the most successful citizen organization results from involvements in EDS processes occur when:

1. The organization decides to participate in an EDS process based on a careful assessment of its goals in a specific dispute, its strategy for achieving change in this situation, and an assessment of its power and other resources.

2. The organization's leaders and representatives understand the EDS processes and have the requisite skills: strategizing to achieve change, negotiation and problem-solving, constituency-building, and group communication, particularly when there are distinct differences in interests and a history of conflict between the groups.

3. The organizations and their involved leaders and members select skilled representatives, commit the resources to enable these representatives to be effective in the EDS process, continue organizational communication during the process of the EDS deliberations and involve the organization in deciding to support any agreements that come out of the EDS process, and involve the organization in implementing such agreements.

4. The organization involves itself in implementation of the agreements arrived at through the EDS process, while at the same time continuing to work on its goals for change, including strategizing and acting on new problems, issues, and disputes.

Citizen organizations—including those focused on natural resources and the environment—need to plan and strategize how to protect and if possible enhance their organizational strengths as they encounter EDS processes. As always, achieving a meaningful voice for citizens in planning and decision-making is challenging regardless of the process. Sometimes it will require the difficult decision to not be a participant in an EDS process or even to seek to prevent an EDS process from occurring because it will be detrimental to a citizen organization's ability to maintain its goals, obtain resources, and exercise influence. Often, in these situations, other parties to the dispute and officials who are not involved in the dispute will be advocating the use of an EDS process. Saying no in such a situation is always difficult.

In other situations, citizen organizations will decide that participating in an EDS process is the best way of fulfilling their interests and goals in relation to the ongoing dispute. Here, too, there should be a concern for maintaining organizational strength while participating in an EDS process. An organization must take deliberate actions to use the EDS process advantageously and to prevent the process from diverting the group from its basic tasks and goals.

This chapter is divided into four sections. The first section focuses on how the citizen organization develops its change strategy and defines its interests in relation to an EDS process. This strategizing is essential for deciding whether or not to participate in an EDS process as well as how to proceed if an organization decides to be involved.

The second section focuses on the needed power and resources for citizen organizations to participate in an EDS process. This process of using conflict to bring about change, like other change processes, requires a citizen organization to develop and use its power through effectively managing its resources.

The third section describes the role of the organization's representative(s) and the involvement of its members in an EDS process. Providing for these essential activities is a critical part of a citizen organization's participation in a dispute settlement process and for many organizations represents new and often unfamiliar tasks.

The final section concerns what citizen and environmental organizations need to do after an EDS agreement has been finalized. An intentional organizational transition requires assessing the organization's power resulting from its participation in the EDS process and planning for its next actions.

Developing Strategy and Defining Interests

Citizen organizations exist to bring about change in decisions and actions. Organizations working on environmental problems need to be sure that participating in an EDS process is the most effective and preferred means for achieving the organization's goals for both its members and for the

environment. To make such a determination requires that the citizen organization purposefully develop its strategy for change. Such a strategy
specifies how the organization, given its goals and the conflicting goals of
other organizations, will act to influence decisions and actions.

Selecting an Appropriate Change Strategy

Citizen organizations should begin the process of strategizing for change in
relation to a particular dispute and its issues by asking themselves, "What
is our goal? What changes do we desire? What are the appropriate tactics
for getting there?" The answers to the above questions clearly influence a
citizen group's choice of strategies. In addition, a group's perceptions of
environmental conflict and appropriate means for achieving social change
will affect its assessment of possible change strategies.

EDS is just one of a host of strategies that can be employed by citizen
groups to effect change. Typical strategies used by citizen organizations
include electoral challenges, mass protest, lawsuits, lobbying, use of grass
roots power, consciousness-raising, and/or education. However, a group's
understanding of conflict and change will predispose citizen groups to the
use of certain strategies to enable them to reach their goals. For example,
a group that sees conflict as arising from class differences will pursue mass
protest as an essential step in increasing awareness of the need for change
and as one way of mobilizing power.

A group's attitude toward conflict also will influence their choice of means
and ends. For example, some groups dislike conflict and perceive it as a
waste of time. Perspective 1 described in the first chapter emphasizes shared
values and interests. Such an understanding often could lead to the use of
collaborative tactics (such as EDS) and education that rest on persuasion
and problem-solving. Most of the citizen organizations involved in the seven
case studies, while having different understandings of environmental conflict, were comfortable with the collaborative, consensus-based approach
inherent in EDS.

In contrast, Perspective 3 recognizes basic conflicts of interest that ne-
cessitate strong advocacy of one's own interest by means of adversarial
strategies and tactics. Such a perspective would predispose a group to prefer
interest-group lobbying, confrontational tactics, and mobilizing groups of
individuals to create the power to force change. Groups espousing such an
orientation would be less comfortable participating in EDS and sometimes
unwilling to engage in this process. Gerald Cormick, a professional mediator
who has been facilitating EDS processes for over fifteen years, has noted
that:

> people join environmental groups because they feel very strongly about an
> issue. And to go out and negotiate seems like a weakness. It's a real risk
> for environmental leaders. (Steinhart 1984, 12)

Similarly, Patrick Parenteau, while a counsel for the National Wildlife Federation, pointed out, that: "Often, our constituents view mediation as the coward's way out. They say, 'We want a lawsuit' " (Steinhart 1984, 10).

In the case studies presented here, there were a few citizen organizations that did not participate in the EDS process because the consensus-based approach did not fit the groups' perspectives toward conflict and purposes in the particular disputes. For example, in the Wisconsin groundwater case, the state's major environmental organization did not participate in the policy dialogue process. Instead, the group chose to rely on other strategies that they thought would be more effective in achieving their purposes in this conflict.

Citizen organizations also can use a mixture of strategies. Strategists may combine long-term consensual values with short-term adversarial tactics, or long-term adversarial values with collaborative tactics in the short term. The key is for citizen strategists to be clear about their group's values, understanding of conflict and change, and goals, and to recognize that it is possible to utilize a variety of diverse strategies to achieve different goals.

The decision to participate in an EDS process can itself be a strategic response. Blocked entry to decision-making was a principal contribution to powerlessness for the majority of citizen groups represented in the case studies. For example, citizens in the Sand Lakes and San Juan cases felt that the traditional system was inadequate to address their concerns. In both cases, management decisions were being made in a process that provided inadequate opportunities for input and influence by citizens. The EDS process was part of a strategy by these citizen organizations to open natural resource management decision-making to citizen input.

Is There Room for Compromise?   If there is not room for compromise around a citizen group's goals for a particular dispute, participation in EDS potentially can lead to co-optation, or wasted time and resources. Citizens should do their own internal assessment before an EDS process begins or during any exploratory meetings that occur before the EDS process begins. This initial analysis may prevent wasted time discussing disputes that can only be dealt with in court or with other more adversarial strategies. For example, in the Pig's Eye case, an attempted mediation ended after four meetings, in part because one of the parties saw no possibility for negotiating their position and walked out; no systematic check of negotiable issues had been done prior to beginning this EDS process.

It can be difficult to know whether there is room for negotiation prior to meeting with the other parties. Often positions that do not appear negotiable at first are amenable to negotiations when the interests of the involved parties are communicated and understood. Participants often do not recognize the complexity of each other's interests and opportunities inherent in the disputed issues. Consequently, the facilitator and the participants should check to determine the potential negotiability on any issue that will be discussed once the EDS process is underway. For example, in the San Juan case, a mediator team would not agree to consult on an EDS negotiation until after interviewing every major stakeholder in the conflict. During the interviews, they asked the representatives if there were any issues that were nonnegotiable. Though it can often be difficult to distinguish areas that could be negotiable, these experienced mediators did an assessment of negotiation potential and only then agreed to lead the negotiation process.

Maintaining Options. If an environmental or citizen organization decides to participate in an EDS process, convenors, facilitators, and mediators will nevertheless encourage citizens to maintain other strategic options while they continue negotiating in good faith. It appears that citizen groups that abandoned their adversarial strategies—lawsuits, petitions, demonstrations—when they began negotiating through the EDS process were less effective than citizen groups that did not. Maintaining several strategic options helped give citizens flexibility and power during the EDS process. Knowing that the negotiations were not the sole possibility for influencing decisions allowed the representatives freedom to negotiate because it was the best way to achieve the group's interests, not because it was the only. way. Having another strategy option also can increase the citizen's power if it keeps the other parties negotiating because they prefer the EDS process to other strategies that could be pursued by environmental and citizen organizations. The only caution that came from citizen representatives was to be prudent in the use or threatened use of another strategy during the EDS process. Other parties can walk out if they feel citizen organizations are not negotiating in good faith but are merely participating to buy time or establish an opening to use a different strategy.

The cases illustrate several examples of the successful use of alternatives to the EDS process. During the Sand Lakes process, one of the citizen groups, Northern Michigan Environmental Action Council (NMEAC), agreed to withhold their petitions for "wild area" designation until the outcome of the negotiations was clear. This step created leverage for the citizens and kept another option open by leaving the petitions as a possible tactic to be used as part of a more adversarial strategy. All the parties agreed to this stipulation on the condition that NMEAC negotiate in good faith during the process. The NMEAC members believed this arrangement maintained their "people power" and contributed to the Department of Natural Resources's willingness to continue negotiations over each point in the Sand Lakes Quiet Area management plan. They felt the department preferred a negotiated agreement to fighting a local petition drive, and therefore negotiated to prevent the latter option.

The citizens in the San Juan case hired a lawyer to investigate the administrative and legal options for stopping road construction and timber cutting. The lawyer's suggestion to use an EDS process was accepted by the citizens, but they retained his ongoing legal counsel in the event that it became necessary to pursue a lawsuit. This citizen group did not enter the negotiation sessions without a fallback strategy should the EDS process not meet their goals. In both the San Juan and Sand Lakes cases, the groups also conducted a community education strategy concurrently with the EDS process to keep public debate and attention alive and local residents informed.

On the other hand, citizens in the Pig's Eye case were less successful at maintaining their options. The Pig's Eye Coalition (PEC) felt they had won a decisive battle when the Minnesota Environmental Quality Board (EQB) rejected a plan for barge slips at Mississippi River Mile 834.0, and sent the Critical Areas Plan back to the St. Paul Planning Department. They felt the decision affirmed their struggle to site a county park along this unique inner-city heron rookery. When the St. Paul Planning Department called for a mediation of the dispute between the city, barge interests, and PEC, the citizens participated as if this effort would bring a final settlement. They continued to run a public education strategy but neglected other strategies of influence to achieve a final decision based on the favorable EQB decision. The mediation could have resulted in an acceptable agreement for all parties, but the citizens were committed to what turned out to be an unsuccessful process, and they had no alternative strategy to make the EQB decision permanent.

Keeping the Organization Strong

Most citizen and environmental organizations have a broader mission than the specific goals they are pursuing through the EDS negotiations and they need to be able to evaluate how their participation in this dispute settlement process is affecting the organization internally. There are benefits as well as costs from participating in these processes, and representatives and other leaders need to be able to assess these impacts in their own organization. Because a successful EDS program depends upon careful communication and feedback within organizations, the process can strengthen groups internally. The process may force group members to better clarify interests, concerns, and goals within their organization. In addition, group cohesiveness and trust may increase, and the group may develop a clearer sense of organizational mission. The citizen participants in our case studies raised questions other citizen organizations might consider as they decide whether or not and how to participate in EDS processes.

Is the EDS process diverting essential group leadership resources? The Common Ground Task Force was a major time commitment for the citizen representatives. In retrospect, those involved questioned the merits of putting an essential staff person in such a time-consuming process. Many of the involved environmental organizations had other programs that needed attention from the staff; the task force took a disproportionate amount of their time. One representative suggested that in the future, key staff members should not be committed to a lengthy EDS process; rather, a competent member or a second-level staff person should be made responsible for participating in these negotiations. The primary leadership can review the progress of the negotiations but not spend hours in meetings and in preparation for meetings. However, if the dispute is a critical, site-specific issue or a policy matter central to the group's mission, it may merit direct involvement of primary staff.

Is the EDS process serving as a training ground for new leadership? Some groups included new members in the negotiations as a training ground for future leadership. When it is possible to send more than one representative, this level of involvement is especially appropriate. Participation in an EDS process can increase an individual's sense of personal power and motivate him or her to continue in public politics, environmental advocacy, and decision-making. In separate cases, Fitchburg and Pig's Eye, two women took on leadership roles for the first time. A few years later, they ran for their respective city councils and won. The organizing work done on the controversial issue and the participation in the EDS negotiations were their first experiences in environmental decision-making. They credited this experience as having contributed to their personal power and interest in having more permanent decision-making authority.

How is the EDS process meshing with other issues and projects of the organization? The Common Ground organizers felt the two-year, policy-level process meshed well with their organizational goals, although it occasionally eclipsed other projects. This fact was accepted by the board of directors for a period, but eventually they questioned the staff's priorities. To conserve the major resources an EDS process can drain from an organization, leaders need to allocate wisely their time and other organizational resources.

Is the citizen organization's involvement in EDS attracting new members or otherwise affecting the numbers and commitments of the organization's members? EDS processes sometimes can be highly visible and completed in a relatively short time; therefore, they attract attention to the involved citizen organizations. At other times, the EDS process has a very low profile and drags out over a long period. Depending on the strength of these organizations' involvement and the way this participation is profiled in membership recruitment efforts, EDS involvement can help or hurt in attracting new members to an organization. Sometimes, when members perceive their organization's participation in EDS as weakening the group, it can lead to people reducing their commitment or, in the extreme, dropping out of the organization. In the cases we studied, there were no reports of membership dropouts resulting from an EDS process.

Adversarial and Collaborative Strategies

Some groups encountered problems in changing from the adversarial strategies of traditional processes to the collaborative strategies in an EDS process. The citizens' problems came in two areas: the disadvantages of being newcomers to an EDS process, and the incorrect assumption that political power plays do not occur in an EDS process. These disadvantages can affect negatively an organization's strengths.

Some representatives felt that their being invited to participate in the EDS process was a privilege; they were grateful that the government authorities had allowed them to participate. This attitude was dysfunctional during negotiations because they worried more about pushing government representatives too far rather than struggling to advance citizens' interests. It appears that the citizens were afraid the agencies would "take their football and go home." Citizen organizations that felt participation was their right, not a privilege, negotiated with a stronger confidence in their legitimacy and the importance of their interests.

Many citizen representatives had the added disadvantage of being newcomers to face-to-face, multiparty problem-solving and negotiation activities. Although they may have been agile and experienced competitors in the legislative process, or skilled advocates organizing demonstrations, citizen organizations and their representatives sometimes were followers in an unfamiliar collaborative negotiation process. To address this problem, citizen organizations tried to choose representatives with demonstrated negotiation skills, and advised them to balance learning the new process with an assertive protection of the group's interests. This response helped put the citizen representatives on comparable footing with the other representatives, some of whom also had to become familiar with new EDS processes.

In some cases, where the EDS process was perceived uncritically, participants believed the more open, collaborative negotiations would be free of traditional power politics. This perspective can be detrimental to citizen and environmental organizations if they do not recognize that power plays sometimes occur during these negotiation and problem-solving processes. Citizens find that there are still key individuals who will influence the group dynamics. Informal but important negotiations can occur in between formal EDS process meetings. And power plays to force specific agreement rather than open and voluntary decision-making are still possible. Hopefully, a good mediator or facilitator, combined with effective process rules, will minimize power plays and maximize equitable participation and information-focused problem-solving. However, a citizen organization's leadership, representatives, and other strategists need to recognize that EDS processes are not "safe" areas devoid of tactics used in more traditional processes. Effective citizen leaders and representatives approach the EDS process with an openness to collaborate combined with a sophisticated respect for the potentials of manipulation and subtle coercion and the danger of co-optation.

Choosing Not to Participate. Some groups decided against switching from more adversarial strategies to the EDS process and successfully co-ordinated their position outside the EDS process with another group directly participating in the process. In the Wisconsin groundwater case, the Wisconsin Environmental Decade organization played a gadfly role outside the process. Staff members of this organization observed the sessions, lobbied other representatives for specific points in the agreement, and were free to publicly critique the process. This EDS process was somewhat unusual in that the final agreement was in the form of proposed legislation that could still be amended before the full legislature through a group's lobbying efforts. As a result, Wisconsin Environmental Decade's nonparticipation in the EDS process could potentially legitimize their lobbying efforts for a stronger bill where they believed changes were warranted.

Analyzing the Issues and Defining Interests

If a citizen organization, after determining its strategy for achieving change, decides to participate in an EDS process as its best alternative for pursuing the organization's goals, then work is required to analyze the issues in the dispute and define the organization's interests in relation to these issues. This work requires in-depth examination of the disputed issues to be sure they are fully understood and examination of what the citizen organization needs and desires to happen in both the short and long run in relation to the disputed matters. This latter work allows the organization to become clear about the issues and thus able to specify what its interests are in relation to the dispute.

It is important that all parties involved in an EDS process recognize their underlying interests and goals in relation to the dispute. This understanding is especially critical for the citizen party, which often must overcome disadvantages in power and access to decision-making. If the involved citizens can be clear about their basic interests and goals, they can develop a stronger organizational base and negotiation strategy from which to participate in the EDS process. Unfortunately, the dynamics of conflicts often obscure the interests underlying the disputed issues for all parties, including the citizens.

In most cases studied, the citizen organizations did not do an extensive analysis of the issues nor explicit work in defining their interests. Most of the organizations gradually and often reactively analyzed the disputed issues and determined their interests as they created a power base and participated in the EDS process. This lack of preparation may have resulted from these organizations' inexperience with EDS processes.

Often, as the first step in participating in a dispute, citizen groups responded to a long-term environmental problem or reacted to an agency decision with which they did not agree. The issues were either relatively clear and understood from the outset, began with a single concern and expanded to others during the EDS process, or were formed by the EDS process. For some citizen organizations, the issue being disputed was relatively clear from the beginning. A neighborhood group in the Fitchburg case knew from the outset that they needed a potable water supply. The problem of unsafe drinking water was evident; the solution was not. In the NIS case, the individual citizen representatives had done no issue analysis prior to the EDS process. They had a general idea of neighborhood concerns, but at the outset, they had not identified and analyzed interests that might be unique to community members as opposed to the interests of business or city government.

In the Sand Lakes and San Juan cases, the citizens began with a single issue but expanded their concerns as the EDS process progressed. In both instances, the citizens quickly developed a position concerning one aspect of an agency management plan for natural resources. In the Sand Lakes case, the citizens called for no oil and gas drilling; in the San Juan case, no timber harvesting or road construction. These were understandable first reactions to objectionable management plans. There were also clear demands that assisted in mobilizing citizens around a single issue. During the EDS negotiations, both citizen alliances expanded their concerns and widened their interests by moving off the single position and negotiating multiple interests. This ability to expand the negotiations to other issues was due, in part, to the agency jurisdiction and the citizens' ability to identify their interests in more than one way. The agencies involved in the two cases had jurisdiction over the whole management plan, which allowed negotiations to move into other areas without bringing in a new party. Once problem-solving and negotiations began, it was clear in both cases that the citizens wanted to participate in the decision-making on the management plan.

In the Common Ground case, some participating organizations had a well-developed understanding of various issues and related interests and others did not. The uneven level of issue analysis among groups led to certain organizations having a stronger voice, and others, which lacked good issue analysis, being capable only of low-level influence.

Clarity concerning a group's primary interests is a key step in maintaining a strong, cohesive organization, in effective mobilization and application of citizen organizations' resources, and in achieving influence that shapes the outcomes of an EDS process.

Power and Resources

Citizen power can take many forms. In traditional decision-making forums, citizen power is often reactive—the ability to prevent or delay projects or legislation through appeals, litigation, and lobbying. In an EDS process, citizens need to be able to garner economic power, political legitimacy, mobilized constituents, and information and expertise to use proactively to protect their interests.

In some cases, citizens may wield considerable power in the process but not realize that they do, in fact, have influence. In the Sand Lakes controversy, the citizens did not understand power politics. They took a powerless position with the director of the Department of Natural Resources, not realizing that the fact that he was sitting down with them personally to discuss the issue indicated that they did wield some clout. Likewise, the citizens involved with the NIS also had trouble recognizing their potential influence.

Power dynamics can also come into play within the coalition of citizen groups. Wisconsin groundwater citizen participants noted that there were complicated power dynamics within the environmental community. The smaller groups felt overshadowed by the largest environmental organization. There was fragmentation within the environmental community; consequently, they were not as effective in presenting a strong, unified front during negotiations.

Susskind and Cruikshank have found in their experience mediating and researching different types of conflict management processes that power can be quite "fluid":

> You may well sit down at the table with a relatively small and seemingly inadequate measure of power. But that allocation is not fixed. The fact is that there are a number of things you can do to enhance your bargaining power. (1987, 211)

They suggest that groups can bolster their influence in a negotiation-based process "by developing a stronger and more convincing claim that you can do pretty well away from the table." They have also observed a group's power strengthened when that group came up with "an ingenious way of meeting the concerns of the other parties" while still achieving their own concerns (1987, 211).

Similarly, Carpenter and Kennedy have found from their intervention experience that:

> the familiar theoretical argument that a "balance of power" must be achieved before meaningful negotiations can begin seems irrelevant. The issue is not one of "balance" but whether or not one party can influence the behavior of another. (1988, 218)

They believe that parties often "underestimate their own resources for influencing decisions":

Questions about power are indeed essential in analyzing a conflict, and the situation is likely to be much more complicated than comparing balance sheets or counting numbers of lawyers. Attention solely to size of financial resources or legal staffs gives insufficient weight to such intangibles as ingenuity, obstinacy, moral indignation, and standing in court. Seemingly weak parties can achieve instant attention by suing. Anyone can sue. (1988, 216–17)

Economic Power. Citizens need to develop sources of funding to maintain their organization, and sometimes to support the EDS process. Financing is needed to support items such as research, staff, meeting costs, and press work. Citizen organizers commented that prior to the EDS, it is helpful to obtain the financing in conjunction with other resources to create power. Donated services can prove as valuable as cash.

Before the Common Ground process, the Illinois Environmental Council received two $30,000 grants for a two-year EDS process; a foundation interested in the proposed issues, and the lower level of conflict of the policy dialogue, allowed time to write grants and discuss issues. In the San Juan case, the citizen alliance had a millionaire in the group as well as leadership from the local Chamber of Commerce. This group did not mention any problems with financing.

However, not every citizen group was so adequately bankrolled. The Pig's Eye Coalition worked for six years building coalition support. Their fund-raising depended on membership dues, donations, T-shirt sales, and grass roots support. In the NIS case, individual citizens did not have funding or economic power. The EDS process was supported by the town and a foundation grant backing the mediators' involvement.

Political Legitimacy. Citizens need political legitimacy to participate in environmental decision-making; EDS processes are no exception. The type of political allies needed usually will be determined by the issue and the traditional authority responsible for the decision. The San Juan citizens used political clout combined with grass roots support as their major power. They had the backing of local officials, state and national legislators, and members of the governor's staff. Inquiries from several federal legislators demonstrated more political clout than could be mobilized from local support.

Participating in the traditional decision-making process also can lend legitimacy and generate new allies. The Pig's Eye Coalition campaigned to cultivate political allies, and participated in all public forums to influence the decision-making agendas. Their strategists believed the group gained valuable public support by such participation. In the Fitchburg case, the neighborhood group used traditional channels to no avail; however, the citizens found an ally in the Wisconsin Department of Natural Resources (DNR), which agreed to take up their water supply problem. The DNR's political clout and legitimacy were sufficient for decisions concerning the water supply.

People as Resources.   People are often the most important resource for citizen organizers. Economic power and political legitimacy may be difficult to accumulate, but a mobilized constituency can go a long way toward making up the difference. In the San Juan, Sand Lakes, Pig's Eye, and Fitchburg cases, the organizers used grass roots membership to make their concerns a political issue, and to maintain pressure as the dispute developed. Citizens were ready to write letters, attend public hearings, lobby, raise funds, or whatever was required.

Active constituencies also can help generate legitimacy for citizen concerns. In pluralist politics one claim to power is the number of citizens that support an issue. Elected and appointed officials often justify their decisions by claiming public support. If a citizen group can gain a large, active constituency, government officials will be compelled to respond. The citizens in the San Juan case waged a letter-writing campaign by both local citizens and people across the nation who used the area for recreation and vacations. This tactic greatly increased the number of concerned citizens interested in stopping the planned road construction and timber harvesting and swelled the perceived constituency.

Information and Expertise.   A basic requirement for the success of an EDS process is that those involved have equal access to information and technical expertise. Citizen group experience suggests that citizens often feel other parties are privy to information they do not share, that the other parties have technical expertise that is not accessible to or affordable by the citizen group, and that even within the process, citizens feel at a disadvantage in terms of understanding and being able to use the information that is available.

The data suggest several strategies for confronting these problems. Citizen representatives found they had to do two things in order to gain information in a timely and clear fashion. First, citizens used their own expertise to evaluate the information; second, they helped form a legitimate channel by which they received information from all parties in the dispute.

Many groups were able to develop a membership that included individuals with expertise on the key issue. These citizen/experts lent credibility to the group in environmental and legal debates. They also were able to share their understanding of the issue with other members. In most cases, the experts strengthened the group internally and externally.

Finding the appropriate information was often a challenge for citizens. Relevant scientific studies frequently had not been done, legal requirements were vague, and natural resource agencies were slow to hand over information. Before every EDS process studied here, the citizen groups had to do their own information-gathering. Some groups did studies with donated professional services; others hired staff members to write background papers. Most groups spent endless hours searching through records, visiting sites, and "finding out for themselves." One Pig's Eye Coalition member spent eight years attending every Port Authority meeting. Her historical knowledge of barge siting on the river was far more complete than any other participant in the conflict.

Access to information is one of the key obstacles to full participation by citizens in the EDS processes. It is not an insurmountable obstacle, however. From their intervention experience, Susskind and Cruikshank have found that:

> you probably will not have to cede much technical ground. Depending on the nature of the dispute, you may have a surprising supply of firsthand knowledge, as well as access to sympathetic resource people. Search hard within your membership for such resources, or look outside for sympathetic advocates who have technical backgrounds. Has a similar dispute occurred elsewhere? If so, which technical people helped the citizens' cause? Can they help, or at least refer you to someone else who can? (1987, 210)

To effectively fill the gaps in readily accessible information requires that the citizen group realize where these gaps exist and invest time and resources in trying to fill them.

In a majority of the cases studied in this book, the government agency or body had most of the important information needed to make environmental and political decisions. Sometimes there was a general reluctance by the government personnel to release information that had previously been their sole domain. However, citizen representatives within an EDS process had unique leverage that they had not possessed prior to the process. Earlier, they used public hearings, visits to the agency records departments, and the Freedom of Information Act to gain access to important information. During the EDS process, the representatives, by working together, were able to demonstrate the merits of sharing information in order to negotiate an environmentally sound, mutually acceptable agreement. By formalizing and legitimizing the exchange of information, the participants were able to develop an open flow of information.

In the NIS and Fitchburg cases, a traditional government authority figure recognized the EDS process and instructed the respective agencies to provide pertinent information. For the NIS process, the mayor's clout was sufficient to start the exchange of information; however, citizens still encountered some agency resistance to such a group "meddling" in agency affairs. The Wisconsin DNR's authority assisted Fitchburg citizens in acquiring the information they needed from the municipal government involved in their dispute.

Other cases exemplify formalized means of information exchange that could prove helpful for future EDS participants. The Wisconsin groundwater legislative committee used a Technical Advisory Committee to provide background reports, issue analysis, and data investigation at the representatives' request. In the Sand Lakes case, a forest management planner was the citizens' principal access to Michigan Department of Natural Resources information. He supplied the needed documents or brought another DNR official to meetings to answer their questions. In both cases, information exchange was acknowledged as important and a formal mechanism was developed for access and communication.

One reality of environmental problem-solving is that very often needed information does not exist. Either scientific studies are inconclusive or there are no data to help reduce uncertainty about future impacts. Common Ground Task Force members working on wetlands issues had to form their own definition of a "wetland" and found there was very limited information on the extent and quality of Illinois's wetlands.

However, access to information is only the beginning. Gathering information and performing analysis take time, and the representatives may debate numerous interpretations of the data. Many citizens asked experts to join their group or sought the advice of experts in appropriate fields to assist in data clarification. Sympathetic experts were essential for clarifying the unending analyses and documentation that environmental problem-solving can require.

As citizen groups analyzed government information or reports from other parties, they occasionally questioned a document's validity. Independent verification became important in several situations so that citizens could have a clear understanding of the information, and be willing to go forward with negotiations. When the participants have a clear understanding of the information and agree to negotiate from a similar information base, the EDS process can develop a final agreement that not only recognizes multiple interests but also incorporates sophisticated environmental solutions.

Necessary Resources

It appears that most citizen groups involved in EDS processes had a problem with limited time and other resources. Unlike the government or business participants, most citizens were not paid for time devoted to the EDS process. In a few cases, citizen organizations were able to use their paid staff members as representatives. However, their staff members often were overworked and underpaid, making the additional participation in an EDS process a strain. Most citizen and environmental organizations did not find a satisfactory way for dealing with this resource bias. One representative commented that it is wise to "be wary of resource drain from the organization," starting in the very beginning of the EDS process.

Use of Staff, Volunteers, and Other Experts. In retrospect, citizen representatives in the case studies recommended using organizational staff to support volunteer representatives. In several cases, citizens were able to use support staff—lawyers, researchers, administrators—to do needed work between meetings, which alleviated some of the pressure on volunteers. Another option for conserving human resources was to use one representative for several citizen and environmental organizations. If it is clearly stated that the representative is speaking for several organizations, and the organizations have closely shared interests, no power will be lost by this arrangement; then other volunteers and staff members will be free to work on other projects. Such joint representation requires the networking and organization of an alliance or coalition of groups with shared interests and mutual support.

Leadership.   Leadership is an organizational resource that citizen organizations require for any type of action; EDS is no different. The data suggest that wise use of leadership from the beginning of an EDS process was critical to citizen effectiveness. In the Sand Lakes case, a single individual kept the EDS process viable and maintained a mobilized citizen alliance. As an acknowledged leader, she was conscientious in verifying all actions with the other involved citizen groups in order to maintain unity; at the same time, she was free to negotiate for the interests of the alliance. It is likely that without her leadership there would not have been an EDS process. In contrast, in the Wisconsin groundwater case, no environmental citizen leadership emerged during the process, partially due to a split among the state's environmental organizations. In this situation, a formalized public advocate who was part of state government negotiated by default for the environmental interests, but there was substantial citizen group dissatisfaction with the final agreement.

Training.   Often citizens found themselves participating in EDS processes without any prior experience in such processes. They perceived negotiation skills as an important expertise that they needed to develop. Citizen representatives who were not experienced in lobbying, legal negotiations, or business bargaining were at a distinct disadvantage. While government or industry representatives had often used negotiations in their careers, many citizens found they had to learn the tempo and skills required in the negotiations that comprised many of the EDS processes. In low-intensity disputes, there was time to gain experience during the process while minimizing the loss of effectiveness in representing the citizens' interests. However, it appears that the inexperienced negotiators in high-intensity disputes were not as successful in representing their interests as the more experienced business representatives.

To address these inequities in negotiation skill levels, citizens can rely on previously experienced negotiators, or they can acquire new skills through training. EDS training can be an effective response to the imbalance in negotiators' skills. Training prior to participating in an EDS process also can be helpful in that (1) it allows all representatives to fully participate from the beginning of the process, (2) the group of representatives in the EDS process spends less meeting time learning the process, and (3) in high-intensity disputes, training can lessen the possibility of co-optation due to inexperience.

One example of a training program implemented before the actual EDS process commences is that used by the U.S. Environmental Protection Agency in their negotiated rule-making program. All participants in negotiations over a specific rule are invited to attend an eight-hour training session that occurs before the first full negotiation meeting. The objectives of this training are:

1. To educate participants about the fundamentals of negotiations;

2. To improve the participants' awareness of the dynamics of disputes;

3. To develop negotiating skills, bargaining strategies, and negotiating style; and

4. To demonstrate ways to apply these skills in the upcoming session. (Schneider and Tohn, 1985)

Without preliminary training, the EDS process participants will have to learn through experience, and this learning can only occur with the passage of time. In every case studied here, the citizen participants had to learn by doing. In the Common Ground process, there was a marked change between the first and second years in how much the group accomplished. The representatives felt they used the six meetings of the first year to learn the process and really accomplished the substance of the work in the second year. In the San Juan case, the mediators orchestrated the first sessions, but only needed to offer occasional comments during the second day, when participants were familiar with the process.

EDS process training can take many forms; the case studies illustrate several examples. In the Common Ground process, training occurred on the first day of the meetings and lasted a few hours. In the San Juan case, the facilitators used a preliminary interview with each participant to: (1) determine if there was room for compromise, (2) explain the process and answer any questions, and (3) ask if there were any suggested changes in the process. Consultants for the Sand Lakes citizens' organizations advised and trained the citizens throughout the process. The consultants periodically reviewed the process with the leaders of the citizen alliance and developed appropriate strategies for the next phase. This approach trained the citizens but the citizens controlled the training content and direction.

Several facilitators noted that training involved more than a focus on negotiations and often included developing an "attitude" for EDS as much as it involved skill acquisition. For problem-solving processes, training helped groups shift from a competitive, adversarial orientation to a collaborative one. Participants had to develop familiarity and comfort analyzing problems, discussing the differing interests of the involved parties, and compromising for a mutually acceptable agreement rather than conquering for a win. Even where negotiation was the predominant mode of interaction, participants had to learn a "cautious openness." The citizens we interviewed focused their comments about training toward what was needed by the individuals directly representing their organizations in the EDS process. However, it is our observation that for effective citizen organization participation, the total membership of citizen organizations involved in EDS processes need at least some amount of training to inform them about these processes and the roles to be played by members, leaders, and representatives.

Carpenter and Kennedy suggest several other ways in addition to training that can help alleviate the difficulties posed by these differences in negotiating abilities. They stress that enforcement of ground rules is one critical way to keep all participants' behavior in check and all parties operating on at least one level of equality. In addition, they caution all parties against "moving too quickly" in the process:

> Time must be built into a conflict management strategy for bringing the parties along in the negotiation process. Especially when participants are aware that they are less experienced than others, they will and should be sensitive to any efforts to push them into accepting proposals they have not had ample time to consider. (1988, 236)

Finally they note that paying attention to the representative's constituents is another way to ensure that a less-skilled participant is not being swayed from his or her group's true interest:

> If representatives are inexperienced, it is a safe assumption that the other people in their groups are at least as inexperienced as they are. There is a serious danger that participants will get too far ahead of their constituents as they gain knowledge about the process and begin to adjust their positions. (1988, 236)

Using Coalitions and Networks

Networking and coalition-building can significantly contribute to citizen power and effectiveness in EDS processes. Groups often used coalitions to consolidate their resources in the beginning of a process, and to support their strategies during the EDS process. The coalitions were able to keep the citizen constituency mobilized around the disputed issues, and provided an essential vehicle for communication between different citizen interests.

Managing a coalition places additional demands on organizations—again in terms of time, energy, and money. Not only must citizen representatives devote time to problem-solving sessions within their own organizations and within the actual group of disputants, but also with members of other citizen groups in order to maintain the strength and unity of the coalition. For example, in the San Juan dispute, the Vallecito group almost fell apart the first day; they had assumed that they all shared the same interests. When they discovered rifts within the coalition, they had to call an emergency meeting to uncover and clarify their mutual interest, and then develop an acceptable joint strategy.

Maintaining a mobilized constituency can be difficult during a long negotiation process. As Susskind and Cruikshank have observed:

> The power of coalitions is enormous—provided, of course, that the members of the coalition share a commitment to the same outcome. Remember that coalitions may ebb and flow during a negotiation. You must constantly check to be certain that your coalition is holding together. (1987, 212)

If the representatives and the leadership of a citizen or environmental organization are focused on the process itself, the everyday communication and other maintenance tasks, required to keep an organization effective, can be neglected. In the Sand Lakes case, citizen representatives commented that when meetings were spread out over months, their memberships became less enthusiastic about the negotiation process and, in a few cases, drifted away due to neglect. If an EDS process is addressing a complex and drawn-out dispute, the citizen groups will not be able to afford a gradual loss of members' interest and commitment. Their representatives will require support from an active constituency to demonstrate the importance of the citizen interests and the reality of their power. Effective networking and coalition organizing can help overcome some of these problems.

In the Pig's Eye case, the citizen organizers used a coalition of forty organizations to maintain the mobilized constituency. The coalition was based on a core of individuals from each group who were dedicated to the Pig's Eye Coalition's (PEC) goal. With a newsletter, PEC meetings, and fund-raisers, these people kept the issue alive in their respective organizations. As the coalition grew, people joined PEC as members and provided a rejuvenating force for continued work. Thus, PEC not only combined various organizational resources for united power, but also provided an ongoing mobilization strategy, bringing new members into the coalition. Either a formal coalition or a loose alliance of citizen organizations can support an active constituency during an EDS process. However, organizations will have to develop an effective networking strategy and have individuals in each organization committed to the disputed issues, the negotiation and problem-solving process, and to mobilizing their respective memberships.

Networking among citizens in the EDS process encourages communication and analysis of disputed issues and the citizens' interests, thereby strengthening the citizens' ability to do effective problem-solving and negotiation. It also helps protect citizens from any divisive situations that may arise during heated debate. In the San Juan case, citizen participants from several organizations entered the process with the impression that they shared a common understanding of the disputed issues; during the first day of negotiations, unexpected differences in understanding and goals began to appear. Fortunately for the citizens, there was time to hold a special caucus to work out the differences and consolidate power before a continuation of the negotiations.

One example of effective networking is the organizing that Peta Williams did with the citizen groups involved in negotiating the Sand Lakes Quiet Area management plan. She determined that open communication and periodic review were the best means for achieving unity among the numerous citizen interests and concerns about the Quiet Area. The EDS process as it evolved was as much a negotiation among the involved citizen organizations as it was between the citizens and the Michigan Department of Natural Resources. Peta Williams worked to make sure all interested parties expressed their concerns during the meetings, and that the total group discussed how particular needs could be addressed. She spent hours calling representatives who missed a meeting, asking them to review any decisions; this information-sharing also provided continuity, so they could participate fully in the next meeting. Connections, the organization from which Williams worked, sent out an agenda before meetings so citizens could prepare. Minutes were typed up and sent out for the coalition's citizen representatives to review the issues that had been discussed and to affirm their decisions. In addition to keeping the alliance together, the citizens established a network of contacts in the Michigan Department of Natural Resources and local governments. These contacts provided background information, gave the citizens insight into the views held by the other stakeholders, and built a network of allies. Overall, networking held the citizen alliance together, created power for these citizen organizations, and provided information on the larger political context that could be used for future issue work.

Impacts of Public Perceptions

It is important that citizens recognize how they are being perceived by the public, traditional decision-makers, and other stakeholders. In some situations, citizen organizations needed to make their names known before being recognized as powerful interests in a particular dispute. In other cases, groups and individuals had to struggle against a perception that they were overly emotional, unreasonable, inappropriately meddling, or "only a single-interest group." Before the Pig's Eye mediation, the citizen coalition confronted repeated industry propaganda that depicted the citizens as an "unreasonable, antibusiness organization." In the Wisconsin groundwater case, the citizen organizations were viewed as ineffectually organized without the "staying power" required to participate in legislative policy-making. In both cases, recognizing their current image helped the citizens strategize for actions to change their image and increase their power in the conflict. In several cases, citizens were able to use expertise and leadership to change the misperceptions of other stakeholders.

Dynamics outside the process are also critical for citizen organizations operating in the larger political arena. In general, the EDS process will be observed by public and private interests alike; any process that affects existing influence and decision-making will not be ignored. External parties will support or challenge the process and its participants depending on their interests and fears. This broader context must be of concern to the participating citizen organizations as well as the other stakeholders.

In the more complicated and polarized situations, some outside groups were not in accord with the final agreement and criticized participating organizations for their involvement. Citizen leaders, representatives, and other strategists had to recognize this possibility and adjust their networking strategies accordingly. However, for the most part, participation in an EDS process improved the citizen group's public image because the groups were recognized as being knowledgeable on the issues and willing to work for a potential solution.

In some cases, the public may not be aware that the EDS process is taking place. EDS processes are usually not flashy events that attract publicity. Unless there is a well-planned media campaign, the press will not cover many negotiations, and public awareness could be minimal. Citizen organizers commented that for an organization building its membership through public action, such anonymity could be deadly.

Citizens in some cases designed an active media campaign to influence media coverage and public opinion. The Sand Lakes citizen representatives called in stories to reporters and sent press releases to local newspapers during the process. One of the Common Ground Task Force objectives was to work through the press to influence public opinion on environmental and agricultural issues. The staff's press work enabled them to present the issues and describe their concerns in the best possible light.

Overall, the EDS participants felt that public opinion supported negotiations due to the widely held value of "talking things over." Press interests followed the same logic. However, reporters usually showed minimal interest in the EDS process until a final agreement was reached. In one case, the press response went beyond disinterest and actually blocked coverage. The NIS policy dialogue was intended to encourage public involvement; the process created dialogue among citizens, businesses, and government about the city of Malden's development problems. Press coverage was an essential means for informing the community, but the mediator's staff was repeatedly ignored by the local newspaper. Claiming limited finances and questionable news value, the editors did not assist in making the NIS process a community event. In retrospect, the NIS staff believe their image as "outsiders" was detrimental to achieving a sense of community ownership. In such cases, local participants in the EDS process should run a media campaign, using their contacts and knowledge to gain news coverage of the dialogue.

Government officials may watch the process from afar because they have an interest in the outcome or because they are considering using an EDS process. The San Juan negotiations were closely watched by the governor's staff, state and federal legislators, and the state fish and wildlife agency. Citizen organizations can use this exposure to their advantage and make gains for their constituency.

Parties that will be affected by the final outcome also may be watching the process, and in some cases challenging it. During the NIS process, Malden 2000, a "group of profit-oriented, pro-development business people," began a parallel forum designed to discuss and promote development in the city. Citizen participants in the NIS process saw it as a challenge to the policy dialogue; in contrast, the NIS facilitator felt it was "a positive by-product of the NIS . . . because it means the NIS has woken up the alligator." In the Common Ground case, the Illinois Farm Bureau declined an invitation to participate in the process, but they did keep track of the negotiations and the final lobbying plans. As the most influential farm lobby in Illinois, the bureau was interested in any consolidation of interests that would result in future lobbying strength.

Citizens also need to assess how the issue is perceived by the public and other stakeholders. Assessing the issue's image can help citizen organizations create a favorable public perception of their interests. Before the San Juan and Sand Lakes negotiations, public land management plan development followed a seemingly obscure government agency planning path. Very few citizens were aware of the plans, much less the details that became controversial. In both cases, the citizen groups had to create a political controversy. There was no "issue" until the organizers and members created one. This "issue creation" was also evident in the Fitchburg case. With newspaper articles, local site visits, public meetings, phone notification, leaflets, posters in business windows, radio broadcasts, and organizational newsletters, the citizen groups demonstrated their dissatisfactions and made the conflict a public, political issue.

For citizen organizations in the Wisconsin groundwater case, the issue was a high priority for the legislator. They did not have to make groundwater regulation a political issue. Instead, the citizens responded to the legislator's "framing of the issue." Citizens in this case had to acknowledge the current public perception of the issue and seek to change it during the EDS process.

Representation and Member Involvement

The Representative's Role

A well-defined role for the citizen representative is necessary to help maintain internal organizational strength and cohesiveness, as well as the organization's power within the EDS process. The data suggest three variables that appear important in shaping this role: the pressure of representation, continuity, and leadership.

The pressure of representation can become very great for a citizen volunteer and for the organization struggling to support the representative. Participation often requires numerous hours and significant information analysis. To reduce these pressures, some citizen representatives worked as a team. With two or three people attending meetings, they were able to divide tasks roughly among a speaker who presented the organization's interests and addressed questions, a listener who also observed the interactions between parties, and a notetaker to provide a record of interactions for reference and analysis as subsequent strategies were planned. Using three people to do the work made the task more viable for these representatives.

Caucusing with representatives of other, similar interests during the process also can assist the citizen representatives. In the San Juan and NIS cases, the facilitators suggested that like parties caucus to share information and clarify their interests. Citizen representatives felt this interaction helped form solidarity and strengthened their ability to analyze the issue.

Both facilitators and participants commented that continuity in citizen representation is advantageous to the process and the involved citizen organizations. In the Common Ground process, there was very little turnover in representation. One organizer felt this stability was a critical factor in the level of trust that evolved and the amount of work the group was able to do. Everyone in the process participated in the initial phases of communication that provided the needed trust and groundwork for issue agreements. The group did not have to begin a relationship with a new representative or bring them up to speed on the evolution of the negotiated issues.

Leadership among representatives is another important factor that influences the citizen representative's role. Leadership usually was derived from three sources: expertise, personal power, and previous power relationships. In some cases, experts took or were given leadership on environmental points relative to their expertise. In the Common Ground and San Juan cases, the participants deferred to specific experts to guide the discussion and frame the technical portion of the agreements. During the Common Ground process, the Audubon representative had the greatest knowledge of wetlands. The participants used his knowledge to develop their definition of a wetland.

In the NIS case, the citizen team experienced a form of leadership derived from personal power. After the first few meetings, Ed Ciavarro decided to "take the citizen team under his wing" and serve as their chairperson. He felt his experience in business negotiations had prepared him for leadership in the group, a skill the other citizen members lacked. Ciavarro's large build and forceful speaking voice also assisted him in presenting the citizens' interests in the EDS process. The other team members acknowledged his leadership skills and supported his guidance.

Representatives in other cases took control because of previous power relationships or official positions. In the Wisconsin groundwater case, leadership in the negotiations came from the political power base that had been the basis of lobbying on the issue in traditional forums. A few legislators, one industry consultant, and various agency personnel led the EDS process and suggested the factors necessary for a sound groundwater bill. Leadership of this type is not uncommon; however, citizen representatives may want to work toward shared leadership in an EDS process. The data from all of our cases suggest that citizen representatives who took a more active leadership role within the EDS process were better able to protect their organizations' interests.

Maintaining Constituency Involvement

Part of the organizational cost in an alternative process is the time and energy spent to maintain interaction with constituents. Representatives from citizen groups may have to devote their energies not only to participating in the actual problem-solving sessions, but also within their own organizations to maintain group cohesiveness and support for negotiated agreements. Often group members who are not on the problem-solving team do not understand the need for certain compromises and concessions. Thus, the citizen representatives must educate and win over their own supporters in order to preserve their personal credibility within the organization as well as within the alternative process.

Wisconsin groundwater citizen participants felt that maintaining constituency support was challenging; in particular, it was tricky explaining trade-offs to those who had not participated in the problem-solving sessions. Likewise, Common Ground citizen participants indicated that constituent interaction and education were difficult. Representatives often had to compete with other meeting agenda items and newsletter articles for feedback and support. NIS citizen participants had difficulties overcoming apathy in the community to generate support and enthusiasm for the process.

Citizen representatives in the cases studied in this book stressed unsatisfactory contact with their "membership" as a major weakness of their strategies and something they would definitely need to improve if they ever participated in an EDS process again. Communicating with their constituency can be an uphill struggle for citizens. Often there are competing agendas for constituency time, and the EDS process can become isolated from a citizen organization's ongoing work. Even groups formed around a single issue can have poor communication resulting in a badly informed constituency. Often this leads to lack of support for the agreement reached in the negotiation process, which in turn can reduce support for the citizen organization.

In a case involving an attempt to develop a compromise proposal for comprehensive national oil shale legislation, an EDS process severely backfired because of the apparent poor communication between the environmental representative and his constituency and because of a weak coalition of interests on the side of the environmental interests. Through a process of direct negotiations between individuals representing the oil shale industry, state and local governments, and environmental interests, a full year of meetings was consumed in developing mutually agreeable wording for a bill that could be presented to Congress. At the last minute, after a proposed final agreement had been distributed, the environmental interest representative was pulled from the negotiations and the process was denounced by his organization (Marston 1984).

While the individual speaking for the environmental interests in these oil shale negotiations thought he had the support of his organization and others and thought they were following in concert, as it turns out they were not.

This case illustrates the critical importance of communication, coalition building, and ensuring the adequacy and appropriateness of your representative in order to prove your trustworthiness at the table. One individual representing the Exxon Corporation commented, "The troubling question is: Who does represent the environmental community? It calls into question whether it's reasonable to include the environmental community in the future in such efforts."

The industry interests' main concern was not so much that the environmental groups rejected the proposal, but in the words of the Rocky Mountain Oil and Gas Association representative:

> The bad faith is that they went through the process with someone supposedly representing them and then pulled him out. We get to our last meeting, and Kevin Markey is no longer representing them. But he sat there for a year.
>
> My perception is that the environmentalists didn't negotiate in good faith. They repudiated the efforts of their representatives at the 12th hour. I'm angry. I think we've been had.

The environmental representative's colleagues felt that he was being manipulated and were dissatisfied with specific negotiated results six months into the one-year negotiations. But they failed to take action until the negotiations were on the eve of being completed. The environmental groups do put some of the blame for this outcome on themselves. Because environmental groups operate with limited staff and resources, everyone clearly cannot be everywhere at the same time. One National Wildlife Federation representative commented, "We should have jumped in on this earlier. This [oil shale] was not a top priority for us."

And a Colorado Wildlife Federation representative similarly said, "Groups like us depended on Kevin; we didn't have the time. We're concerned that there was a major effort and that trust among three major entities—and concerned that it was undercut largely by people not on the scene."

The result is a lot of hard feelings, a lot of seemingly wasted time and energy by all participants, and the unlikelihood of these groups ever to negotiate effectively these issues in the future. The process has also tainted the future involvement of these state and commodity interest group representatives with environmental organizations more generally.

Ann Montgomery, a citizen representing Oregon's Natural History Society, who participated in successful negotiations over several timber sale proposals in Oregon's Willamette National Forest, has this advice for other citizens pursuing an EDS process:

1. Be able to work within your own group to reach a consensus before you approach the other party.

2. Be willing to work with the other party to learn their values and processes. If you don't understand each other, communication is blocked and negotiation is hopeless.

3. Keep your main goal in mind; don't get sidetracked on less important issues.

4. Keep a record of all meetings. Immediately write down the position as it is formulated so all can see it and consider it. It provides physical evidence of the process. It also enables all to be sure that they are clear about what is being agreed upon (Mason and Desmond 1983).

Similarly, her colleague in these negotiations, Ben Ross, advised that:

> you need to build a consensus among your own group early on so you can present a united front at the start. In the usual approach to public involvement, groups submit comments independently of each other and the Forest Service has to try to recognize the differences between them.

Setting up a communication link between the representatives and the constituency can serve several purposes. A representative may need to verify decisions or agreements with his or her membership. For example, in the Common Ground case, the Illinois South Project (ISP) representative set aside time for the ISP staff to read every agreement before accepting it. This provision was necessary because the organization worked by consensus and needed everyone's approval.

Communication can keep a representative sensitive, responsive, and accountable to his or her organization's interests rather than caught up in pressure to reach agreement in the EDS process. Meetings of the representative and leadership with a subgroup of the organization also can serve as a sounding board on ideas and arguments for future negotiating sessions. One representative mentioned that he never felt so isolated as when he participated in the EDS process; the reality of decentralized, volunteer work left him making decisions with very little feedback from the organization he was representing. Next time, he suggests the environmental citizen organization create a task force on the EDS process to provide support and consultation to the representative and information exchange between the representative and the rest of the organization.

Communication channels are not only helpful for the representative, but they can also be critical for the organization and its supporting constituency. Communication between the representative and the constituency helps to maintain organizational mobilization and information. Communications can educate members about the issues being negotiated in the EDS process and the organization's interests. Former participants often found that understanding and analysis evolved among the representatives in the EDS process, but their constituencies did not share this new understanding. The membership continued to view the issue as it was analyzed before the process began.

Susskind and Cruikshank have frequently seen this divergence in understanding of the issues and potential solutions arise between a representative and his or her constituency. To avoid this problem, they stress that all participants understand that:

> You begin as the spokesperson for your group's interests. Gradually, as you gain an understanding of the other side's interests, you become a spokesperson for the work of the group. You may well realize that your group's initial aspirations were unreasonable. But, without help, your group will not grasp this. The interactions between you and your membership that were adequate at the beginning of the process may no longer suffice. Consider additional meetings or periodic published reports to your membership. Make sure they can easily reach you—to ask questions or to express disappointment. (1987, 209–10)

In order to prevent factions from developing within the involved environmental and citizen organizations, it is essential that representatives communicate with members throughout the EDS process. To share their new analyses of the issues, representatives have used meeting reports, newsletters, and in one case a conference on the EDS process and the final agreements. These mechanisms created dialogue that was beneficial for all. The representatives were able to clarify their stance by explaining the issue, and the membership served as a check on the representatives, reducing the chance that the group's interests were not being addressed adequately.

Such ongoing dialogue also may reduce the chances of an organization backing out on an agreement in the final moments of the process. Differences can be identified early in the process, rather than in response to a final document that the group may be forced to reject. In the Wisconsin groundwater case, the special legislative committee representatives were expected to return to their constituencies and fight for the agreement. They were asked to argue strongly against any major changes their organization might develop and advocate in the subsequent legislative sessions. This advocacy was important because the authors, representatives in the EDS process, viewed the agreement as a finely balanced document resulting in a fragile "consensus" of divergent interests.

In summary, it appears that ongoing communication can educate the constituency, support the representative, maintain organizational cohesiveness, possibly preclude a last-minute withdrawal by an uninformed organization, and increase members' support for the final agreement.

After the EDS Process

An assessment of citizen effectiveness in the EDS process should include an evaluation of citizen power at the end of the process as groups move on to new projects.

Assessing Citizen Effectiveness

It appears that citizen organizations in the case studies had mixed experiences in using their power. Some groups gained increased political legitimacy, but they also used a tremendous amount of leadership time. Some citizens improved their access and influence to decision-making for the issues discussed in the EDS process, but it is not certain whether this new influence will transfer to other issues. Finally, in a few cases, the experience empowered individuals to continue participating in politics, but whole groups stayed at their original, pre-EDS process level of participation.

Organizers may find they gained organizational strength and increased political legitimacy by participating in an EDS process. For example, the NIS citizens discussed town policy with government and business leaders in an atmosphere of legitimate participation, where previously they had been uninvolved. The Pig's Eye Coalition (PEC) gained an improved public image and increased political power because PEC had participated in negotiations in good faith while the barge interests had "walked out of the process." After the EDS process, PEC's adversarial strategies were more acceptable to the public because PEC had attempted negotiations. PEC used this argument during subsequent political lobbying to gain legitimacy for their position. In the San Juan case, the citizens went from being a nonentity in Forest Service decision-making to being a significant, organized force that influenced management decisions.

Citizen power also can be assessed by reviewing citizen effectiveness in the established decision-making process after the EDS process ends. Power may be demonstrated through new points of entry to decision-making and/ or a new consciousness of the citizens' unique interests. To create new entry points in established decision-making channels, citizens will need to continue their pressure on the traditional authorities. For example, a few of the Common Ground organizations' representatives lobbied the Illinois Agriculture Department until a Citizens Wetlands Task Force was formed to advise on the Illinois Wetlands Inventory; out of twenty task force members, six were from Common Ground organizations. In two other cases, a few individuals were empowered by their involvement in the EDS process; they became active in citywide politics and eventually ran for city council. However, their representative organizations did not greatly alter their political participation following the experience with the EDS process.

Assessing the citizens' power following an EDS process is important in that it can affect the citizen group's selection of its next project as well as strategies it is willing to use in the future. Citizens with ongoing concerns were best served by remaining powerful after the official EDS process had ended. This longer-term involvement may be easier for larger citizen groups because they have an organizational structure to support long-term planning. However, the data suggest that any group can consolidate power if it decides early in the EDS process that continuity is a priority for monitoring implementation of agreements and for planning future projects.

Continuing the EDS Process

Once the EDS process is completed, citizens should evaluate what else ought to be done to achieve their interests. The range of options is from "Do nothing, our objectives were met," to "Now that the first agreement is reached, we need to design the main strategy," and options that fall between these two extremes. In other words, the next step may be to acknowledge that the organization's goals have been entirely satisfied, or it may be to move from the initial agreement to a more long-term and more comprehensive strategy for achieving additional desired changes. In the Fitchburg case, citizens ended their involvement in the water supply problem when the new system was installed. In the Common Ground case, participants found agreement between agricultural and environmental groups on three issues: soil erosion control measures, wetlands protection, and farmland preservation. However, they had to continue with joint lobbying of the state government bodies and education on the issues for their respective constituencies.

For the Sand Lakes citizens, whether to continue the citizen alliance was not a planned decision but instead a matter of attrition due to busy personal schedules and commitments to other groups. On reflection, several representatives felt they missed an opportunity to consolidate their power and make a long-term change in the Michigan DNR's public participation policies. In contrast, citizens in the San Juan case used the momentum of the negotiations to build a strong, ongoing local group concerned with all of the management decisions in the San Juan National Forest. Citizens who want to continue their role in decision-making and sustain their power will need to plan its transfer to the next project, as the San Juan citizens did, and move on to developing new strategies for their next issue.

It appears that whether or not the involved organizations and representatives continued with lobbying efforts had less to do with their satisfaction with the EDS agreement than it did with how the issue meshed with the citizen organizations' total program. The issues' "fit" with organizations' ongoing projects determined whether groups only voiced support or became actively involved after the EDS process. In general, if a strong informal network is developed and the issues are central to a group's ongoing agenda, it is possible to build the necessary follow-up strategies. In the Common Ground case, out of fifteen groups, three or four had wetlands programs and picked up the leadership roles in lobbying for the Common Ground wetlands agreement. Other groups found soil erosion more consistent with their total program and lobbied principally for the soil erosion agreement.

Citizen groups have to be aware of strategic considerations as they move from the collaborative process back to adversarial politics. Some representatives felt there could be a loss of power if citizens did not address this critical shift. Critics of EDS processes felt an agreement from a consensus process actually compromised future possibilities for organized protest. They commented that once a consensus agreement was reached, the public and other participants are predisposed to believe there will be no future conflict. Thus, leaders and organizers may want to plan carefully necessary adversarial strategies. If they cannot make a public case for why adversarial strategies are necessary, the citizens could be caught in an unfavorable position. EDS proponents argue that the benefits of a mutually acceptable agreement are worth these strategic risks.

Conclusion

Environmental citizen organizations are important parties in environmental and natural resource conflicts and as such need to be able to use effectively a wide array of strategies and tactics for achieving the changes that they desire. EDS is a strategy that is gaining increased attention and use because of the willingness of government and business to be involved sometimes in the face-to-face problem-solving and negotiation of EDS processes.

The research reported here represents an early step in work to better understand the dynamics of EDS processes and to better describe, from the perspective of environmental citizen organizations, the situation, options, problems, and likely outcomes from deliberate and selective participation in these processes of conflict management. As with any change strategy, information and skill are required for effective use of the involved ideas and actions.

Three case studies follow this chapter, all highlighting organizational issues that confront citizen groups who participate in an EDS process.

The Sand Lakes Quiet Area issue-based negotiations case study describes the efforts of a citizen group to protect the wilderness characteristics of this state land in Michigan. Through persistence and a variety of strategies, the citizens were able to encourage a collaborative interaction with the state Department of Natural Resources in developing the management plan for this area and responding to proposed oil and gas drilling there.

The Pig's Eye attempted mediation case study illustrates a concerted effort by a coalition of forty citizen groups to protect a heron rookery along the Mississippi River. While the mediation failed, the citizen coalition nonetheless benefited from its participation in the process. Their experience illustrates several issues that any organization must confront in deciding whether or not to participate in an EDS process and how to participate once there.

Finally, the Wisconsin groundwater legislation negotiation case describes a hybrid dispute settlement process: part consensus-building, part politics-as-usual. It raises key concerns about representation and coalition-building that citizen groups must be aware of when entering into negotiations in the legislative arena.

References

Carpenter, Susan, and W. J. D. Kennedy. *Managing Public Disputes: A Practical Guide to Handling Conflict and Reaching Agreements.* San Francisco: Jossey-Bass, 1988.

Marston, Ed. "Industry and Government Charge Environmentalists with Bad Faith Negotiating." *High Country News* (April 7, 1984): 12–13.

Mason, Jerry, and Jack Desmond. "The Land-Use Fight That Didn't Happen." *American Forests* 89, no. 11 (1983): 17–56.

Schneider, Peter, and Ellen Tohn. "Success in Negotiating Environmental Regulations. *Environmental Impact Assessment Review* 5, no. 1 (March 1985): 71–78.

Steinhart, Peter. "Talking It Over." *Audubon* 86, no. 1 (January 1984): 8–14.

Susskind, Lawrence, and Jeffrey Cruikshank. *Breaking the Impasse: Consensual Approaches to Resolving Public Disputes.* New York: Basic Books, 1987.

CASE STUDY 5:
Sand Lakes Quiet Area
Issue-Based Negotiation

Kristen C. Nelson

This case study presents an issue-based negotiation between a coalition of citizen groups and representatives of the Michigan Department of Natural Resources over management of a state Quiet Area known as Sand Lakes. As is the case with many environmental dispute settlement processes, the Sand Lakes Quiet Area negotiations gradually evolved as the site-specific dispute heightened. The citizens used their influence at the state level to initiate a dialogue with agency representatives and to keep them at the bargaining table. The process allowed a more creative package of solutions to be developed than would likely have been proposed by the agency on its own. The citizens relied heavily on outside process and strategy consultants to help them through the process, in making decisions and in setting strategy. It was facilitated by a well-respected member of the citizen coalition, and it allowed the discussion to expand from a dispute over a single oil and gas well to larger issues in developing the area's overall management plan. While the oil company representative was not present during the negotiations, the citizens' persistence and the willingness of the agency representatives to act as go-between allowed the process to succeed and the oil company to support its conclusions.

The case study looks at organizational issues from the perspective of all three major parties involved. It addresses the following key organizational questions:

Encouraging an EDS Process to Evolve. What are some ways in which to encourage a traditional decision-making structure to evolve into a dispute settlement process that accommodates collaborative problem-solving? How can an active citizen group provide the forum within which a more productive, two-way dialogue can occur? What are some ways in which a citizen group can build their power and influence such that decision-makers must listen to them?

Managing a Coalition. How might a citizen coalition achieve and maintain internal cohesiveness or "one voice" in the dispute settlement process? How might internal communication and trust be fostered within the coalition? How might internal negotiations be accommodated? How and when should a key spokesperson be selected for some meetings or issues in order to minimize the burden on all groups?

Acquiring Necessary Resources.   How might you harness the resources, expertise, and political influence that the citizen organizations and/ or their individual members have access to? When might it be advisable to seek the advice and feedback from individuals or organizations with expertise in collaborative dispute settlement processes? How might having a staff available to handle administrative matters ease the process?

Participation.   What can you do if one party chooses not to participate?

Personal Emotions.   How might representatives separate their own emotions and opinions from the position of the organization he or she is representing?

Assessing Ongoing Involvement.   Should you stay involved in the issue once agreement is reached within the dispute settlement process? How might you do so? What resources do you need to monitor implementation of an agreement reached in the EDS process? What might be the likely course of events if you choose not to stay involved?

Unless otherwise noted, information and quotes in this case are from the author's personal interviews with the participants.

The Chronology

The Beginning of Sand Lakes Quiet Area

On July 13, 1973, the state of Michigan Natural Resources Commission dedicated the Sand Lakes Quiet Area. The Department of Natural Resources (DNR) personnel and representatives of local citizen groups had worked together for several years to create an area of "Michigan lands for fulfilling a recreational experience of solitude" (Michigan Department of Natural Resources 1973). Because motorized recreational vehicles increasingly had dominated the use of Michigan's state lands, hikers, cross-country skiers, and "sports people" had argued for a unique area providing quiet recreational activities.

Ned Caveney and Dan Bonner, Traverse City DNR foresters, and other DNR personnel suggested an area, seven miles west of Kalkaska, Michigan, that "still retain(ed) a natural wilderness aspect" (Michigan Department of Natural Resources 1973). This 2,775 acres of state-owned land had within its boundaries many microenvironments: small pothole marshes, fourteen small lakes, rolling hills, and a variety of forest cover. Caveney and others developed the 1973 Quiet Area management plan around the management objective "to provide the opportunity for forest recreation of the highest quality. While recreation is not the only activity or resource to be managed on the area, it is the most important. Proper management calls for as little development as possible" (Michigan Department of Natural Resources 1973). The plan describes the conditions for forestry, fisheries, wildlife, and hydrocarbon development. These activities had to reflect the spirit of the Quiet Area; they were to harmonize with a "peaceful haven," an "experience of solitude," a place "closed to motorized vehicles," and a "refuge from noise, disturbing activities, and unsightliness."

For seven years, financial constraints limited active DNR management of the Quiet Area. During this time, while visible land management practices were absent, public use of the area increased. Quiet Area visitors became accustomed to recreation that did not compete with other uses. However, during these years, hydrocarbon development grew in the surrounding state lands. In 1967, all state lands had been leased for hydrocarbon development on a ten-year contract. The drilling plan for the Sand Lakes Quiet Area was a sequential plan with slant drilling from outside the area boundaries. When the leases came up for renewal in 1977, the Northern Michigan Exploration Company (Nomeco), requested an extension for all its leases, including the Whitewater Section 24—a tract of land in the Sand Lakes Quiet Area. The DNR granted the extension but changed the lease terms from development to nondevelopment. A nondevelopment lease allows consideration of surface drilling only if there is a probability of drainage of oil and gas from state land. This decision regarding surface drilling on a nondevelopment lease can only be made by the Michigan Natural Resources Commission (NRC). The policy-making NRC has overview responsibility for all DNR programs.

Nomeco Applies for a New Hydrocarbon Lease

In October 1980, Nomeco's field division recommended exploration of Section 24, but the nondevelopment lease prevented the DNR from issuing a drilling permit. After much consultation with the DNR Lands Division and the DNR Geological Survey Division, Nomeco applied to the NRC for a change in lease status. The DNR personnel reviewed countless options and conditions for drilling, then recommended reclassification of the Section 24 lease. The DNR identified one drilling site that offered the least possible environmental damage. They designated eleven construction and maintenance stipulations under which the well could be drilled. This recommendation went to the Natural Resources Commission. In cases of lease reclassification, the NRC has sole decision-making power. Following standard procedure, the NRC held public hearings on the reclassification issue at their November 1980 meeting. A decision was scheduled for the following month.

Traverse City area residents were surprised by the possibility of drilling in the Quiet Area. Many environmentally minded citizens had worked diligently for the Quiet Area dedication in 1973 and felt hydrocarbon development was incompatible with the Quiet Area philosophy and stated objectives. Some people heard about the proposed well from the newspaper, others learned of it by talking with the local DNR field staff. The unanimous response by members of this group was disbelief, confusion, and anger.

Quiet Area Users Attempt to Halt the Well

Peta Williams, a long-time environmental advocate, wrote a letter to the NRC members and the DNR director calling for a denial of lease reclassification. Her interest stemmed from an early public support of the Quiet Area's creation. Williams's position as president of Connections, a nonprofit organization dedicated to involving citizens in the local and state decision-making process concerning environmental issues, served as a vehicle for challenging this decision. She spoke for many local people in her plea to maintain the "wild area experience" and to "stay true to the spirit of the original Quiet Area" plan. Williams lobbied then DNR director, Dr. Howard Tanner, through letters and phone calls. She repeatedly mentioned the citizen/environmental organizations that were opposed to changing the lease status and identified the possible repercussions associated with a hasty decision. As an alternative to an NRC ruling, Williams offered Connections as host for a meeting between local citizens and Dr. Tanner to discuss concerns over Quiet Area drilling. She felt the DNR needed input from primary users and suggested face-to-face dialogue as a positive option. The next day, Howard Tanner temporarily withdrew the lease reclassification from the NRC agenda and agreed to meet with concerned citizens. He had been unaware of this controversy and believed further consideration was in order. Whenever possible, Tanner wanted to deal with conflicting interests before the DNR took decisive actions; previous environmental conflicts had erupted into after-the-fact battles in court and the legislature. Tanner believed the DNR should take into consideration public opinion and encourage participation. Earlier, multiple party negotiations on Michigan oil and gas policy issues had developed satisfactory compromise plans with broad-based support.

Other citizen organizations in the region, in addition to Connections, were reacting to the threat of surface drilling in the Quiet Area. In a continuing public service effort, the Ski Trails Action Committee held a highly publicized "Quiet Area Trail Grooming Day" about the time Tanner was considering a meeting in Traverse City (Traverse City *Record Eagle*, December 10, 1980). The group's purpose was to work along with the local

DNR personnel to maintain the trails, parking lots, and some facilities in the Quiet Area. The Trail Day was an attempt to focus on the Quiet Area's value as a "near wilderness experience." Helen Milliken, the governor's wife, lent her support to the activities. She focused the press attention on the importance of protecting the spirit of the Quiet Area. This publicity calling for preservation of a unique recreation area brought the Quiet Area into the public's eye.

Another organization, Northern Michigan Environmental Action Council (NMEAC), began a petition drive on February 6 to dedicate Sand Lakes Quiet Area as a "natural or wild area under the Michigan Wilderness and Natural Areas Act of 1972." Because of development restrictions in the act, designation would eliminate any possibility of hydrocarbon exploration. The petition drive focused publicity on the drilling and identified broad-based support for a "wild area" designation. It confronted the DNR's management plans head-on. There appeared to be no sentiment within the department to move management closer to a wild areas plan; DNR field staff and planners strongly supported a multiple use plan.

Tanner Meets with the Citizen Representatives

As the groups organized activities to halt the well, they also attended the meeting initiated by Connections. On February 20, 1981, Howard Tanner and several DNR staff met with a group of concerned citizens selected by Connections's staff. Williams knew most of the people working on environmental issues as many of them had worked together on past projects and local events. The meeting's objectives, according to Williams, were to "explain users' concerns to Tanner, to listen to his thoughts, and to explore possible solutions." In facilitating this meeting, Connections took the first step toward their organizational goal of developing "better communications between our decision-makers and us who live with their decisions." Connections was also interested in building their organization and increasing their perceived legitimacy by the Department of Natural Resources and local environmental groups. The following representatives attended the meeting:

Citizen Representatives

Norman Brokaw	Sierra Club
Ross Childs	Grand Traverse County
Jim Hall	Ski Trails Action Committee
John Ammar	Ski Trails Action Committee
Neil Hoch	Northern Michigan Environmental Action Council
Sally Olsen	Northern Michigan Environmental Action Council
June Janis	Michigan Inventory Advisory Committee
June Mason	Audubon Club

Ford Kellum	Audubon Club
Sally Wilhelm	Michigan Trail Riders Association
Rogers Williams	Traverse Bay Regional Planning Commission
Gordon Hayward	Traverse Bay Regional Planning Commission

Invited but not
attending:

Grant Trigger	Michigan Environmental Council
Helen Milliken	governor's wife
Ken Sikkema	Western Michigan Environmental Action Council

DNR Participants

Howard Tanner	DNR director
Allen Crabtree	Environmental Enforcement—Lansing Office
Barney Chase	Forest Management—Traverse City Office
Bernie Hubbard	Forest Management—Traverse City Office

Invited but not
attending:

| Don Inman | governor's office |

Connections Staff

Peta Williams	facilitator
Jim Olsen	legal adviser
Peg Kauffman	recorder

Connections invited Nomeco to send a representative, but John Hamel, district land manager, declined. Hamel explained his decision, commenting:

> We didn't attend the meeting in Traverse City because we felt we shouldn't be there. We'd only take abuse. I let others fight that battle . . . I don't know about the environmental issues. I couldn't answer any of the questions and I'd rather the DNR work out with the other parties what their [citizen] interests are.

Reflecting later, one citizen representative thought Nomeco chose the "smart option." They pointed to the history of conflict between industry and environmentalists as ample reason for Nomeco to avoid "unnecessary interaction." Peta Williams had other hopes. Though she understood Nomeco's response, it eliminated the possibility of face-to-face discussion among all the stakeholders and possibly threatened a mutually acceptable solution.

The DNR director met with twelve environmental and citizen group representatives. This exploratory meeting gave Tanner insight into citizen interests not addressed in the limited management activities in the Quiet Area. Since the citizen representatives did not collaborate prior to this meeting, their comments came from many fronts. Initial concern about surface drilling expanded into multiple issues on appropriate management practices. One observer found it confusing to have one issue presented and then dropped as the group moved on to the next issue—jumping from forest practices to the original philosophy of the Quiet Area. He interpreted Tanner's agreement to attend the meeting as "just letting the citizens blow off steam." Other participants felt successful in merely getting the DNR director up to Traverse City. They believed a strong protest from a variety of interests would force Tanner to respond with more than the standard bureaucratic channels.

Dr. Tanner answered many questions but deferred any specific commitments until he could consult with DNR personnel. He did suggest an expansion of Sand Lakes Quiet Area as an answer to some concerns. Peta Williams was encouraged by the meeting, which had successfully brought together a wide variety of dissenting voices. This gathering suggested an approach that could be used to negotiate an acceptable solution. Citizens asked for input into the decision about whether or not to drill in the Quiet Area and requested participation in planning the management of Sand Lakes Quiet Area. The ball was now in Tanner's court; he needed to provide a process for public input.

In the meantime, Northern Michigan Environmental Action Council (NMEAC) completed their petition drive calling for the Quiet Area's dedication as a "wild area." With over fifteen hundred signatures, NMEAC organizers felt supported and confident about their resistance to the proposed surface drilling. Working for a "wild area" dedication would take considerable political organizing. The Michigan Wilderness and Natural Areas Board, which had the authority to make these decisions, was not functioning. As a result, neither the DNR nor NMEAC could receive a hearing for wilderness dedication. NMEAC board members decided to wait until Tanner presented his option for resolving the present conflicts. At that point, they would decide on a strategy for using the petitions, if it proved necessary.

How Do You Define "Quiet Area"?

Tanner instructed DNR staff to follow through with the Traverse City group. One month later, in March 1981, Connections facilitated another meeting between DNR personnel and citizen representatives. The citizen organizations decided that Connections would serve as the representative umbrella. They believed it was the best way to represent citizen interest in this situation because (1) Connections had many contacts in state government, (2) Connections had credibility as an organization that shared work and leadership as a result of the community forums it had sponsored earlier, and (3) under this umbrella, strategies would be mutually set. Jerry Thiede, DNR forest management planner, spent the afternoon explaining DNR management practices and listening to the citizens' critique. Much of the meeting was spent clarifying misunderstandings, but gradually the critical differences emerged. Much contention pivoted on the definition of a Quiet Area. The DNR interpreted Quiet Area as a "nonmotorized, dispersed recreation area." Their emphasis was on nonmotorized recreation, an activity that did not exclude oil/gas drilling or other management actions. The quiet recreation users approached the definition from a preservationist perspective, emphasizing the "wilderness experience" as the most valued quality. The arguments concerning a wide variety of management options centered on this philosophical difference.

During the meeting, Jerry Thiede acknowledged that the conflict expanded well beyond the issue of hydrocarbon development. Connections wanted discussion on a variety of management issues rather than solely on surface drilling. The DNR staff mentioned that the Quiet Area was scheduled for an operations inventory leading to its next ten-year management plan. With this much public concern, Thiede recommended that the group consider the entire management plan for Sand Lakes Quiet Area.

The following commitments were made at the end of the meeting. Connections agreed to convene and facilitate all meetings between the local citizens and the DNR. As the process evolved, the citizen members trusted Peta Williams to facilitate the meetings instead of bringing in a third party facilitator. They felt her dual role of facilitator and participant could be manageable. Connections would also serve as the local contact for the DNR. The citizens decided to participate in discussions leading to an acceptable management plan. NMEAC agreed to withhold the petitions until the outcome of the discussions. At that time, they would decide whether to continue pushing for a "wild area" dedication.

As Connections considered the approaching discussions, they sought the advice of Dr. Patricia Bidol, from the School of Natural Resources at the University of Michigan. Bidol served as a sounding board for questions on organizational and negotiation dynamics that confronted the citizen groups. Within this arrangement, Dr. Bidol assisted Peta Williams in developing an "issue-based negotiation" process. She encouraged the citizens to (1) "assess the goals, power, and past history for each stakeholder," and (2) to "develop strategies and tactics that help [citizens] format the alternative environmental conflict management process in a way that makes sense for them and fits into the ongoing traditional processes." The first assumption of this process was that citizens do not have carte blanche in creating the process but have to mesh with the traditional systems. According to Bidol, "implementation is more likely if the outcome [of negotiations] is connected to an agency."

The second assumption within this process was that the old citizen group leaves "other options [strategies] open and does not cut them out as possible plans for future use." For Peta Williams and Patricia Bidol, the main tenet of this consulting style allowed for the citizens to do their own process development and outcome negotiation. This informal relationship continued throughout the process.

Department of Natural Resources Task Force Is Formed

One month later, DNR director Tanner established the DNR Sand Lakes Quiet Area Task Force (DNRTF) to review the 1973 management plan. The task force was instructed to "include consideration of alternate management options, alternate boundaries, natural area status, etc. Full opportunity for public and oil company (Lessee) input should be provided" (Michigan Department of Natural Resources, October 1981). Jerry Thiede was appointed chair and charged with coordinating the DNR divisions for internal negotiations and incorporating public input. Along with Thiede, the following DNR personnel represented the DNR divisions on the DNRTF.

Jerry Thiede	Forest Management
Ray Schofield	Wildlife
Allen Crabtree	Geological Survey
Bob Borak	Forest Management
Mike Bricker	Geological Survey
David Freed	Lands

Advisers

Bill McClay	Fisheries
Dennis Vitton	Forest Management

Tanner held all actions on Nomeco's lease reclassification request until the task force report was submitted. Nomeco recognized that the DNR director had the power to hold up a lease reclassification and decided to work with the DNR to clear the way for a drilling permit. To begin the review process, Thiede initiated the DNR operations inventory for Sand Lakes Quiet Area asking field staff to propose management options. The staff considered the input from the Traverse City discussions as they planned trail placement, timber harvests, and so forth.

For the next two years, the DNR, Nomeco, and the citizens referred to the process as "negotiations," "discussions," and "public input." Patricia Bidol, Citizens Task Force adviser, called it "issues-based negotiations." The most common term used by all parties was "negotiations," but everyone's meaning was different. At no time were the parties negotiating in the same manner as labor negotiations or formal environmental mediations. The DNR maintained their control and authority, never giving up their power over the final decision. Some participants referred to these negotiations as formal discussions with the DNR. Others felt the DNR had committed to negotiating around management issues and was required to include the citizen position. Taking these various interpretations of negotiation into account, the Sand Lakes alternative management process evolved as a series of discussions prior to negotiations over the differences between two reports; the DNRTF report and the CTF report, a counterproposal. After these negotiations, the DNR authored a final Sand Lakes Quiet Area management plan, presenting it to the Michigan Natural Resource Commission for approval.

Prenegotiation Information-Gathering

In the beginning of the process, the citizens were encouraged by the task force formation. This structural response to their criticism offered a glimmer of hope for change. From April to September 1981, the DNRTF worked as a mediating force between Nomeco's interests, the citizen interests, and the DNR division interests. Initially, Jerry Thiede wanted to bring all of the parties together. The citizens agreed to meet, but Nomeco wanted to work solely through the DNR. Nomeco's John Hamel felt the long-established communication ties with the DNR Lands Division staff would better serve the company: "They understood our problems and they understood the environmentalist's problems." This relationship set the communication dynamics for the remainder of the process. Thiede worked with the DNR Lands Division and Nomeco on leasing contracts. He consulted the DNR personnel for their recommendations on forestry, fisheries, wildlife, and recreation management options. Finally, he met with the citizen representatives to collect their opinions about Quiet Area management.

For three months, the citizens waited for a response to their suggestions. As one participant said, "After talking with Thiede we waited. Nothing came out of Lansing very quickly, but waiting was better than drilling." The DNRTF was in the process of negotiating internally over Sand Lakes management issues. Within the DNR divisions, there was considerable concern that management expertise be given precedence in planning and that unrepresented user groups such as anglers and hunters be provided for in the plan (see "Evaluation of the Settlement" section below for details). A number of DNR managers thought that natural resources in the area should drive the management plan.

In October 1981, the DNRTF submitted a "Report to the Director" on Sand Lakes Quiet Area management. This report gave an overview of current programs and proposed a program for each issue area: Fisheries; Roads, Trails, and Campgrounds; Forest and Wildlife; Hydrocarbon Development; and Boundary Relocation. In December, it was sent to Connections for reactions.

Seeking a Citizen Consensus

Peta Williams brought the citizen representatives together to critique the proposed management plan. During January 1982, the citizens went through a process comparable to the DNRTF's. These diverse interests negotiated among themselves in an attempt to reach a common response. Initial organizational positions such as "no well" evolved into new identifiable interests and issues as the coalition formed. These joint interests went beyond the singular positions held in the beginning. Each representative had specific positions important to their constituents. Some groups wanted no forest management practices, others felt limited forestry would be acceptable. On camping issues, one participant wanted to eliminate all camping from the Quiet Area, while others supported natural areas camping. Throughout the discussion, the facilitator, Peta Williams, kept the focus on issues rather than hardened positions of individual opinions.

In three confrontational but collaborative meetings, they reached a consensus on several issues. The citizens criticized the DNR report for eliminating most of the Quiet Area philosophy that had been written into the 1973 plan. The DNRTF felt their plan was more "action oriented" in an attempt to put the 1973 philosophy on a concrete footing. The new management plan was a technical document that identified "nonmotorized recreation" as the key value. Some of the original supporters of the Quiet Area proposal were shocked at the new report's lack of spirit. They saw it as a technical management plan that omitted the philosophy of the 1973 dedication. The citizen representatives asked Connections to rewrite the DNRTF report incorporating all points made during the group meetings.

They also officially formed the Citizens Task Force (CTF) to author the response. On February 4, 1982 a rewritten document—"The Citizens Task Force Report"—reached the DNR director's desk.

Negotiations Over the Different Reports

The DNRTF and the CTF began negotiations over the differences in the two reports. From February to October 1982, these groups met to sell their ideas, modify sections of the report, and identify potential compromises. Initially, the DNRTF and the CTF met as full groups, but by August only the DNRTF chair and Peta Williams were meeting over disputed issues. At the same time, Thiede was communicating with the Nomeco and AMOCO oil companies concerning their role in the negotiated plan. AMOCO held several development leases in the Quiet Area that the DNR wanted changed to nondevelopment.

The CTF continually struggled for internal consensus as each exchange brought new issues to the table. The organizational diversity within the CTF contributed to the variety of salient issues. In the summer of 1982,

Bonnie Anderson, an organizational consultant and student of Dr. Bidol's, worked with Connections to facilitate the coalition-building. As negotiations became more specific, the informal process used in earlier meetings did not address the group's needs. Anderson and Williams worked to keep all of the representatives informed, committed, and participating. She helped Williams strategize by "keeping the details in perspective and collaborating on meeting plans." After every counterproposal from the DNRTF, the group had to discuss the potential compromise and reach a consistent agreement for a response. In the final negotiation sessions, Williams was officially delegated to represent the CTF interests, a role that until then had been filled on an informal basis.

The Final Agreement

The 1983 Sand Lakes Quiet Area management plan reflected negotiation of seven issues: definition of SLQA purpose; hydrocarbon development; boundary relocation; fisheries; road, trails, and campground; forest and wildlife management; buffer zones. The DNR's initial positions were presented in the DNR report to the director, October 1981. In response to the DNRTF positions, the CTF members prepared a modified report to the director in February 1982. Nomeco's interests were represented during discussions between Jerry Thiede, DNRTF chair, and John Hamel of Nomeco. After numerous discussions, these initial positions evolved into a mutually acceptable plan.

Definition of SLQA Purpose and Philosophy

In a cut-and-dried management statement, the DNRTF proposed the SLQA key value as "nonmotorized, dispersed recreation." Using this statement to guide all management "would not necessarily exclude other uses, but would limit them to levels which do not conflict seriously" (Michigan Department of Natural Resources, April 16, 1981). Management would include hydrocarbons, wildlife, fisheries, forestry, and other recreation. As long as hydrocarbon development was allowed, Nomeco supported this key value and offered no other suggestions.

The CTF members, many of whom supported the 1973 SLQA proposal, were appalled at the technical language that ignored all of the "poetry" and philosophy in the 1973 management plan. They believed management of the Quiet Area should center on "quietness and wilderness." Many people felt the spirit and philosophy of this area must be encouraged and expanded. They rewrote the DNR report by including eight statements of purpose from the 1973 version, adding that "incompatible activities should be prohibited," and requested a future definition of "overuse" for monitoring the multiple uses in the Quiet Area. In the final agreement, the key value for the Quiet Area is "as a nonmotorized, dispersed recreation area" that modifies all other uses to the point that they do not impair the primary use. The language from the 1973 management plan is included in the 1983 plan.

The Issues

Hydrocarbon Development

Hydrocarbon development was the issue that began the conflict. Nomeco wanted a lease change for Section 24, SLQA, from nondevelopment to development and DNR permission to drill. The DNR supported the Section 24 lease change but required eleven environmental restrictions with the permit to drill for hydrocarbons. The DNRTF recommended changing the five remaining development leases to nondevelopment leases for all land within the Quiet Area; keeping hydrocarbon leasing in nondevelopment for the life of the Quiet Area. An alternative DNRTF proposal was to request a promise from Nomeco not to do any surface drilling in the Quiet Area. The CTF report proposed no lease changes for Section 24 and no hydrocarbon development in the Quiet Area.

One of the final issues settled between the stakeholders was hydrocarbon development. It was the only reason Nomeco was involved and it was the catalyst for CTF concerns. As negotiations evolved, the parties expanded their interests, realizing there were several issues that could contribute to a mutually acceptable plan. When the 1983 SLQA management plan went to the Natural Resource Commission for approval, the hydrocarbon settlement stated that the lease for ten acres in Section 24 would be changed from nondevelopment to development and the permit to drill would be issued with eleven strengthened environmental restrictions. The language in the lease change cautions against any precedent-setting and points out the uniqueness of this leasing change.

A critical change for the CTF involved other leases. Five development leases, three belonging to Nomeco and two belonging to AMOCO, were changed to nondevelopment. This change accomplished a no-drill policy for the life of the Quiet Area designation.

Boundary Relocation

Enlarging the Quiet Area was one of the possibilities proposed by Howard Tanner, the DNR director, in his meeting with Traverse City citizens. Tanner discussed many boundary options. CTF members suggested extending the southwest boundary to include the Boardman River in the Quiet Area. DNR representatives believed it would be difficult to patrol a Boardman River boundary and this proposal would also require the closing of a county road. Instead, they called for the addition of two hundred acres of state-owned land in Section 35 (southwest boundary) that would maintain the integrity of the Quiet Area and facilitate enforcement. The final agreement settled on the DNR proposal that provided an area wholly contained within county roads. There was also an intention written into the report that two privately owned land parcels within the Quiet Area boundaries be acquired by the DNR when possible. (As with many of the following issues, Nomeco expressed no interest and no position.)

Fisheries

The DNR report called for continued fisheries management in Guernsey Lake and the Sand Lakes with DNR use of existing motorized roads and motorboats. Public use of gasoline engines was banned on Sand Lakes and a maximum of 7.5-horsepower motor on Guernsey Lake was allowed. CTF members proposed the elimination of all motorboats on Guernsey Lake and the Sand Lakes. They also proposed that a user survey be done for all Quiet Area lakes.

The final agreement reflected the DNR's position but changed the Guernsey Lake's motor requirements to "slow, no wake speed." A DNR manager explained that this was a more easily enforced management policy because "most anglers would not want to buy a 7.5 horsepower just to fish Guernsey Lake and DNR personnel can identify a speedboat wake from a distance."

Roads, Trails, and Campgrounds

The DNR report required that all trails and roads be maintained for hiking, cross-country skiing, and management needs and that "public motorized access to Guernsey Lake Campground" be continued. The CTF response eliminated public motorized access and called for "limited management use" of the trails and roads. The DNR proposed that Guernsey Lake Campground and the walk-in sites at the Sand Lakes should be maintained. They wanted primitive campsite rehabilitation, suggesting that the establishment of fire-rings might be necessary at the walk-in sites to prevent resource damage. The CTF report proposed no Guernsey Lake Campground expansion and suggested maintenance of existing Sand Lakes sites unless overuse occurred. They recommended that a permitting system or prohibition of dispersed camping should be considered by management personnel.

The final agreement followed the DNR suggestions, adding that when the Guernsey Lake Campground is "in need of major renovation, an evaluation should be done to determine the suitability of maintaining the campground in its present form" (Michigan Department of Natural Resources, December 21, 1982). It also mentioned campsite deterioration at the Sand Lakes that needed to be addressed by the field staff. As a result of negotiations, one more stipulation was included in the final report. The DNR agreed that a groomed snowmobile trail on the northern boundary would be moved further north, leaving the existing trail for horseback riding, skiing, and hiking. As part of the hydrocarbon development, Nomeco was willing to pay the cost (up to $2,000) of moving the trail and use the abandoned trail/road for any transportation into the Section 24 oil well. CTF members advocated this arrangement because it moved snowmobile noise farther from the heart of the Quiet Area.

Forest and Wildlife Management

The DNR report initially proposed full forest and wildlife management programs to "maintain the diversity of habitats and species associated with the Quiet Area." It recognized that the key value, quiet recreation, should be considered in every forest management project. The CTF first responded that forest management should be selective cutting but no clear-cutting or new planting. There were many heated discussions between the two parties as they tried to negotiate the interests of resource harvesting and management versus the interests of minimal impact and quiet. The final agreement provided for a full management plan in wildlife maintenance and timber harvesting. Special note was made that all projects would be reviewed with the key value in mind and modified in order to minimize the impact on the aesthetic and recreational aspects of the Quiet Area. DNR personnel agreed to reduce the size of their clear-cuts from forty acres to twenty acres (ten acres if economically feasible) in an attempt to meet the key value.

Buffer Zone

The last issue came from the CTF report. It recommended establishing a buffer zone surrounding the Quiet Area to reduce noise. The report encouraged local municipalities to adopt complementary controls and information campaigns about the importance of the Quiet Area. These suggestions were not included in the final report, but the DNR did respond with an informal agreement. Jerry Thiede, DNRTF chair, agreed that management of state lands surrounding the Quiet Area would "take into consideration the Area's key value by using the *influence zone* concept established for DNR boundary management."

These seven issues were proposed, discussed, and negotiated throughout 1982. The DNRTF submitted the revised report to the Natural Resources Commission for information purposes in December 1982, even though an entirely negotiated settlement had not been reached. The NRC decision was scheduled for January 1983, over two years after Nomeco had first requested a lease reclassification. The CTF members had to decide whether to support the plan or to oppose it at the NRC public hearing. Those members in attendance at the last CTF meeting believed the plan incorporated enough of their concerns to merit support. Until the last meeting, the CTF members were not sure if an internal agreement would be reached. When the plan came to the floor, one CTF member spoke in favor of it and the process by which it was achieved. Another CTF member spoke protesting the surface drilling but did not attempt to block the total plan. Finally, Jim Olsen of Connections summarized the support behind this joint agreement. The next day, the NRC approved the Sand Lakes Quiet Area management plan, commending the DNRTF for its diligent work in public participation and decision-making.

A brief chronology only skims the surface of process dynamics and lessons learned. The participants in the Sand Lakes Quiet Area issue-based negotiations have, to varying degrees, analyzed their own involvement. The remaining text will focus on the particular observations made by the three major parties: the Citizens Task Force, DNR personnel, and Nomeco. These observations are structured to shed light on effective participation of citizen organizations in issue-based negotiations.

Assessing Citizen Task Force Dynamics in Issue-Based Negotiations

Internal Relations

Connections had a major task in front of them; from many disparate groups, one voice had to arise. Every group had specific concerns with the Quiet Area and varying abilities to compromise on their positions. Though the citizen representatives came together in protest over the oil leasing, the interests soon expanded to include site-specific and policy concerns.

Hopes and Ideas

All members were opposed to the oil leasing; some would even have lain down in front of bulldozers to stop the drilling. Down to the last few months, the group refused to compromise on the oil well. The Sierra Club's Norman Brokaw was concerned about precedent-setting if the oil lease terms were changed. The Michigan Sierra Club's major concern was protection of the Great Lakes. Any oil leasing in the Quiet Area might set precedent for further leasing along Lake Michigan. Audubon's June Mason and Ford Kellum saw no need for extensive forest and wildlife management practices. They believed that species diversity would continue without formal management practices. In their opinion, a natural area needed to be as free of human interference as possible. NMEAC, with representatives Sally Olsen and Neil Hoch, was just starting out as an organization. Their preservationist and environmental watchdog goals quickly got them involved in the Quiet Area negotiations. Sally Wilhelm, Michigan Trail Riders Association, wanted to maintain a quiet recreation area for horseback riding. If that meant working on the entire management plan, she was willing to do it. Jim Hall and John Ammar, from the Ski Trails Action Committee, stood strongly opposed to the oil well. The committee had been working with the local DNR staff to maintain the trails for skiing and they found the idea of oil drilling, oil trucks, and oil roads in a quiet area infuriating. The Traverse Bay Regional Planning Commission felt "the DNR was not managing the area true to the intent from 1973." They saw the oil well conflict as "a way to get at this problem of defining a Quiet Area . . . a prototype which needs special management techniques." Peta Williams was interested in creating policy changes in the DNR treatment of special places such as the Quiet Area. Williams's experience as a member of the Michigan Environmental Review Board and the Michigan Oil and Gas Board left her dissatisfied with the DNR's planning approach in these areas. The debate within the Citizens Task Force ranged from policy issues to opinions on which stand of trees to cut. One participant commented on the CTF meeting, "At first everyone was feeling one another out. There was no goal to the meeting . . . it was difficult for me because I was unclear what we could discuss, only oil or other issues too. Everyone had their own agenda."

Building Trust

Working together requires a mutual commitment to cooperation. For CTF members, this commitment stemmed from a common bond of trust. Each CTF member had a long history of commitment to environmental issues, and there was an obvious dedication to preserving the environment. This background gave them positive grounding for cooperation. In particular, individuals had worked to support "their Quiet Area." Everyone knew each other and based their mutual trust on years of living alongside one another. The local environmental networks created a climate for compromise. As one CTF member commented, "We knew each other and we knew the background of Sand Lakes Quiet Area."

Connections had considerable practical experience in citizen and government interaction. Over the course of the Sand Lakes case, they had to develop additional technical skills in group process, including information exchange and meeting facilitation, to reinforce the members' trust. Information was shared with all participants. Memos were distributed announcing meetings or describing the agreements verified after each meeting. These administrative details worked to keep information flowing. The group learned not to let trust levels disintegrate as a result of inadequate information-sharing. The facilitator strived to maintain this trust in every discussion. A citizen participant commented, "One positive thing is that within the group there was a minimum of animosity due to the atmosphere the facilitator set up . . . there was room for everyone to speak." Peta Williams guided the discussions so that all had a voice and few individual opinions dominated the process. At times, facilitation was not easy—"We environmentalists can get pretty emotional sometimes"—but the group struggled for joint action.

Working for Combined Strength

The struggle to maintain a joint response became most intense as the CTF began compromising from their first CTF report, a position statement that rewrote the DNRTF report. Each organizational representative was responsible to their constituency's interests. As CTF considered allowing some forest management practices or agreeing to the surface drilling, some organizations threatened to withdraw from the coalition. These representatives used the power of their participation and the consequences of its withdrawal to move the CTF position closer to their interests. At these moments, individual organizational autonomy appeared more appealing than a coalition position based on compromise. Each representative had to consider whether the combined strength of eleven organizations could obtain more for the Quiet Area than independent strategies consistent with individual organizational goals.

Consensus was reached through struggle that included moments of disagreement as well as periods of cooperation. One participant remembered the CTF meetings as "our own conflict management process." Emphatic opinions were expressed, but divisive fighting was avoided. In the final meetings, a consensus was formed by a "strong majority." One dissenting representative did not attend the last meeting, when the final position was accepted. This action demonstrated his dissenting position but did not block the group from reaching a consensual agreement on the final position. The CTF members reached the final agreement in an attempt to protect "their Quiet Area . . . a symbol for why people lived up there anyway."

Relationships with Other Stakeholders

The citizen representatives were surprised by the DNR's responsiveness to their concerns. On a local level, Bernie Hubbard, DNR forest manager, had solid ties to the Ski Trails Action Committee and the Audubon Club. Their relationship had been very collaborative because Bernie recognized the importance of sharing DNR plans with the local users. He was the closest DNR representative to the public and had an excellent reputation for open communication.

At the regional- and state-level DNR, citizen representatives believed some employees were responsive, but, in general, DNR response was resistance to citizen input. When discussions began, it appeared to some CTF members that a few DNR managers were put off by a perceived encroachment on their expertise areas. Many environmentalists believed the differences stemmed less from a level of expertise than from a differing set of values. For them, the DNR staff valued managing more than preserving. DNR personnel's inherent interest in a well-managed environment left little room for the option of leaving everything alone.

At the state level, Jerry Thiede, DNRTF chair, was a critical factor in the negotiation's success. All of the citizen representatives felt he listened well and shared information in a collaborative problem-solving way. As negotiations became more specific and points of disagreement clearer, Thiede maintained the lines of communication, never closing off attempts at compromise. Underlying the attitude of many citizens was a feeling that "Lansing makes the decisions from on high, we live with them." This assessment did not change dramatically, but the work with Thiede and the DNRTF offered hope for a new relationship.

Power and DNR Responsiveness

The DNR responsiveness did not occur in a vacuum; many factors encouraged this behavior. Connections and the environmental organizations used their power to force a DNR response. Peta Williams used her political contacts to get Tanner's attention and to highlight the issue for the NRC. She formerly served on the Michigan Environmental Review Board (MERB) when Howard Tanner was the MERB chairperson. As one citizen representative observed, "Peta is especially good. She knew Howard Tanner personally. She would call him up and say, 'Howard, I don't like this.' I couldn't do that, I don't know Tanner." Williams also had a long-standing relationship with state government, including an acquaintance with Governor Milliken. Though no direct reference was ever made to these relationships, it can be surmised that this was not unknown to the DNR director. The political contacts extended beyond Williams. CTF members had worked in environmental circles for many years, serving on committees, authoring legislation, and supporting candidates. These contacts became useful when the members needed special attention on this issue.

Publicity added public awareness to the political contacts and kept the pressure on the DNR to respond. The symbolic nature of this conflict over the state's only Quiet Area kept the media interested. Media attention maintained the urgency of the Quiet Area conflict, not allowing it to be ignored by the busy DNR department chiefs. Moreover, publicity kept the public interested. This broad public awareness and concern were powerful attractions for the state bureaucracy's attention.

Finally, NMEAC's petitions were used as bargaining leverage to bring the DNR to the table. This offensive move increased the group's political clout. Some in the DNR did not want to be perceived as "antiwilderness" by fighting the petition drive. Such an action would be bad public relations for an agency charged with protecting Michigan's natural resources. With petitions in pocket, NMEAC had an option in addition to the DNRTF process. They could have organized a public campaign for the more restrictive "natural area" dedication or even sued the DNR. Political contacts, publicity, and a potential movement for "natural area" dedication, all contributed to the DNR's responsiveness.

The DNR Role

Several CTF members questioned the role DNR personnel chose in developing the Sand Lakes Quiet Area management plan. They asked: Should the DNR be mediator, participant, protector, government servant, or expert manager? They saw conflicts in the DNR attempting to mediate a solution at the same time they were representing DNR management interests. The DNR definitely had a stake in the outcome of the negotiations. Yet, they held onto the powerful position of mediator—appearing to arbitrate between the environmentalist interests and the oil company interests. One participant likened it to "playing God." The DNR controlled the process rules and the outcome. Some citizens felt the DNR's willingness to allow public input was commendable—a good step forward from past procedures. Other citizens challenged the DNR to go a step further and assume public input as an obligation.

The Silent Party

Another stakeholder in the Quiet Area negotiations was Nomeco. The oil company made a strategic decision in the beginning not to participate in three-way negotiations. John Hamel of Nomeco did not want direct confrontation and felt the DNR could better evaluate environmental issues. They opted for using the standard lines of communication with the DNR Lands Division. Hamel felt this relationship had been satisfactory in the past and would serve them for any future interactions. DNR staff had worked closely with Nomeco in past leasing and permitting processes. The citizen representatives accepted this arrangement as a condition for the negotiation, although hoping for Nomeco's participation. At the early stages when Nomeco declined direct participation, most people felt the CTF did not have the leverage to force Nomeco "to the table." CTF members identified the DNR role as a buffer for the company—pointing to it as a sign of Nomeco's political power.

Connection's staff were disappointed that a negotiation between all the stakeholders was not possible but recognized the history between environmentalists and industry representatives that precluded it. One CTF member commented, "As environmentalists we have a preconceived notion that oil companies are bad but I have found that the smaller ones just need to know what our needs are to be able to respond." As a small state-run oil company,

Nomeco had the sympathy of some CTF members and the skepticism of others. The only response Nomeco gave the CTF was implied in the final negotiated agreement: drilling in Section 24 under strengthened environmental guidelines, funding for moving a snowmobile trail off the northern Quiet Area boundary, and an agreement to reclassify all their leases within Quiet Area boundaries from development to nondevelopment.

Evaluation of the Settlement

"We compromised . . . we compromised the goal of no oil well," said Sally Olsen of NMEAC. "It wasn't a complete win but on the overall preservation, yes, in the long run, we got our goal." For the CTF, there were two key issues involved in this dispute: (1) who gets input to DNR decisions and how it is done; and (2) the Quiet Area management plan. On the first issue, everyone in the coalition felt successful and hopeful. They had challenged the standard DNR procedure and gotten an acceptable process for decision-making. The new plan was a product of multiple parties negotiating for their interests. For them, this form of conflict management was superior to costly litigation and time-consuming legislation as a way of settling disputes. With this issue-based negotiation, the DNR acknowledged the more active role citizens are demanding in decision-making. Passive public support of DNR expertise is a thing of the past. The CTF was generally pleased with the process for decision-making—at least the door was open.

In retrospect, Peta Williams identified an "entry problem" that should have been addressed:

> It didn't dawn on me until later but the problem was when it was opened up to negotiation of the management plan. Negotiation on a management plan isn't the right process. What you [DNR] should do is go to the users of the Quiet Area and ask for participation in the planning. By connecting it to the negotiation of the oil lease we make it an adversarial process rather than a participatory one.

Williams identifies a matter of attitude—adversarial versus participatory. She admitted that participation by multiple interests will obviously have its heated moments but noted the difference in the posturing in the two processes. In the future, the DNR has the chance for a great deal of support and involvement in their planning process. All of the participants learned from this negotiation, but its adversarial tone should not have carried over to other management planning processes. Sand Lakes contributed to a structure for improved citizen participation. Since the Sand Lakes negotiations, the statewide Forest Land Management Plan includes improved guidelines for incorporating citizen participation. In the long run, that participation will support the CTF's interests in the Quiet Area.

The second goal focused on the management plan. Everyone agrees that an oil well within the Quiet Area boundaries was a compromise. But this single well, whether only exploratory for six months or producing for twenty years, was in exchange for (1) five development leases reclassified as nondevelopment with the stipulation that they will remain in nondevelopment for the life of the Quiet Area, (2) an additional two hundred acres in the Quiet Area boundaries, (3) a snowmobile trail moved north of the Quiet Area boundary, (4) an *influence zone* around the Quiet Area, where activities are modified to limit noise, and (5) maintenance of the 1973 language stressing "solitude," "peaceful recreation," and "wilderness experience."

The CTF originally wanted no motorboating in the Quiet Area and no timber harvesting, but the DNR refused to institute these provisions. They did agree to a "slow, no wake" requirement on Guernsey Lake. Future forest practices will place emphasis on the key value of quiet recreation in an aesthetic environment—timber cuts will be limited to an average of twenty acres and temporary harvesting roads will be restored. Despite the unmet conditions, the CTF members are pleased with the overall agreement. According to Patricia Bidol, "They participated in a process that demonstrated that nonadversarial conflict resolution offers an opportunity to deal with broad issues rather than narrow points of disagreement or law, as well as an opportunity to keep persevering until a solution is found to as many issues as possible."

Conclusion

As the Citizens Task Force members reflected back on the negotiation process, several critical points were noted that influenced the possibilities of success. In the Quiet Area issue-based negotiations, these factors were process legitimacy, power relationships, representation, participant roles, coalition development, resources, communication with constituents, and information.

Process Legitimacy

Connections and the CTF members pushed the DNR to develop a process that would legitimize citizen involvement in planning. Evolution of the DNRTF set a precedent for future citizen involvement that could lead to a new forum for decision-making with representation from groups that voice an interest in participating and are acceptable to the DNR. Participants are unanimous in their assessment that this process is far preferable to current battles in court or bureaucratic hearings. As June Mason and Walter Hastings of the Audubon Society put it, "It is better than a hearing where you express your views, but it is someone else's decision."

The DNR director's initiation of this particular process was certainly one condition for its success—he encouraged the process and supported the final agreement. If the negotiation had been outside of the existing administrative structure, its legitimacy may have been questioned. According to Dr. Bidol, the current decision-making powers need to recognize the process for it to be ultimately successful. In this case the DNR, in other cases the courts, municipal government, executive offices, or institutions could serve as a legitimizing power.

Political Power as a Reality

The CTF used political power to focus DNR attention on the Quiet Area controversy. Nomeco used its power to control their own involvement in the negotiation, and the DNR used its power to control the process. All parties used the available power at their disposal to influence the outcome.

One observer of the process felt the CTF members never fully acknowledged this exchange of power politics: "They didn't understand their power. Tanner had come down to meet with them. . . . But they still took a powerless position. You could tell from the things they'd say." A CTF member commented that many participants were fearful of challenging the DNR's process for decision-making, that they were "playing the DNR's game" and not creating one of their own. She believed they were often reactive rather than proactive and "never recognized the power politics that goes on with a state agency." Another representative resolved to use his organizational contacts more the next time he participates in a similar process. He noted that everyone represented a strong environmental or civic organization, "we were not just individuals" trying to do something. In summary, several citizens felt the power of organizations working in coalition could have been greatly enhanced. In the beginning, CTF members often felt as though they were dealing with a vague series of actions and reactions to DNR positions. Increased clarity in strategy decisions during the following month improved their use of the power at their disposal.

Is Everyone at the Table and for Whom Are They Speaking?

Gordon Hayward, Traverse Bay Regional Planning Commission representative, focused on a principal factor in successful negotiations—consistent and well-defined representation: "My personal problem was on who to represent . . . my own views, or the Commission's." The CTF members occasionally found themselves expressing personal opinions from a strong emotional commitment to the Quiet Area. Often they had to distinguish between individual opinion and their organization's position. Most participants felt the negotiations proved most fruitful when an organization's interests were represented. The organizational support gave legitimacy to arguments and kept the process from deteriorating into a series of soapbox speeches.

On a broader representation level, CTF learned that all primary stake-holders in the conflict should be included in the negotiations. Full partici-pation will lead to a more comprehensive settlement and will avert the chance of a major challenge to the agreement. The Quiet Area negotiations neared the end before CTF members realized there had been no represen-tation from Kalkaska County (a county surrounding a large portion of the Quiet Area.) The DNR went outside of the process and negotiated a separate but consistent agreement with Kalkaska County representatives. The fa-cilitators learned that identifying all of the potential stakeholders in the beginning would contribute to the most comprehensive settlement.

The Results

The DNR is a large state agency with a wide variety of responsibilities. It is organized into a number of very specialized subunits. The tendency is for agency personnel to be primarily responsible only for problem solutions within their specific area of expertise. While agency members are generally committed to sound management, an agency staff member stated that it takes an "extraordinary person to look beyond their division to department-wide problems."

Changing the planning process had two major impacts. It opened up DNR planning to citizen input and it forced the DNR to face the internal differences between divisions. In many ways, the DNRTF had to go through the same consensus-building process as the CTF. The inconsistencies and conflict positions between divisions were negotiated in the DNRTF, some for the first time.

Another process dynamic occurred in the negotiation relationship be-tween the CTF and DNRTF. Instead of eleven citizen groups lobbying the agency and participating in negotiations, the DNR interacted with one coalition, the Citizens Task Force. Connections accepted responsibility for building a consensus among the varying groups. The DNR did not have to juggle multiple citizen positions. By focusing on a single group, they had less conflict to address. It also ensured that the issues being discussed had substantial backing. The statements developed by CTF had the support of at least eleven organizations. Thiede did not have to question whether a point represented only the individual lobbyist's interest. The coordinated citizen response streamlined the process significantly.

Thiede mentioned that a further advantage for the DNR is that the "people begin to understand there are respected organizations that want different management strategies." During discussions, respect between parties builds, similarities are emphasized, and differences have to be acknowledged. No longer does the DNR have to serve as an interpreter of user differences.

The Citizens Task Force has not done formal monitoring of the man-agement plan's implementation partly due to the fact that CTF disbanded immediately after the NRC hearings. In some cases, CTF representatives have not even seen a copy of the final agreement. During the last few days, most participants were tired and overextended. No one identified the monitoring role as an important part of the agreement. Implementation was left to DNR self-monitoring. As citizen representatives reflect, they realize a formal monitoring role should have been addressed early on in the process. It could have been a part of the total agreement. In this process, they negotiated an acceptable management plan on paper and had no way to ensure it would become a reality. Although no formal monitoring process was designed, many of the local environmentalists use the Quiet Area regularly. If there is any glaring deviation from the negotiated settlement, it will be noticed. So an informal monitoring takes place on a regular basis. In addition, the trust built between the DNR and the CTF gives some participants reason to believe that the DNR will notify the citizen organizations if any changes need to be made in an area in which no formal agreement exists.

Interviews

Department of Natural Resources
Jerry Thiede   June 22, 1984
                                                  July 16, 1984
Bill McClay   June 27, 1984
Bernie Hubbard   July 13, 1984
William Mahalak   July 13, 1984
Robert Borak   July 16, 1984

Northern Michigan Exploration Company (Nomeco)
John Hamel   June 26, 1984

Citizens Task Force
Bonnie Anderson   February 14, 1984
                                                  February 10, 1985
Peta Williams   June 20, 1984
June Mason   June 28, 1984
Gordon Hayward   June 28, 1984
Norman Brokaw   July 10, 1984
James Hall   July 16, 1984
Sally Olsen   July 17, 1984
Dr. Patricia Bidol   February 3, 1984

Draft Case Study Readers
Bonnie Anderson
Jerry Thiede
Peta Williams

References

Brokaw, Norman T., Chair, Little Traverse Group, Sierra Club, Memo to Sand Lakes Quiet Area Meeting, February 20, 1981.

Michigan Department of Natural Resources, proposal for Sand Lakes Quiet Area; Memorandum to the Director, June 20, 1973.

Michigan Department of Natural Resources, Interoffice Communication: Sand Lakes Quiet Area Task Force, Howard A. Tanner, Director, April 16, 1981.

Michigan Department of Natural Resources, Report to the Director: Sand Lakes Quiet Area, DNRTF, Jerry Thiede, Chair, Department of Natural Resources, October 1981.

Michigan Department of Natural Resources, Memo, February 24 Meeting with Traverse City Groups Concerned with Sand Lakes Quiet Area, February 1982.

Michigan Department of Natural Resources, Sand Lakes Quiet Area: Management Plan, Memorandum to the Natural Resource Commission, December 21, 1982.

Sand Lakes Quiet Area, Citizens Task Force Documents; Internal Memos, Meeting Notices, and Agendas, February 1981 to December 1983.

Sand Lakes Quiet Area, Report to the Director: Citizens Task Force, February 1982.

The Traverse City Record-Eagle

> "Group Tries to Save Ski Trails," Katherine J. Hall, September 10, 1980.

> "State to Act in Sand Lakes Drilling Dispute," Katherine J. Hall, November 3, 1980, p. 4.

> "Volunteers Groom Cross-Country Trails," Sand Lakes Quiet Area, December 10, 1980.

> "Testimony to Be Heard Thursday," December 23, 1980.

> "Environmental Group's Methods Show Promise," A Page of Opinion, March 19, 1981.

> "Quiet Area Oil Trade-off Offered," Katherine J. Hall, February 25, 1982.

> "Group Helps Negotiate Quiet Area Solution," Peta Williams, The Forum, January 24, 1983.

Williams, Mrs. Peta. Letter to Natural Resource Commissioners, November 28, 1980.

CASE STUDY 6:
Pig's Eye Attempted Mediation

Kristen C. Nelson

The Pig's Eye mediation case study presents an unsuccessful mediation attempt between a coalition of environmental groups, barge interests, and local authorities over development along the Mississippi River in St. Paul, Minnesota. In this case, two critical precursors to effective collaboration were never satisfied: the role of the third party mediator was never clearly established and ground rules for the process were never agreed upon by the parties involved. Additionally, the citizen coalition did not keep other options alive while they participated in the process and were unprepared when it collapsed. Nonetheless, because the citizens did participate in good faith while other parties did not, public and government respect for the citizen organizations and their position was enhanced. While the mediation failed, the process strengthened the citizen organizations and gave them greater credibility and legitimacy.

Some of the key organizational issues this case study illustrates include:

Managing a Coalition.   What strategies might be used in developing an effective coalition and then building a resource base to support this coalition's efforts? What issues will be confronted in maintaining communication with the constituents of the diverse groups involved? How should specific responsibilities be assigned to the active leaders representing the individual groups within the coalition? What factors should be considered in the debate within the coalition about whether or not to participate in the dispute settlement process?

Maintaining Options.   Why is it important that citizen groups keep a close watch on the traditional, political decision-making arena as well as on the progress of the dispute settlement process? How might they do so?

Unless otherwise noted, information and quotes in this case are from the author's interviews with the participants.

The History

In 1978, the St. Paul Port Authority proposed a massive dredge-and-fill project on the Mississippi River. The project called for dredging fifty to one hundred acres to create off-channel barge fleeting on the Mississippi River's banks near Pig's Eye Lake at an area referred to as River Mile 834.0. In the early 1960s, three out of seven barge slips had been constructed in the area. However, the development permit had expired in 1965, before the project was completed. At that time, the project was not a priority for the Port Authority (the Port) and the permit was not reissued.

In 1978, the Port decided to start the project again. They wanted to dredge soil from the project to be used to fill in one hundred acres of wetlands farther down the river. The filled-in area would then be developed for industrial and commercial expansion at what would be called Red Rock Industrial Park. While the Red Rock Industrial project was their primary interest, the Port also had leasing authority for the barge slips that would be developed in the dredged area. Twin City Barge (TC) of St. Paul was interested in leasing the proposed slips and wanted to arrange contract details with the Port. As a result, the Port began contract talks with TC Barge and the Upper Mississippi Waterways Association (UMWA) in March 1978.

A variety of environmental, citizen, and sports groups opposed the new dredging at River Mile 834.0 from its inception. They claimed it would destroy a valuable wetland, harm a nearby heron/egret rookery, and pollute the river. As an alternative, they wanted the Port Authority to turn over the land along River Mile 834.0 to St. Paul for a county park. Their objectives were to develop a recreational area and to designate the only inner-city heron rookery in the Midwest as a scientific and natural area.

These groups were not new to River Mile 834.0; the St. Paul League of Women Voters and Minnesota Environmental Control Citizens Association (MECCA) had been advocating a park there since 1973. At that time, their concern was a proposal by the Port to build a coal-transfer terminal for Northern States Power (NSP) Company. NSP proposed hauling coal by rail from Montana and then loading it on barges from this transfer terminal for shipment to riverfront power plants. However, the Minnesota Pollution Control Agency saw the project as inappropriate for that site. The agency denied a permit to build and the proposal died in 1975.

Four years later, the Port Authority, backed by the barge interests, shifted its proposal to barge fleeting at River Mile 834.0 The UMWA and TC Barge had long contended that new barge fleeting was sorely needed for Upper Mississippi commerce. Without this expansion, they predicted that major economic hardships would result for the shipping industry and its customer.

The Critical Areas Plan

Though the Pig's Eye conflict was waged at city, county, and state levels, the primary focal point for action came around the development of a Mississippi River Critical Areas Plan (MRCP) for the St. Paul riverfront. After the state's Critical Areas Act passed in 1975, then-governor Anderson designated eighty miles of the Mississippi River between the towns of Anoka and Hastings as environmentally sensitive. This designation directly affected the Port's dredging proposal.

The act required a balancing of uses in planning for or developing rivers designated as critical. It established a process by which MRCPs were to be designed and development decisions made. The act specified that all decisions had to be consistent with this plan.

The governor designated the existing Minnesota Environmental Quality Board (EQB) as the Critical Areas monitor. EQB's membership was comprised of seven state agency heads and four citizens appointed by the governor. In this case, the EQB created standards for the Critical Area Plans and set up interim guidelines to protect these areas until plans were completed. These guildelines remained in effect until the jurisdictions along the river had submitted acceptable plans. Twenty-four municipalities developed plans for EQB review. If the EQB was not satisfied with any proposed plan, it could veto it, returning the entire plan to the municipality with EQB suggestions for amendment.

The St. Paul Critical Areas Plan

The St. Paul Planning Commission was responsible for developing St. Paul's Critical Areas Plan. Once completed, this proposed plan was to be forwarded to the City Council for passage before being sent to the EQB. Many times, Planning Commission reports are approved by the City Council without modification.

In developing specific plans, the Planning Commission often forms a citizens' task force representing groups likely to be affected by the plan. This task force serves in an advisory role to the Planning Commission and also assists the Planning Commission staff in developing draft plans to be forwarded to the commission. A sunset clause disbands these task forces as soon as the Planning Commission reviews a plan and forwards it to the City Council. Such a task force was formed for the MRCP. Some observers felt the Citizens Advisory Task Force for the River Corridor MRCP had a bias toward environmental interests. There was no navigational industry involvement because the invited industry representatives chose not to participate. They believed that directly lobbying the commission was a more advantageous strategy. Although there were no commercial navigational industries involved, many other industrial interests were represented such as Northern States Power, Burlington Northern Railroad, and Chicago Milwaukee Railroad.

Some participants believed that the proenvironmental leanings of the task force resulted in a draft MRCP, sent to the Planning Commission by the citizens' advisory group, which did not include the Pig's Eye barge slips at River Mile 834.0. This decision not to include the barge slips did not settle the debate, however. It only shifted everyone's efforts to the Planning Commission forum, where industry interests lobbied for inclusion of barge slips. One observer commented, "Environmental groups at [this] time didn't know enough to lobby, although heavy lobbying was done by barge interests, including taking the Planning Commission on a barge tour of the area."

According to Erv Timm, UMWA executive vice-president, the UMWA pushed approval of the dredging project through the Planning Commission: "I worked very hard lobbying on an individual basis with each member. There was even lobbying between members once I had convinced somebody. It was a hard fight." To the Pig's Eye Coalition's surprise, the slips were included in the final plan approved by the Planning Commission in November 1978 and forwarded to the City Council. Most MRCP Citizens Task Force members were furious. However, due to the sunset clause, they were unable to do anything as a task force. In anger, many members joined a coalition of groups fighting the barge slips.

At this point, UMWA and St. Paul League of Women Voters lobbied the City Council, explaining their representative concerns about the MRCP. On December 7, 1978, the council "did not want to make a determination regarding the environmental effect of the dredge and fill project." They stated the plan had to be reviewed and approved by a number of different agencies before the project could begin. The lobbying groups criticized the council members for "passing the buck" rather than making a tough political decision. After two months of agency review, the St. Paul City Council approved the MRCP—including the barge slips. Erv Timm attributes this outcome to the UMWA lobbying efforts: "George [Latimer, the mayor] is a realist as is the rest of the City Council. The mayor came to our support; we had done everything we could." Timm had been working to get an out-of-state barge company to give up their slip-leasing rights along the River Mile 834.0. Giving up these leases would have allowed an unrestricted view from the existing recreation area, no barges would be parked in that spot on the river. Timm concludes, "We set it up so that council members asked me if I had done anything to work toward a solution. I pointed out all this work. They were happy. The Pig's Eye Coalition just about took his [the mayor's] head off when he included the Pig's Eye slips."

The Pig's Eye Coalition

St. Paul Audubon, St. Paul League of Women Voters, and MECCA formed the Pig's Eye Coalition (PEC) in February 1979. The groups had become increasingly frustrated with the limitations of their individual effectiveness.

In one member's words, through the PEC they "gained greater strength" by recruiting other environmental and citizen groups for a united struggle against River Mile 834.0 barge fleeting.

The coalition formed after careful planning by Peggy Lynch of the League of Women Voters, Kiki Sonnen, an Audubon member, and other organizational representatives. The League of Women Voters of Minnesota agreed to participate primarily because Peggy Lynch, a LWV board member, recommended the strategy. As Lynch explained:

> We had been involved in a few coalitions previously which we had to back out of. We had had problems with coalitions not having information and doing a poor job. But they [LWV] went with this coalition because they knew I had the same value about information the LWV does and they trusted my involvement.

Lynch reported to the St. Paul LWV, the Council of Metropolitan Area Leagues, and the LWV of Minnesota. Before agreeing to any coalition statements, she cleared them with every LWV board. Two LWV chapters involved in the coalition deferred to the LWV Council's judgment in order to speed up the decision-making process.

Other organizations did not become as involved in reviewing PEC's decisions. According to Lynch, "Some of the groups in the coalition really didn't care about what we did, so we didn't have to check in. . . . The LWV needed to know more—if a group needed to have a lot of information I made sure it happened but some didn't care."

When Lynch and Sonnen asked an organization to join the Pig's Eye Coalition, they first asked to use the organization's name as a supporter. Second, they asked for people to help organize, and third, they asked for money. According to Lynch, "We did it in that order and different groups did any combination of those things. After deciding the level of participation their organization was willing to make, the leadership of every organization left the planning and negotiating to the primary organizers."

The PEC went to fifty different meetings, presenting their case to all potential allies. After the St. Paul City Council approved the plan, it was then reviewed by the Ramsey County Board of Commissioners; Metropolitan Parks and Open Space Commission; Metropolitan Council; and, lastly, the Environmental Quality Board.

The Next Step: Environmental Quality Board

The ballpark shifted now as the plan was forwarded to the Environmental Quality Board. The St. Paul MRCP was presented to the EQB on February 21, 1980, with 725 recommendations for review and approval. The Pig's Eye barge slip proposal became the only point of contention.

While the industry position had been favored by the City Council, the environmentalists' turn came with the state. The EQB served as an extension of the governor's office, with all its power. Several of the participants believed the state's position is the most sensitive to environmental issues, whereas the local jurisdictions are more concerned with jobs and tax revenues. As Kiki Sonnen, PEC president, said, "It was like a *deus ex machina*. The EQB attorney argued for every one of our points. We had never directly lobbied him but it was like he was working for us." On February 21, 1980, the EQB ruled in support of PEC's position. It instructed the city of St. Paul to:

> not recommend any development of a fleeting basin along Pig's Eye peninsula at approximate river mile 834.0 until detailed environmental analysis of alternative fleeting sites and environmental impacts associated with those sites has been completed and until an amendment to this plan had been sought from and approved by the Environmental Quality Board. (Minnesota Environmental Quality Board 1980)

In so doing, the EQB rejected the Pig's Eye dredging project as it was then presented. They requested analysis of alternative fleeting and a detailed process description for the barge slip development of River Mile 834.0. Rick Wiederhorn, St. Paul Planning Department staff, was responsible for writing the amendment. He interpreted his task in these terms: "The theory was that the City needed to change the process. We had been very brief in our description of the Pig's Eye development. They just wanted to see more. They didn't think we knew what we were doing. I knew we had to get all the conflicting groups together to solve this one." PEC was elated; they felt they had won their point. Their feeling was that this further review would show the EQB that the project was inappropriate and that alternative sites could be found. The UMWA was angered that a state committee was regulating federal waterways. With the plan once again in their hands, the City Planning Department was stymied.

Mediation as a Step Toward Resolution

In February 1980, Jim Bellus, St. Paul Planning Department, called Ronnie Brooks of the Center for Environmental Conflict Resolution, a nonprofit organization dedicated to using conflict management techniques in environmental problem-solving. Ronnie Brooks had been involved with state and local government for many years. She had served on the then former governor Perpich's staff, and as a consultant for city governments. She also had previously been on the EQB board. The Planning Department needed some place to start so they asked her for suggestions.

Ronnie Brooks was currently on contract to the mayor of St. Paul to facilitate the implementation of St. Paul's innovative negotiated investment strategy (NIS). The NIS process "seeks to use negotiations to organize and direct public and private investments in a city to solve its problems and maintain a healthy economy" (*Nation's Cities Weekly* 1979). The process brought together local, state, and federal representatives for negotiations over several months, to develop specific plans to meet these local needs as well as to satisfy broad national and regional objectives.

In St. Paul, a three-point agenda was outlined by the NIS to achieve this goal:

1. Lowertown Development: "Use public funds to stimulate major private investment" in redeveloping this underused district.

2. Energy Park: Develop a 250-acre site "for high-density, energy-efficient housing and for industrial and commercial facilities to accommodate energy research, manufacturing and production."

3. Mississippi River Corridor: "Replace the haphazard pattern of riverfront development with carefully managed residential, industrial and recreational development" (*Nation's Cities Weekly* 1979).

Any Pig's Eye compromise attempt would likely affect this third objective. As a result, Ronnie Brooks was concerned that the Pig's Eye conflict be successfully resolved.

The NIS was generally considered a successful negotiation between the local, state, and federal interests and the local private sector. Some NIS participants, including Ronnie Brooks, believed that mediating the Pig's Eye problem would help accomplish the third NIS objective. Brooks encouraged the Planning Department to "get everybody together and see if there was room for negotiations." As a result, Jim Bellus invited the major conflicting parties and other significant interests to discuss the situation and explore mediation. The Planning Department needed a solution to the Pig's Eye conflict. They were interested in trying to achieve a workable compromise on the barge fleeting issue. One participant believed mediation was instituted because "the City and the Port Authority had a major setback at the EQB, and it was the mayor's hope that some agreement could be reached between the parties involved."

The conflicting parties considered participation from different vantage points. After receiving Bellus's call, the Pig's Eye Coalition met to consider participation in the proposed mediation. Some members strongly supported the idea, but others were skeptical, considering it a political trick. The more skeptical members argued that the normal decision-making channels had already produced a positive outcome. They suggested that PEC graciously refuse participation. Another perspective within the group encouraged mediation, however: "At that point we were feeling magnanimous . . . we felt the poor barge company must be pretty out of it. We knew there were other slip possibilities so we thought we could help out in identifying them." This latter perspective eventually prevailed. The more skeptical PEC members gradually supported the mediation. According to Sonnen, they had decided that it would be politically unwise to refuse an invitation from the mayor's office.

As a coalition, PEC had the backing of forty organizations, which supported the work of a small group of activists. PEC's decision to participate was made by four to six primary organizers, after receiving input from a few of their supporting organizations. This form of delegated authority was to remain the pattern throughout the mediation. The member organizations lent their legitimacy and constituency numbers to one goal: developing Pig's Eye Riverfront Park at River Mile 834.0. The organizers made all decisions, set negotiation strategy, and responded to alternative proposals. Peggy Lynch explains her strategy for maintaining coalition unity:

> We were able to stay together. That is one thing I am very proud of . . . we lost no groups from anger, conflict, or doing the wrong thing. . . . I was careful to stick to the specific objective around the Pig's Eye issue. We were asked often to work on one issue or another, or support a rally of some kind but I said no. The coalition groups all supported the one objective and had not agreed to work together on anything else.

Don Dunshee and Bob Sprafka, both of the St. Paul Port Authority, responded to the mayor's request for attendance. In conversations, many implied that when the mayor's office asks for participation, few agencies refuse. Regardless, they were not optimistic about mediation possibilities. Some participants reported that, historically, the Port had been a very powerful agency independent of City Council control and supported by its own tax base. Consequently, they preferred to minimize involvement with the city's Planning Department.

The UMWA and the Twin City Barge Company agreed to participate at the Port Authority's encouragement, but the UMWA entered the negotiations with a very skeptical attitude. The UMWA board of directors was evaluating political and legal strategies to promote barge slip development and fight city/state interference in federal waterways issues (Timm 1980). They instructed Erv Timm, UMWA executive vice-president and former Chamber of Commerce chairman, to attend the first meeting. Working in unison with UMWA, Jack and Dick Lambert of TC Barge attended, representing the principal fleeting company. Erv Timm describes the UMWA perspective as they entered the mediation:

> I was a frustrated person in Minnesota. Environmentalists are driving business out of the state. The so-called Pig's Eye problem was more than that site. It was all about development of the Upper Mississippi. The mediation was to look at alternatives. We went ahead and participated with all seriousness. It was important for us to educate these people that every alternative had been considered.

The major negotiation parties in this process were:

1. *The City of St. Paul.* Planning Department—represented by Jim Bellus, Planning Department director, and Rick Wiederhorn, Planning Department staff member. The Planning Department staff were responsible for the entire MRCP. They served as meeting facilitators and sources of information for participants in the negotiations.

   Port Authority—represented by Bob Sprafka and Don Dunshee, Port Authority staff members. The Port is responsible for the riverfront development. They would be responsible for developing and leasing the fleeting basin at River Mile 834.0 and for leasing the new industrial park.

   Ronnie Brooks—Brooks initially helped the group with process questions and agenda setting; in this capacity, she was perceived as the third party facilitator. There was also a belief held by some participants that she represented the mayor's office. Working for the mayor, she was not perceived as a neutral third party by all participants.

2. *Pig's Eye Coalition.* Represented by Kiki Sonnen, PEC president; Peggy Lynch, League of Women Voters; Merrill Robinson, MECCA; and Tom Diamond, District I Community Council (where Pig's Eye was located). The PEC represented forty organizations that advocated park development at River Mile 834.0.

3. *Upper Mississippi Waterways Association.* Represented by Erv Timm, UMWA executive vice-president. The UMWA is a major barge interest lobbying organization at the local, state, and federal level. Its board of directors include representatives from internationally influential commodity industries such as Continental Grain, Cargill, and Northern States Power.

4. *Twin City Barge Company.* Represented by Jack Lambert, founder and chairman of the TC Barge board of directors and principal stockholder. Twin City Barge was an independent, family-owned barge construction and fleeting company. Jack Lambert is considered by some the father of commercial navigation in the area.

Other participants observed or offered information. While they had a stake in the issues to be discussed, they were not major conflicting parties. These representatives were from the Park and Recreation Division, Ramsey County Parks, District I Community Council, Continental Grain Company, Cargo Carriers, and the Grain Terminal Association.

The parties agreed to sit down and talk in the attempt to mediate this particular environmental dispute. A significant difference between the parties was their perception of the process and the process facilitator. This differing perception influenced the process tremendously. The PEC representatives believed from the first meeting that some form of mediation was in process. They were confused as to Ronnie Brooks's role, describing her interchangeably as facilitator, mediator, and mayor's representative. Despite this confusion, the dominant perception was that they were involved in a mediation process. The Planning Department carried this same perception but believed the process was much more informal. The barge interests referred to the process as "mediation" but treated each meeting as a separate discussion. They recognized Brooks as the process facilitator but apparently never agreed to the process rules. Ronnie Brooks described the process as initial discussions between conflicting parties to assess the possibility of mediation. These differing perceptions directly affected the participants' attitude toward the attempted mediation and its eventual outcome.

The Attempted Mediation Process

Jim Bellus, Planning Department director, convened the first of four meetings between these different interests. All four meetings were held between April 7 and April 21, 1980, during an extended noon hour. As the agency director, Bellus had responsibility for the MRCP and spearheaded the attempted mediation process. Ronnie Brooks advised Bellus in the mediation process. She attempted to help the Planning Department find out "what people wanted and what could be done." Her efforts throughout this process were somewhat strained, however, because of the conflicts between her ties to the mayor's office and her assistance in facilitating the process. Participants were confused as to what she intended her role to be.

The process objectives and rules were outlined in the April 7 meeting minutes:

- "Purpose—to develop a compromise on the barge fleeting issues discussed in the development of the River Corridor Plan. A joint position agreed to by all had a good chance of being accepted." (There was strong political backing from the mayor's office for the compromise attempt.)

- "State, regional, and federal agencies would be kept apprised of the group's activities but would not be considered major actors in a St. Paul decision-making process." (St. Paul was responsible for the MRCP. They also wanted to reinforce their claim to planning authority within city limits.)

- "It was the representative's responsibility to keep their constituency aware of actions."

- "Attendance of representatives should be constant for the sake of continuity."

- "Decisions would be by consensus of the group, no votes would be taken."

In this first meeting, the participants agreed to discuss four issues.

1. *Off-channel basins.* The Pig's Eye proposal was in an off-channel basin, not located along the main river channel. The Port maintained they had been gradually removing on-channel fleeting in an attempt to clean up the overpopulated riverbank. The barge interests wanted to maintain all of the on-channel sites. PEC did not believe the Port was removing on-channel fleeting. Lynch explains, "When the MRCP was first being presented, the Port listed five on-channel fleeting sites they expected to lose within the next few years. The PEC maintained that the projected loss of these sites for ninety-nine barges was misinformation. The Port gradually stopped projecting these losses, and they still use all of them to this day."

2. *Red Rock Industrial Park.* The Port wanted to use the cheap fill from the Pig's Eye dredging at the proposed Red Rock site. Their primary interest was development of this area.

3. *Pending fleeting permits.* Several fleeting permits were coming up for review during the mediation. The Port was responsible for renewing any permits under a barge slip lease. Twin City Barge was very interested in seeing the permitting process speeded up. They also wanted a renewed temporary permit for storage of 120 barges that were in production. They wanted space on Pig's Eye Lake for that purpose. The Planning Department and PEC felt this request for temporary fleeting on Pig's Eye Lake was very "sneaky." According to the Planning Department, these issues aggravated the discussions.

4. *Pig's Eye Regional Park.* PEC wanted a regional park at River Mile 834.0 There had been some discussion about park development at the city level. A few acres were already controlled by the Parks Department. According to the NIS agreement signed in December 1979, the Port was to turn over a "majority" of land they owned in this area to the city for parks (approximately twelve hundred acres).

During the first meeting, the group decided to inventory past, existing, and potential fleeting sites. They agreed that "the City lacks the jurisdiction to recommend specific alternative sites or alternatives to fleeting outside the City limits." As a result, they limited their discussion to fleeting recom-

mendations in St. Paul with some reference to "the larger scale problem."
This agreement set the boundaries for proposing alternative siting.

Summing up this first meeting, Ronnie Brooks reminded the group that
agreement on the compromise process was for the benefit of all. She believed
all necessary technical information was present and would not change. In
the meeting minutes, Brooks argued that continued debate would prove
fruitless. The meeting minutes state that "the group *appeared* to agree on
the desirability of compromise" (emphasis in minutes). In preparation for
the next meeting, each interest group was asked to prepare a draft compromise statement on the issues identified.

Rick Wiederhorn was "optimistic" after the first meeting: "People agreed
to talk in a rational manner for the first time. The history [of the issue] was
a series of name calling—excellent name calling. I thought there was a way
out. We had already agreed on a process for environmental testing of the
basin. We were getting good vibrations from Ronnie Brooks. PEC was
optimistic. They had a victory at the EQB. This time they came across as
real statesmen in a way they had never done before. Up until then, they
were definitely not statesmen." He did note, however, that the barge industry was "confident their position would prevail . . . maybe they lost at
the EQB but they were going to win in the end. They had the attitude that
'We've got a good lawyer so . . .' The Port was exasperated but also
convinced it would be hard to get Red Rock."

PEC observers strongly disagreed with Wiederhorn's summary of the
conflict. They believed PEC and all of its affiliated organizations conducted
themselves very well, always being "careful to state all [their] facts and
[their] sources." As an example, Peggy Lynch cited EQB chairman Art
Sidner's commendation of PEC because of the professional way they presented their position. In contrast, she recalls Jack Lambert's strategy of
"taking" quarter-page ads in the newspapers that condemned environmentalists before key votes on the Critical Areas Plan.

On April 11, the participants met for the second time and presented their
draft compromise positions. PEC went first—an unwise negotiating strategy
that they later regretted. They "thought everyone would pretty much lay
their cards on the table" and were disappointed when that did not happen.
PEC held to their position of no dredging at River Mile 834.0 and requested
park development on the site. They added a list of five potential fleeting
sites: new slips or the refurbishing of old slips that would be environmentally
acceptable. Prior to this meeting, Peggy Lynch and Merrill Robinson had
done considerable investigation with on-site research and historical riverfront documentation. They were well versed on the particulars of each site.
In her work for the League of Women Voters, Peggy Lynch had attended
every Port Authority hearing during the previous eight years; not much
slipped by her.

Jim Lambert presented comments for Twin City Barge regarding the Environmental Quality Board's findings on River Mile 834.0. Lambert wanted to continue with the traditional development decision-making process involving the Army Corps of Engineers for dredge/fill projects. He contended that the "EIS process called for under Corps of Engineer regulations contemplates both environmental analysis and a consideration of alternatives" and that the present negotiations were therefore unnecessary (Meeting minutes, April 11, 1980). This positioning by Twin City Barge and UMWA persisted throughout the attempted mediation.

As Jim Bellus stated, the UMWA's position did not represent the type of position from which a negotiation of acceptable alternatives in St. Paul would take place. Erv Timm questioned the city's authority to approve fleeting and affect navigation on the federal waterway. The city Planning Department responded that the city's recommendation, while not formally binding, was critical as a practical matter. History had demonstrated that the Corps of Engineers rarely approves permits when the local community objects to them.

All parties felt that there was a great deal of rhetoric in every meeting. It was generally agreed that the facilitator did her best to stop people from "giving their speeches over and over again," but one PEC negotiator became very frustrated with the process and with the facilitator: "That didn't stop Erv Timm. He'd talk on and on which, of course, made us angry. We'd listen to Ronnie and stop our positioning and Timm would just keep on blabbing. Finally, Ronnie didn't even try to stop him." PEC began to feel resentful about the process and the asymmetrical response to the facilitator's requests. In another situation, relating to the draft compromise positions, it was observed that "Ronnie gave us assignments to do between meetings. We'd come back like good little students, all prepared for the meeting. The barge company didn't do any of the tasks . . . so Erv would begin his speech."

Ronnie Brooks played a strong facilitating role at the next meeting on April 18. She clarified the points of difference after an item-by-item review of all alternative sites and then suggested a series of negotiations. The negotiations did not happen. The waterways interests questioned the value of the compromise process when the final decisions were to be made elsewhere.

After Brooks attempted to explain the advantages of working at developing a joint position, Timm presented a letter to the city Planning Department participants. It stated that the UMWA would continue to work within the compromise process but that a parallel legal action was being initiated to prohibit the EQB from enforcing its order. PEC was mildly surprised by the UMWA's statement but remained confident in the EQB decision. Summing up the meeting, Brooks suggested that the process be abandoned if the next meeting was not productive in beginning a negotiated settlement. The UMWA had not modified its position in public or private. She suggested that "those unwilling to negotiate should question the advisability of coming" (Meeting minutes, April 18, 1980).

Each party left this third meeting feeling frustrated. The UMWA felt it had already evaluated potential fleeting sites. Each proposed site had been reviewed, each time with the conclusion that the development obstacles proposed were too great to overcome. As Timm commented, "If we knew of potential barge fleeting sites that were operationally, economically and environmentally feasible, we would quickly advance them." PEC, too, was frustrated. They would not move off their position on River Mile 834.0, but they felt they stood alone in mediation and had compromised in many other sites.

The final meeting on April 23 began with a cleanup of old business and further position descriptions. PEC continued to advocate a park at River Mile 834.0 and supported all other fleeting sites except for two—834.0 and 835.0 on-channel. By withholding these sites, PEC hoped to bolster their negotiating position. They agreed to consider the site when the Port Authority turned River Mile 834.0 over for park purposes. The Port, however, did not want to close out its options. They said that they would turn the land over only after studies indicated that it was not an appropriate fleeting site. The UMWA pressed for basins at River Mile 834.0 and called for the Army Corps EIS process to proceed.

After much discussion, it was apparent that negotiations had stalled. Participants decided to return to the formal planning process. Planning Commission meetings on amendments to the River Corridor Plan, MRCP, were to be announced in the future. The alternative mediation process was recessed indefinitely. PEC's Kiki Sonnen remembers the final meeting in this way: "We were sitting there and Ronnie Brooks had just stated people's positions. Erv Timm packed up his things saying, 'We have no authority to authorize this and we're not interested,' he walked out." Erv Timm describes his perceptions of the mediation process, perceptions that clearly impeded its success:

> That was a joke. She [Brooks] came in with this conflict resolution stuff. There was no resolution. The barge industry couldn't compromise. We were far too short on barge fleeting as it is; the barge industry needs room for fleeting. We serve as a shipper and as a storage warehouse. We were in even more trouble because we had lost over 400 slips in the past few years. Barge slips are being taken away to make room for other taxable industries. All along we were saying OK we won't fight this one because we were promised Pig's Eye to replace the lost slips. Then, all of a sudden it's an environmental issue. There is no possibility of compromise.

The Planning Department was caught in the middle. They had 724 other approved MRCP recommendations at stake and an unanswered charge from the EQB. They felt the only way to get things moving was to find something the groups could agree on. Rick Wiederhorn asked Ronnie Brooks to call each participant and see if there was any room for negotiation. All of the parties declined a further attempt at mediation. She asked if they could agree on doing an EIS for River Mile 834.0 and use the information gathered to determine the fleeting acceptability. PEC refused; any form of development was not acceptable to them.

The PEC organizers believed the Port Authority and the industry representatives had no intention of negotiating from the beginning. Peggy Lynch identifies this as the single reason the attempted mediation failed. She believes mediator Ronnie Brooks should "have been able to assess the situation better and realize that they [the Port and the industry representatives] were not intending to negotiate." Ronnie Brooks also noted that the lack of "intent to negotiate" on the part of industry was the key factor in blocking any mediation from starting. PEC organizers notified their supporting organizations of the failed negotiations through meeting reports and newsletters. In reflection, several organizational leaders felt a mediation could have worked, but in the future they would be more cautious as to whom they agreed to negotiate with—"if they were honest maybe."

Outcome and Ongoing Relationships

In May 1980, Twin City Barge Company sued the city of St. Paul for restricting federal waterways. At this time, it was apparent to most observers that the planning commissioners and the Port Authority were fed up. Rick Wiederhorn, riverfront planning staff, felt Twin City Barge Company had isolated themselves from any city agency support by filing this suit.

PEC strategically used the failed negotiations to their advantage. They blamed the city and the barge interests for "tricking" them. They were able to paint themselves as open and willing to negotiate. As Sonnen noted, "In one way it worked well . . . until then we received comments like—you've got good points but what are your alternatives? We could come back with the fact that we had found 99 possible alternate sites and were stabbed in the back!" The city Planning Department agreed with PEC. They felt the UMWA and TC Barge had not negotiated in good faith. In general, the parties used the process in their overall strategy to stop or start River Mile 834.0 fleeting development. All participants felt the attempted mediation had failed because there was no compromise position; some felt the barge industry never intended to negotiate.

After mediation was abandoned, Rick Wiederhorn decided to follow the EQB directive literally. He "massaged the language" of the River Mile 834.0 proposal by expanding the review process description and then presenting the project with more sensitivity to the environmental impacts. The amendment passed the City Council and the EQB.

At the same time, the PEC sent five hundred petition signatures to the EQB requesting an EIS for cumulative on-channel fleeting. EQB consideration of PEC's request lasted over two years and though the request was denied, the strategy did serve to stall the MRCP. The environmental organizers felt their coalition was "extremely effective" in maintaining this strategy and found few disadvantages to working together. One organizer commented, "Someone on the EQB board said they could not get over all the power we had by coordinating all our groups in testifying, etc. The whole year would not have happened without the coalition." After a year's delay, the St. Paul's Critical Areas Plan was approved; the Port was given permission to begin the EIS for River Mile 834.0.

In 1982 and 1983, Twin City Barge Company fell on hard economic times. In the fall of 1983, Twin City Barge Company sold out its remaining barge operations. Because the Port was interested in cheap fill and only minimally in barge fleeting, as the economic advantages of the project disappeared, the Port Authority support was withdrawn. The estimated project cost had risen more than $2.5 million, in addition to the $1 million for an EIS. The total cost was estimated at $16 million to $24.2 million for the Port Authority (*Minneapolis Star and Tribune*, February 22, 1984).

On February 21, 1984, the St. Paul Port Authority dropped its proposal for a fleeting basin at River Mile 834.0 and turned over the remaining land to the city of St. Paul. Regardless, barge fleeting is still controversial in St. Paul. The Upper Mississippi Waterways Association believes city restrictions on river development are squeezing the lifeblood out of the industry and Upper Midwest commerce. Since 1981, the UMWA and the Minnesota Agri-Growth Council have had a lawsuit against two state agencies and the city of St. Paul pending in U.S. District Court. They contend that the defendants are violating federal interstate commerce laws by restricting barge fleeting in the metropolitan area. According to Erv Timm, "The primary issue [in this lawsuit] is interstate commerce—whether a state has the right to interfere with interstate commerce. You know that this idea is one of the founding principles of our law. However, there has been a new environmental law which is untested. This is the first attempt to find out whether a state can restrict commerce because of an environmental or citizen issue." The environmental interests disagreed. The Pig's Eye Coalition (with the National Audubon Society, Sierra Club, and Izaak Walton League) was an intervenor for the defense, contending that joint federal, state, and local jurisdiction results in balanced decisions. (In August 1984, the UMWA and the consortium of agribusinesses had dropped the lawsuit.) PEC is also petitioning the Minnesota Department of Natural Resources to designate scientific and natural area standing for the heron rookery.

Interviews

Kiki Sonnen	February 8, 1984
Ronnie Brooks	April 5, 1984
Erv Timm	April 7, 1984
Rick Wiederhorn	April 9, 1984
Peggy Lynch	September 17, 1984

Draft Case Study Readers
Ronnie Brooks
Peggy Lynch

References

Audubon Action, "Victory for Pig's Eye," June 1984.
Meeting minutes, Pig's Eye Compromise:
    April 7, 1980.
    April 11, 1980.
    April 18, 1980.
    April 23, 1980.
Minneapolis Star and Tribune; Metro News, "Barge Basin Plan Sunk; Rookery Saved," February 22, 1984.
Minnesota Environmental Quality Board Finding of Fact, Conclusions of Law and Order, February 21, 1980.
Nation's Cities Weekly, "Negotiating the City's Future: A Report on Experimental Plan for Pooling Urban Investments and Bargaining to Coordinate Policy Goals," November 26, 1979.
PEC Press; Newsletter of the Pig's Eye Coalition, March 1984, August 1984.
Timm, Erv, Executive Vice-President of the Upper Mississippi Waterways Association. Letter to James Bellus, Planning Division Director, April 18, 1980.

Case Study 7:
Wisconsin Groundwater Legislation Negotiations

Sharon L. Edgar

The Wisconsin groundwater legislation committee process was a hybrid consensus process mixing the realities of political bargaining with the need for broad-based support if any effective groundwater legislation was to be enacted. The process was instituted and facilitated by a state legislator and involved all sides of the groundwater protection issue. The case presents an interesting process, one providing citizens an opportunity to be involved in the legislative development arena rather than solely in lobbying once a bill has been introduced to the legislature.

While the case was unusual in structure, its analysis holds particularly important lessons for citizen groups participating in any environmental dispute settlement process. The citizen representatives in this committee process encountered considerable difficulties because of the time and amount of detailed information involved. Other individuals participated as part of their jobs and often had staff support to keep them organized and informed. The case illustrates how important it is for a citizen organization to select an appropriate representative for a dispute settlement process. In this instance, an individual with considerable political savvy and aggressiveness was needed yet not present. Furthermore, in a politically based process such as this one, it is important to mobilize a strong constituency outside the process in order to maximize influence and keep key issues on the agenda. In this instance, the environmental community was fragmented and hence was not as effective as it might otherwise have been.

This case is very different from the EDS processes described elsewhere in this book. But the hybrid process (part politics, part consensus-building) bears analysis because it is an effort to problem-solve involving multiple parties. It is not inconceivable that citizen organizations will find themselves in a position of deciding whether or not to participate in such a process. Some of the key organizational issues it raises include:

Participation. What if you choose not to participate in the EDS process? What are the ramifications to your organization as well as to the other organizations that are participating? What options does your organization have and where do the disputed issues fit on your agenda? What are the risks of letting someone else (another interest group or a government agency) represent your interests? Who could most appropriately represent your group and does he or she have the skills necessary to participate effectively?

Resource Commitment. What resources will you need in order to participate in the EDS process and how might they best be acquired?

Coalition-Building. How might coalition-building bolster your power and influence within the process? How will you effectively coordinate your activities with those of the other groups? What are your options if other groups refuse to join in the coalition?

Communication. How might you build effective communication back to your constituents in order to keep them abreast of the progress being made as well as to get their support behind the final product so that it succeeds?

Unless otherwise noted, information and quotes in this case are from the author's personal interviews with the participants.

Beginnings of a Groundwater Special Committee

In the late 1970s, the special committees were used to tackle environmental issues. Representative Mary Lou Munts, an environmental leader and chair of the Assembly Environmental Resources Committee, chaired many of the special committees dealing with environmental issues using a "consensus" approach to policy formulation. Although used previously, the "consensus" process became a focus of public attention when it helped to develop mining legislation and regulations in 1976 and 1977. Use of consensus was brought to the mining process by Representative Munts and supported by major mining companies in the state who were looking for the certainty and security that legislation mutually agreed upon by business, environmental groups, and government agencies would offer them. The mining process took several years and resulted in a number of innovative laws and regulations that were considered major breakthroughs in state environmental legislation.

Munts continued to use a consensus approach in special committees and other ad hoc groups throughout the late 1970s and early 1980s. In 1980, groundwater contamination was emerging as a major environmental issue in the state. Proposed increases in mining activity was posing threats to groundwater resources. The relationship between groundwater and these mining activities surfaced as an issue in the development of mining rules in the late 1970s. In addition, groundwater contamination problems were being identified around the state as a result of pesticide use and solid waste landfill leakage. Wisconsin did not have any specific, comprehensive groundwater protection legislation and existing legislation giving the Wisconsin Department of Natural Resources general responsibility for groundwater was not being aggressively implemented. New and more specific legislation was needed. Munts, environmental leaders, and others realized that a case-by-case approach to the individual contamination situations (mining, pesticides, and landfills) would not be productive. In an amendment to a solid and hazardous waste law passed by the state legislature, the Legislative Council was requested to establish a special committee on groundwater. Munts also requested a special committee in a personal letter to the council.

In January 1982, the Legislative Council appointed two senators, six representatives, and eight public members to the Special Committee on Groundwater Management. This one committee would tackle all of the groundwater issues. Unlike past special committees, which dealt with environmental regulation that affected only industry, the Groundwater Committee also included agricultural interests in addition to the environmental community, making it a much more complex undertaking. The Legislative Council gave the Special Committee the following mandate: "Study and submit recommendations necessary to establish the goals and objectives of the state's groundwater management policy" (Wisconsin Legislative Council Report No. 25, 1983). The Committee's aim was to develop a comprehensive groundwater management law that would offer broad groundwater protection.

In addition to the full Committee, the Legislative Council established a seven-member, nonvoting Technical Advisory Committee (TAC). The TAC was chaired by Linda Bochert, executive assistant to the secretary of the Wisconsin Department of Natural Resources, and included representatives from several state agencies, the University of Wisconsin, and the Public Intervenor's Office. Its role was to provide the Committee with agency input including: the agency perspective on the groundwater problem, existing agency capability to deal with the problem, and regulatory needs and options for groundwater protection. Later in the process, a smaller Subcommittee on Compensation was also formed. This Subcommittee will be discussed in more detail later. Legislative Council staff provided legislative, legal, research, and administrative assistance for the entire Committee process.

The Special Committee on Groundwater Management met for the first time on April 26, 1982. After nine full Committee sessions, seventeen TAC meetings, and fifteen Subcommittee sessions, a bill was voted out of the Committee in June 1983. Although the Special Committee no longer existed as a formal, organized unit upon completion of its bill, key Committee participants continued to work with Representative Munts in the subsequent stages of legislative development. For the most part, however, this paper is concerned with the organized Committee process that took place between April 1982 and June 1983.

The sixteen-member Committee was chaired by Representative Munts and, in addition to seven other legislators, the Committee included eight public members:

Roger Cliff	Wisconsin Farm Bureau legislative representative.
James Derouin	Wisconsin Association of Manufacturers and Commerce, lobbyist/lawyer.
Terry Kakida	Citizens for a Better Environment, aquatic biologist/director of research.
Myron Ehrhardt	Citizen/farmer, Township chairman, Oakfield, WI.
James Hoffman	Professor, University of Wisconsin, Oshkosh, hydrogeologist.
Lonnie Krogwold	Wisconsin Potato and Vegetable Growers Association, farmer.
Tom Kunes	Residuals Management and Technology, private consultant.
Douglas Mormann	Portage County local health official.

The Special Committee bill contained two major provisions: (1) a progressive, two-tiered standards program with both enforcement standards and preventive action limits and a strict enforcement program designating the Wisconsin Department of Natural Resources as the lead agency; and (2) a compensation program for contaminated private wells (Wisconsin Legislative Council Report No. 25, 1983). This main frame was left intact in the legislature but was amended. Key members of the Special Committee worked with legislators in the Standing Committee stage and within the full legislature to amend the Special Committee bill and satisfy additional political interests. (The Environmental Resources Committee—a Standing Committee in the State Assembly—should not be confused with the Special Committee. Unless otherwise noted, reference to "the Committee" means the Special Committee.) Additions made in the Standing Committee included: (1) an environmental repair program, or "mini-superfund" for the cleanup of dangerously contaminated sites and facilities; (2) a laboratory certification program; (3) an elaboration of the bill's impact on the solid waste industry; and (4) an extensive monitoring program (Wisconsin Legislative Council Staff 1984). No significant changes were made in floor debate except for a provision shifting responsibility for the animal waste management program from the Department of Natural Resources to the Department of Agriculture. The latter provision was vetoed by the governor when the final bill was signed into law in May 1984.

The "Consensus" Process Defined

An understanding of the Groundwater Committee first requires clear comprehension of how Wisconsin legislators have used the term "consensus." This section will provide this understanding, using information from interviews and other correspondence with Representative Mary Lou Munts.

In Wisconsin, "consensus" means group negotiations in a process that is still very much characterized by legislative politics. Representative Munts, the primary force behind the Groundwater Committee, describes consensus as the essence of the legislative process. Thus, she sees the use of a "consensus" approach in legislative decision-making as very natural and logical. Munts used the special committee framework to more effectively and consciously build the consensus that is needed to develop and pass legislation. Her special committees brought together the broadest range of interests she could achieve and opened the doors to individuals who might not otherwise have access to these early legislative discussions. The special committees and other ad hoc groups that Munts chaired with her consensus approach were continually prodded toward agreement. For Munts, using a consensus approach meant stressing the need for consensus to her committee members and helping them along by pressuring for cooperation and compromise and highlighting small agreements as encouragement for the group.

Munts used consensus as a meeting process in the Groundwater Committee. Meetings were orchestrated in "Quaker-like" fashion, with voting restricted to the final vote required by the Legislative Council to accept the bill at the end of the process. According to Munts, the consensus process differed from normal bilateral negotiations between legislator and interest group lobbyist because it brought a broader range of affected interests together to negotiate as a group and work toward a collective agreement. The Committee process also differed from normal legislative politics in that Munts tried to involve people who were not necessarily key lobbyists. Despite these differences, the Committee was still a component of Wisconsin's normal legislative process, and, thus, was characterized by political bargaining and traditional power dynamics. The result was a hybrid process: part consensus and part typical legislative politics.

Public members were selected by Munts to approximate the interests with a major stake in the issue that would be able to help or hinder the Special Committee product in the legislature. In the case of groundwater, the major interests that needed to be represented were business and industry, agriculture and the environmental community. In addition, Munts selected persons who were or could become comfortable with working in a consensus framework and who would have the time to produce a collective opinion and then support it throughout the legislative process.

While it was hoped that the Groundwater Committee would achieve a complete consensus, Munts reminded the group that the Committee was only the first round in the overall legislative process. Therefore, it was not necessary for the Committee to achieve a complete consensus because any issues or interests not satisfactorily addressed by the Committee bill would continue to be worked on in her Standing Committee before being introduced to the entire legislature for debate.

Although some of Munts's past special committees produced bills that moved through the legislature virtually unchanged, the Groundwater Committee did not result in a consensus bill, either internally or externally. Internally, the bill was not "consensus" because it was not 100 percent agreeable to all Committee members. The bill was voted out of the Special Committee by a ten to three majority vote (three members were absent at the final meeting). Even though three Committee members were not satisfied with the bill and another three were not present to express their position, the bill was still forwarded by the Committee to the legislature. Externally, the bill was not "consensus" because it was later expanded by Munts and a few key Special Committee members in the Environmental Resources (Standing) Committee in order to satisfy interests who were displeased with the Committee bill. As Munts stated, "The Committee product is only a consensus of the participants, but if they have been well chosen, [they] may mirror the major actions of the legislative process so that a bill receives agreement relatively easily. [However] the resulting product may or may not be a consensus as far as the broader body-politic is concerned." The Committee bill had to be amended and further refined to achieve a consensus in the "broader body-politic."

Committee Dynamics and Key Actors

The groundwater consensus process is very difficult to document. Although minutes were taken at every Special Committee meeting, the minutes reveal little in actual dynamics between participants or indicate how decisions were made and agreements reached. What the minutes do indicate is that full Committee meetings were not decision-making forums, but were instead used to present and exchange information and discuss and debate broad issues. Committee meetings were open to the public, and representatives from many different organizations attended either to speak before the Committee or to observe. A brief public comment period was usually allowed at the end of Committee meetings, although this method of public participation was not significant. Therefore, much of the meeting time was spent hearing presentations from the public and outside speakers. In addition, the Legislative Council staff and TAC members presented the full Committee with legal and technical information, both through oral testimony and written reports and memoranda that were presented at the meetings (Wisconsin Legislative Council, Summary of Proceedings, Special Committee on Groundwater Management).

Most of the actual decision-making and fine-tuning of the bill took place outside of full Committee meetings in informal discussions between members and in smaller work groups. Proposals prepared by the TAC often provided a firm base for the Committee to build on. In addition to the TAC, another Subcommittee accounted for a majority of the bill's formulation. This formal Subcommittee, the Subcommittee on Compensation for Groundwater Damages (hereinafter referred to as the Subcommittee), was formed in August, about midway through the process. Munts established the Subcommittee to form a smaller nucleus of individuals to tackle the complex technical and legal issues facing the full Committee.

By establishing the Subcommittee, Munts purposely altered the composition of the Committee to develop a more "skilled and productive work group." Aside from herself and a fellow environmental legislator, Representative Thomas Crawford, Munts brought two public members from the full Committee—Roger Cliff (agriculture) and James Derouin (industry)—and four TAC members to the Subcommittee. These four TAC members—Linda Bochert of the WDNR, Dr. Henry Anderson of the Department of Health and Social Services, Orlo R. Ehart of the Department of Agriculture, Trade and Consumer Protection, and Thomas Dawson from the Public Intervenor's Office—were given a broader role when they were brought into the Subcommittee. For Thomas Dawson, in particular, this expanded role enabled him to become more influential in the overall Committee process. Although a limited number of participants were formally assigned to the Subcommittee and its working groups, Subcommittee meetings were open to participation from all Committee members and also open to the general public. Nonetheless, establishing the Subcommittee altered the Committee's power dynamics, putting some public members in a more influential position than others.

In theory, the Subcommittee was established to consider methods of compensation for groundwater damage. In practice, however, the Subcommittee dealt with a variety of issues, including standard setting. The Subcommittee, and informal working groups that spun off from it, made most of the incremental decisions in the process that added up to the final Special Committee bill. The Subcommittee, the TAC, and the Council staff drafted actual language and specific provisions of the proposed bill.

As chair, Munts had significant influence over the process. Munts saw her role as catalyst, facilitator, and process manager, not as a negotiating party. Her power within the process not only came into play at the outset, through defining the process and determining participation, but also as she continued to influence the process throughout the life of the Committee.

Because her orientation was that of an elected official, Munts shaped the power dynamics of the Committee to maintain the support of politically important interests.

Of particular importance to Munts and to the success of any groundwater legislation was the support of agriculture. Agricultural interests had killed environmental legislation in the past and were considered the primary force that proponents of strong groundwater protection would have to confront. In response to this perceived threat of opposition, Munts made a special effort to involve agricultural public members in discussions and decision-making. Because Roger Cliff of the Farm Bureau represented a large and possibly opposing constituency, he wielded considerable power. According to Munts, the agricultural representatives never "signed on in blood" to the Committee bill, but instead gave their "uneasy support."

In addition to Cliff, public member James Derouin, of the Association of Manufacturers and Commerce, was also a significant power broker in the process. As the primary industry representative, Derouin brought considerable constituency power with him into the negotiations. A highly skilled and talented negotiator, Derouin was one of the most influential public members.

The environmental perspective was represented by public intervenor Thomas Dawson and public members Terry Kakida and Professor James Hoffman, a groundwater expert and Sierra Club activist. The public intervenor's office consists of two environmental lawyers situated in the Wisconsin Department of Justice, who watchdog the Department of Natural Resources. They are charged by law with protecting "public rights" in the waters and other natural resources of the state and they provide legal assistance to citizens with environmental problems. By placing Dawson, a nonvoting TAC member, on the Subcommittee, Munts put him in a position of considerably more influence. Dawson became the primary environmental representative, since, on the whole, the environmental citizen groups did not play a strong role in developing the Committee bill. Kakida, director of research for Citizens for a Better Environment, did not support the Special Committee bill and voted against it. James Derouin, of the Wisconsin Association of Manufacturers and Commerce, also voted against the bill but later changed his vote after several minor changes were made. The other dissenting vote was Representative Thomas Crawford, a strong environmentalist.

Munts and her key interest group representatives—Thomas Dawson, James Derouin, and Roger Cliff—were not only the moving force in the Committee process, they also continued to be influential throughout the legislative process. When the Special Committee bill left the Committee, it was introduced to the Assembly Environmental Resources Committee by the Legislative Council. There, these four individuals had several obstacles to clear. First, they had to win the support of Representative Jeff

Neubauer, who several months earlier had succeeded Munts as chair of the Environmental Resources Committee when she took a more influential appointment. Neubauer would be responsible for introducing the bill to the legislature; thus, his support was essential.

In addition, Munts, Dawson, Derouin, and Cliff worked with other interest groups to expand the basic bill created in the Special Committee. The four Special Committee members fought to maintain the integrity of "their" bill while adding on new provisions to satisfy the other political interests. By the time the amended bill got to the floor of the legislature, Munts and other legislators from the Special Committee had gathered majority support in both the Assembly and the Senate. Outside the legislature, Dawson, Derouin, and Cliff built support among their interest groups so that the bill going to the full legislature would have a strong backing. Thus, the power positions that emerged in the Special Committee were maintained in the months to follow. In addition, the working relationships that were fused in the Committee process continued to be important in subsequent decision-making forums.

Other than identifying the key actors in the process—Munts, Cliff, Derouin, and Dawson—describing the dynamics of the Committee in an objective, comprehensive manner is nearly impossible. Many of the process's critical dynamics and decisions took place outside the full Committee in the Subcommittee and its working groups and between key individuals. Because of the complex decision-making network, the uneven interaction between participants, and the subtle political bargaining that characterized the process, each member came away with his or her own perception. Depending upon their goals, objectives, and degree of involvement, Committee members focused on different issues and elements of the Committee process and identified different failures and successes. Thus, the most productive and enlightening way to look at the Groundwater Committee is through the eyes of Committee members representing the three different interest areas. The following perspectives are not necessarily the objective "reality" of the process, but are the perceptions of the various participants and the aspects of the process on which they focused.

The Business and Industry Perspective

One of the most influential and skilled participants on the Committee was attorney James Derouin, environmental consultant for the Wisconsin Association of Manufacturers and Commerce (WMC). The WMC is the state's largest trade association of business and industry. It has over 2,800 members and includes both small and large businesses and industries. The WMC maintains a very small permanent staff, hiring lawyers in private practice to represent them in various issue areas. Derouin is the sole environmental lawyer/lobbyist for the WMC. In addition to representing the WMC, Derouin is the environmental lawyer/lobbyist for several other Wisconsin businesses and industries, such as the Wisconsin Paper Council and Union Carbide.

The WMC's goal with all proposed environmental legislation is to seek laws that are "livable, understandable and balanced." When the WMC feels there is a proven need for environmental legislation, they will not take a "knee-jerk opposition" stance, but will instead work with other affected parties to develop reasonable and intelligent laws. While working on environmental legislation, the WMC always seeks a high level of specificity in the law's language. Derouin feels that, in general, federal laws are too vague, letting the "experts," or agency personnel, implement the laws as they see fit. On the contrary, the WMC has always stressed the need for specific legislation—laws that clearly answer all the questions they raise. According to Dawson, it is commonly understood in Wisconsin that, when the WMC participates in the development of legislation, they will advocate a high level of specificity. Since the WMC is a very "desired commodity in all environmental negotiations" because of their immense political clout, Derouin feels that their objective of specific legislation has been accepted as an overall goal in Wisconsin environmental policy-making.

The WMC became involved in groundwater legislation because politically it was an issue the WMC had to deal with. Although there were many sources of groundwater contamination in the state, Derouin felt that the media stressed the role of solid waste sites, thus implicating industry as a prime source and demanding their participation in the solution.

As discussions began to take place and the Committee was formed, Derouin actively helped recruit agricultural representation, in particular Roger Cliff of the Farm Bureau. Derouin did not want to devote time and effort to a package that in turn would either be forced on or opposed by the agricultural community. It was very important to the WMC to work *cooperatively* with agricultural interests.

Prior to the formation of the Groundwater Committee, Derouin had been involved in a key regulation effort surrounding pesticides contamination of groundwater. Pesticide use in the state's central regions, where soils are very sandy and groundwater is abundant and shallow, had led to a serious pollution problem discovered in the summer of 1982. The groundwater in this highly agricultural area has been transformed to "chemical soup," primarily due to the intrusion of the pesticide aldicarb, which is manufactured by Union Carbide's Agricultural Products Division.

As the legal representative for Union Carbide, Derouin began working with the state agency that was taking a leading role in pesticides regulation — the Department of Agriculture. In cooperation with Derouin, the agency began developing a regulatory program for aldicarb. Proposed regulations were completed in fall 1982, and the department began holding public hearings.

Derouin, who was in the hospital for an extended period of time during the hearings, contacted public intervenor Thomas Dawson and Farm Bureau lobbyist Roger Cliff to discuss the regulations and gain their support in making them law. The support of Dawson and Cliff would be vital, since they represented major affected interest groups, the environmental and agricultural communities respectively. The three men worked together in Derouin's hospital room, negotiating out an understanding of mutual support for the pesticides regulations. They "formalized" their support in a joint statement—a set of principles on groundwater/pesticides regulation agreed to by the three primary interest group lobbyists.

Later, when the Groundwater Committee got under way, Derouin introduced their joint statement to the Committee. The statement became a working paper of sorts for the Committee and Derouin felt their previous work together helped the three lobbyists make greater progress in the Committee.

Going into the Groundwater Committee, Derouin did not have a specific agenda, but did have some "bottom lines." First, the WMC would not agree to any type of "zero discharge, zero degradation, or zero impact legislation." Second, the WMC always advocates using numerical standards in regulating contamination problems.

Previous to the Groundwater Committee, Derouin had worked on most of the environmental special committees and was very familiar with Munts's consensus process. Derouin shares Munts's view of consensus and describes consensus as "building a majority—which is the manner in which a legislature gets laws passed." According to Derouin, using a consensus approach in the committees requires that a legislator—either the chair of the House or Senate Natural Resources Committee—take a leading role in pulling together the various interests to negotiate out mutually agreeable legislation.

Derouin compares the success of the consensus process to the failure of the U.S. Congress, which passes "lousy environmental legislation because Congress tries to split the baby among many *fighting* interests" rather than negotiating out mutually acceptable laws. In contrast, in Wisconsin, cooperation is stressed and "obnoxious people who throw themselves out in front of the train [and will not work with the Committee] get run over."

In describing Munts's role as chair of the Groundwater Committee, Derouin said that "without Munts we never would have been able to pull it off." Her political clout, patience, and savvy were instrumental in bringing people together and keeping them together. Since 1975, Munts has been involved in developing over ten environmental laws and Derouin feels that "without her maybe only 30 percent would have been passed." In January 1983, Munts moved from her position as chair of the Environmental Resources Committee to the prestigious and powerful chair of the House Finance Committee. According to Derouin, her personal convictions and legislative etiquette kept her as head of the Groundwater Committee. If she had left, "the bill would have fallen apart."

Derouin identified three skills that were needed to effectively participate in the Committee: (1) participants have to understand the issues technically; (2) participants have to understand the political system and possess a certain amount of political sophistication; and (3) participants must be able to "sell the bill to their constituents." As Derouin said, "You must be able to take the heat of going back to your constituency and selling the end product of the Committee." Derouin had to constantly go back to the WMC and brief standing committees. In addition, he helped WMC members alter sections of the Committee bill they did not support so that he could, in turn, take their suggestions back to the Committee. He also had to meet with other organizations and lobbyists to brief them and solicit their support. Some of these lobbyists represented very conservative corporations with different philosophies from those of Derouin and the WMC.

The WMC supported both the Committee bill and the final bill that emerged from the legislature. Derouin described the two major additions to the Committee bill, the lab certification program and the "mini-superfund program" as ornaments on a Christmas tree. The lab certification program was the DNR's ornament and the "superfund" provision was Jeff Neubauer's ornament. According to Derouin, Neubauer, Munts's replacement as chair of the Environmental Resources Committee, wanted the "superfund" program added to make it "his" bill. Without this claim to ownership of the bill, Neubauer would not have taken on the bill and worked it through the legislature as his role dictated.

Derouin describes the consensus process as a "formalized, structured process which works." He said the groundwater bill was not an easy bill to develop. "It was a breech birth . . . or better yet, a Caesarian section."

The Agricultural Perspective

The agricultural community was primarily represented by the Wisconsin Farm Bureau. Farm Bureau lobbyist Roger Cliff was one of the most influential and prominent public members. Several other public members were also from smaller farm organizations, although they played a much lesser role in the Committee than did Cliff. Included among the agricultural representatives was Myron Ehrhardt, an Oakfield Township farmer. Ehrhardt was the only public member who served as an individual and not a representative of a larger organization.

Roger Cliff and Myron Ehrhardt brought two very different backgrounds to the Groundwater Committee. Representation of agricultural interests on the Committee is described below through the different perspectives of these two individuals.

Roger Cliff

The Farm Bureau is the largest farm organization in Wisconsin and has over forty thousand members. Although the Farm Bureau has participated in several special committees before, it does not always accept the invitation to participate. In the past, the Farm Bureau has declined the offer to join a special committee because it did not want to be "trapped" into decisions it did not like. The bureau's decision to participate depends on the issue. Whenever they feel that there is "room for agreement" in an issue, the Farm Bureau will meet with people both in and outside the agricultural community to try to build "consensus" around the issue. This cooperative approach might include participation in a special committee. However, if they do not see any opportunity for achieving a consensus and feel so strongly about an issue they do not want to negotiate, they will stay out of the committee process and go with what Cliff describes as the traditional route—"line up and take votes."

In assessing the groundwater issue, Cliff decided there was considerable "flexibility" and negotiating room, so he felt comfortable participating. Groundwater is an important issue for the Farm Bureau. According to Cliff, groundwater is "a vital resource to our people . . . their livelihood is dependent upon the groundwater resource." On the other hand, agriculture is seen as a polluter of groundwater. Therefore, the Farm Bureau's interest in groundwater protection legislation was somewhat two-sided. They wanted effective groundwater protection, but not "overregulation." One of many issues that brought groundwater into the legislative arena—contamination of groundwater throughout the central regions of the state with the pesticide aldicarb—was a primary interest area for the Farm Bureau.

According to Cliff, the two major issues with which the Committee dealt were the compensation program and determining the role of the state regulatory agencies. These two issues were of particular importance and personal interest to Representative Munts; therefore, she was heavily involved in the working groups that tackled these issues. When Munts was less interested in a particular issue, she left the Committee members assigned to the working group more to themselves to discuss the issues and make the decisions.

The Farm Bureau supported the Committee bill, and although Cliff felt that a few "bad" amendments were added on in the legislature, they supported the bill that went to the governor's office. Overall, Cliff was satisfied with both the Committee process and the results. He feels that participation in a consensus process as it is structured by the Legislative Council is "nothing out of the ordinary" and not much different from normal lobbying and negotiating. He described the consensus process as "getting those affected together, working out differences, and then getting the bulk of those affected to agree."

In assessing how effectively different organizations participated, Cliff concluded that the public members faced the same obstacles in the Committee process that they would have in the normal legislative politics. Cliff observed "obvious" and "expected" differences in effectiveness and ability to participate. For example, citizen members were not the professionals in the political process that legislators and lobbyists were, putting them at a disadvantage. Agency representatives had a support staff dedicated to the groundwater issue, whereas public members were usually working on several other issues in addition to participating on the Committee. Cliff also felt that some members, like himself, came into the Committee with relatively large memberships/constituencies behind them, giving them a political advantage over other public members.

Myron Ehrhardt

Public member Myron Ehrhardt is a dairy farmer and Township chairman for Oakfield, Wisconsin. Ehrhardt entered the Groundwater Committee fresh out of a lengthy and bitter groundwater pollution problem in his community. Throughout 1979 and 1980, Ehrhardt was one of several community leaders who fought with the Grande Cheese Company. Grande was land-spreading whey and other dairy wastes, causing a local groundwater pollution problem. Citizens organized to deal with the problem, but the local government was unable to bring a resolution. The Wisconsin Department of Natural Resources (DNR) was unreceptive to the local concerns. Finally, the group went to the public intervenor's office. Through the public intervenor and a private environmental attorney hired by the citizens, the problem was finally resolved.

From that conflict, Ehrhardt was asked to serve on a whey rules committee set up within the DNR in the fall of 1981. As the only citizen on the committee, Ehrhardt helped to develop rules for the disposal of whey and dairy waste products. Although all of his concerns were not met in the rules, he did feel that he was able to accomplish some things. It was a learning experience, albeit a very difficult one, because the issues were emotional ones for him. He was the only committee member directly affected by the pollution problems and, therefore, he could not discuss the issues as objectively as other committee members. For example, Ehrhardt was particularly frustrated trying to communicate with the industry's legal counsel, who viewed the problem very differently from the way he did. In addition, Ehrhardt was committing his spare time to the project, and he found it very draining.

Ehrhardt experienced similar frustrations on the Groundwater Committee. Asked to serve because of his recent involvement in the issue and
previous dealings with the public intervenor's office, Ehrhardt went into
the process as the self-proclaimed "maverick." He felt obliged to "represent
the victim [of groundwater pollution] and to wake up people in ivory
towers." Representing the individual farmer and, he felt, his community
as well, Ehrhardt accepted the invitation to participate even though previous
political involvement had been very costly personally as well as in keeping
up his farm. Serving on the Groundwater Committee was a heavy strain
on Ehrhardt. Unlike most other public members who were representing
organized groups and were serving in a professional capacity, Ehrhardt was
an individual. The Committee was not part of his job, but was instead an
obligation he accepted in addition to his job and personal life.

Ehrhardt found the paperwork load to be overwhelming at times. A pile
of reports and memoranda would be handed out each meeting. Ehrhardt
remembers sitting next to Roger Cliff, the lobbyist for the Farm Bureau.
Cliff came to every meeting with a notebook, each report neatly filed and
referenced; whereas Ehrhardt barely had the spare time for the meetings,
let alone the time to organize all the reports. Also, he didn't have the office
support staff that many members had.

In addition, most reports prepared by the Legislative Council and the
TAC were either very technical or written in legal form and jargon. Having
never worked with legislative issues before, Ehrhardt found interpreting
the documents to be extremely difficult and time-consuming. He would
spend most of his Sundays just trying to keep up.

Despite these frustrations, Ehrhardt still found working on the Committee a valuable experience. He felt as though he had equal power with
the other Committee members in that he had a right to speak and air his
views just the same as everyone else. Occasionally, his opinions would be
supported by other members, which gave him a sense of legitimacy and
clout. Ehrhardt went into the Committee expecting a political process with
political power plays. He was not frustrated or surprised to find that, as a
lone citizen, he had less power than others. Ehrhardt saw himself as the
voice of the local people, a role that would mean that he lacked resources,
legal and technical expertise, and organizational abilities. Nevertheless, he
felt that he served a vital role on the Committee. Ehrhardt enjoyed being
able to meet people and talk one on one. He had good dialogues with Roger
Cliff, the Farm Bureau representative, during lunch and breaks.

Ehrhardt was comfortable with the bill, although it was "definitely a
compromise." He had pushed strongly for the well compensation issue and
felt instrumental in getting the compensation program included in the final
Committee bill. Lack of legislative knowledge, organizational capabilities,
and personal time were the major frustrations for Ehrhardt.

The Environmental Perspective

Aside from environmentally oriented legislators, the environmental perspective was represented by two public members and public intervenor Thomas Dawson. The two public members were Terry Kakida, director of research for Citizens for a Better Environment, and Professor James Hoffman, a hydrogeologist from the University of Wisconsin. Munts selected Hoffman and Kakida primarily for their technical expertise. Hoffman played a relatively minor role in the Committee process and even though Kakida's organization was interested in advocating broad policy stipulations, he was not a strong political force, either. As a result, Dawson turned out to be one of the most politically influential environmental interests within the Committee process.

Richelle Lisse of Wisconsin's Environmental Decade, the state's largest environmental group, also played a significant role in the Committee process, although not as a formal participant. Lisse attended most of the Committee meetings, and Decade was highly active in the legislature, working on the final bill that became law.

Thomas Dawson

Dawson describes the public intervenor as "an institutionalized advocate for protecting public rights in the environment." Since the public intervenor is recognized as the environmental voice within state government, he or she "would naturally be considered a key participant in any environmental decision-making process." The public intervenor works closely with environmental citizen groups and Dawson considers these groups to be part of his constituency. He does not, however, feel he can act as a formal representative of the organized environmental community, especially since there are a few environmental organizations in the state Dawson does not "get along with."

As a government representative, rather than a public member, Dawson was placed on the nonvoting Technical Advisory Committee. When Munts arranged the Compensation Subcommittee, she brought Dawson in to represent the environmental perspective, since by that stage in the process he had emerged as the primary environmental representative. The TAC and the Compensation Subcommittee were his "formal role," but throughout the process, Dawson informally worked with the entire Committee.

A major agenda item for Dawson was also one of the "driving forces" making groundwater a legislative issue: the contamination of groundwater resources with the pesticide aldicarb. The aldicarb issue was receiving considerable publicity and was an issue that heavily involved Dawson as public intervenor. His office had been pushing strongly for regulatory action on pesticides and groundwater for some time. He had been communicating with both the agricultural and industry leaders about the pesticides issue.

In July 1981, Dawson wrote an open, public letter to the three state agency secretaries that would be involved in pesticide regulation—agriculture, health and human services, and natural resources. The letter made an intense plea to the agencies to take strong action on the pesticides/groundwater problem. Of the three, only the secretary of agriculture responded, although the Department of Natural Resources already had plenary authority over the groundwater resource.

Dawson began pressuring the Department of Agriculture to adopt as stringent regulation as possible. The agency's activity and Dawson's pressure sparked the interest of James Derouin, of the Wisconsin Association of Manufacturers and Commerce, and Roger Cliff, of the Farm Bureau. As a result, Derouin, Cliff, and Dawson began discussing options for pesticide regulation. The joint statement they developed stressed the need to develop standards. As Dawson stated, "We are all going to live and die by the numbers [standards], therefore, we all need to work together to determine the right numbers."

According to Dawson, the Special Committee "floundered" in the initial months, trying to grab hold of issues, an approach, and a purpose. In October 1982, when the joint statement was completed and Derouin introduced it to the Committee, Dawson felt that the statement provided a needed focus for the Committee. Most of the Committee dialogue already centered around pesticide issues. It was not until the end of the Committee process that the discussions were broadened to consider other contamination problems.

Dawson identified two major obstacles to building the groundwater bill. The first was determining and agreeing upon a "conceptual framework" for groundwater regulation. Since groundwater protection was a relatively new field with no federal legislation to serve as an example, Wisconsin legislators and Committee members had little guidance in developing legislation. "Terms had to be defined," stated Dawson. Terms that had been used in surface water legislation had to be reassessed for groundwater regulation. Questions such as "What *is* groundwater pollution?" . . . "What does 'nondegradation' mean?" . . . and "What constitutes 'no detrimental effect'?" were addressed.

Not only did the Committee need to make "a breakthrough" on defining groundwater pollution, they also had to determine the role of regulatory agencies. "This was another obstacle," Dawson observed. The Wisconsin DNR had been termed "a sleeping giant" by some. Although the DNR had plenary authority over the groundwater resource, the agency was not taking strong regulatory action. Confronting the "*right* and the *duty* of an agency to take action" was a difficult issue for the Committee. The issue was resolved by including a strong enforcement provision in the bill. In the provision, the DNR and other state agencies were mandated to take action upon identifying groundwater contamination. The state agencies would have a nondiscretionary duty to shut down the polluting activity. Dawson considered this provision a major success.

In addition to the mandatory enforcement provision, Dawson strongly supported the two-tiered standards program in the bill. The standards program was also strongly supported by Terry Kakida, Richelle Lisse, and other environmentalists. On the other hand, even though some environmentalists advocated a citizen suit provision, Dawson did not believe the bill should "die" for lack of such a provision. From his understanding of Wisconsin law of standing, Dawson concluded that citizen suits would be allowed without an explicit provision in the bill. Although Dawson pushed for a citizen suit provision in the early stages, when it failed to receive any other political support, he let it go.

Within the Committee process, Dawson, Derouin, and Cliff represented the three primary interests in groundwater—environmental, industry, and agriculture. However, any agreement reached by Committee members could not be the final word. The three representatives were "expected to deliver their clientele" in order to ensure support for the bill from the broader community. They had to go back to their constituencies and "sell" them on the agreement.

For Dawson, it took a lot of selling to gain his clientele's support. Although the environmental community supported the bill on the conceptual level, it was difficult for him to explain how particular provisions of the bill were formulated. As Dawson explained, "The bill was comprised of a series of trade-offs. A real balance had been struck between industry, agriculture and environmental interests." But explaining the nature of and reasons for these compromises to environmental groups who were not party to the negotiations was a complicated task. What appeared to be weaknesses to environmentalists outside the process were, in fact, trade-offs Dawson had made for stronger, more critical provisions in the bill. The trade-offs had to be both explained and justified. In Dawson's eyes, the bill was a "house of cards and if one card was knocked down the whole house would fall down." It was this view of the bill Dawson had to communicate to his constituency.

During the process, there was fragmentation within the environmental community. Not all environmental groups in the state were satisfied with the bill that was being developed in the Special Committee, but Dawson did not feel the fragmentation was serious. When it came to action within the legislature, the critical "mainstream" environmental groups—Wisconsin's Environmental Decade, Sierra Club, and the Audubon Society—were there to support the bill. According to Dawson, the organizations that "screamed" about the bill were smaller, more radical organizations that rarely participated in developing legislation. In the groundwater process, they consistently remained on the "outside" and had little impact on the final bill.

Because the Special Committee bill was a "house of cards" when it reached the legislature, each party to the bill had to fight for the bill as a whole and not just his or her particular interests. "For example," explained Dawson, "if a legislator offered agriculture an amendment that would change the nature of the bill we had all worked toward, each of us would have to fight the amendment." Industry would have to fight off an amendment that would hurt environmentalists and environmentalists would in turn have to fight off an amendment that would hurt industry. An amendment that would help one interest would hurt the entire bill and destroy the Committee's "consensus."

At first, Dawson did not support the Committee bill, but since he was not a voting member of the Special Committee, he was not able to formally voice his opinion. However, using the role he established in the Subcommittee, Dawson worked closely with Representative Munts while the bill was in the Standing Committee and bargained for the amendments that were needed to gain his support. Thus, later in the legislative process, Dawson joined the "consensus" that he was not a part of when the Special Committee bill was voted on in June 1983. According to Dawson, he would not have supported a weak bill. Unlike others on the Committee, Dawson was not willing to make any trade-off to get a bill—*any* bill. Dawson felt that at times during the process some legislators on the Committee pushed too hard for any agreement in order to get a bill. Occasionally, Dawson found himself in situations in which he was the only person not in agreement and there was pressure on him to join the group. He suggested that, in the face of such pressure, it is easy to lose sight of your objectives in the Committee process and he had to work to maintain his vision. "You don't make trade-offs to get a bill, you make trade-offs to get groundwater protection," said Dawson. "You have to keep asking yourself, 'Am I here to get a bill or to protect the groundwater resource?' "

To be effective in the Committee process, Dawson believes you should have a problem-solving orientation. He found James Derouin effective to work with because he was a problem-solver. Derouin did not "talk ideology or rhetoric, but instead helped identify, address and solve problems." In Dawson's opinion, some Committee members were less effective because they would not discuss, negotiate, and problem-solve. They took a "purist" attitude and would, therefore, not interact with traditionally opposing parties.

Terry Kakida

Terry Kakida, aquatic biologist and director of research for the Wisconsin office of Citizens for a Better Environment (CBE), was the only public member formally representing the environmental community. And, although a member of the Sierra Club, Hoffman was not a formal representative of that organization. The Wisconsin CBE is a science/research/public education organization. A major issue area for the organization is increasing effective public participation in environmental decision-making. They do not lobby. CBE is comprised of environmental scientists, researchers, and lawyers. Kakida entered the process with scientific and technical information, but not a strong lobbying/political pressure orientation. He consulted with a CBE attorney throughout the process.

Before accepting the invitation to participate, CBE assessed the Legislative Council's goals to make sure they were consistent with the group's objectives. CBE's goals going into the process were: (1) advocate a policy of nondegradation; (2) stress the need for preventative rather than reactive strategies; and (3) ensure a strong enforcement process.

In general, Kakida was not satisfied with the process or the results. He felt the Subcommittee produced a bill too weak for CBE to support. Contrary to other Committee members, Kakida did not believe "half a loaf was better than none." In terms of the Committee process, Kakida was not satisfied with the representation on the Compensation Subcommittee—namely Munts, Derouin, and Cliff—although he accepted Munts's appointments to the Subcommittee without protest. Although Kakida felt that Thomas Dawson was an effective participant in the Subcommittee, Dawson's agenda was not as stringent as Kakida's. As a result, Kakida felt the Subcommittee's decisions primarily represented the interests of agriculture and industry. For example, the state Pesticide Review Board, an interagency board that had previously had the authority to review pesticide regulation, was denied this power under the groundwater bill—a decision supporting agriculture interests. Metallic mining was exempted from coverage—a decision supporting industry interests.

Kakida felt that many full Committee members were either overwhelmed by the process or oblivious to the workings of the Subcommittee. Thus, Subcommittee decisions were in a sense "slipped past" the full Committee. The paperwork load was so immense that most full Committee members could not keep up with all of the small "deals" being made in the Subcommittee. Subcommittee results would be brought to the full Committee with pleas to support the results because "It took so much work," or because "It's a compromise—a delicate balance," or because "Time is running out." In other words, Kakida felt that the message to the full Committee was "Please, pass the bill." He believed that many members were too confused or unaware to do otherwise.

Kakida realized that the environmental community as a whole and CBE, in particular, did not do well in the Committee process. He did not feel that he lacked lobbying or negotiating skills needed for success, but instead saw the problem as a deficiency in the environmental community. According to Kakida, the environmental community did not have an "agreed upon bottom line." Some groups were interested in *any* bill being passed; others, like CBE, wanted a bill only if it was a strong one. Some groups were interested in only specific groundwater issues such as landfills, and, therefore, had very limited agendas. As the process proceeded, Kakida felt that the various groups were trying to come together and "develop a common thread" to negotiate with, but it was too late. Because the community as a whole did not back CBE or appear to be a cohesive group, they were not the lobbying powers that agriculture and industry were.

In spite of CBE's failure to implement many of their objectives, the group never considered pulling out of the process. Kakida did not feel it was an unreasonable strain on the group or a difficult process to participate in, although relating his experience during the process to his peers was sometimes difficult. Kakida himself often wanted out of the process for personal reasons. Politics, in general, is not something he enjoys.

Richelle Lisse

Wisconsin's Environmental Decade, a major state environmental group, was invited to be a public member on the Groundwater Committee, but the organization declined the invitation for several reasons. First, Decade had participated in the mining "consensus" process and, even though they were satisfied that the mining rules were "the best that could be had at the time," their participation unearthed some misgivings in the environmental community due to fragmentation among Wisconsin environmental groups. Decade is a "mainstream" organization that can find itself in conflict with the more "radical fringe." For example, a particular issue of dispute is the use of numerical standards in pollution control. Whereas Decade advocates the use of stringent standards in environmental regulation, some "radical" groups in the state feel that the use of standards implies an acceptable level of pollution and, therefore, any standard is too liberal.

Decade advocated numerical standards in the mining process. This issue and others placed some strain on the relationship between Decade and other groups. As a result, questions of representation emerged. Both Decade and the public intervenor represented environmental interests on the mining consensus committee, and some groups were not comfortable with that representation. In addition to the concern about whether Decade fairly represented the entire environmental community, Decade had grown from about 700 members in 1976 to 150,000 in 1984. As a result, some groups were also feeling overshadowed by Decade. Decade also decided not to participate because the organization was in a state of transition. Lisse was new to her job as the groundwater specialist.

Lastly, Decade purposely stayed outside of the process to play the "gadfly." According to Lisse, participation in this sort of process implies that you are willing to be "co-opted" to a limited extent in order to produce a compromise bill. Decade wanted to stay out of this round to keep clear vision. By being on the outside of the Committee, Decade could play the role of the critic. Lisse was active during the Committee process, offering a critical analysis of Committee decisions and pointing out holes in the Committee bill. Lisse was even more active in the legislature, working with Munts and other legislators in amending the bill. This role was an effective one for Decade, since most of Decade's criticisms of the Special Committee bill were addressed by the legislature to formulate the final bill. Although Decade did not feel the Special Committee bill adequately reflected environmental interests, they strongly supported the amended bill that went to the governor's office.

Lisse shares Kakida's perception that the environmental community did not wield much power in the Committee process, at least in comparison to agriculture and industry. An environmental citizen representative was not a part of what Lisse termed the Subcommittee "inner circle of influence." The "inner circle" (Dawson, Derouin, Cliff, and Munts) was the group that networked outside the process, making subtle decisions over the phone and in other informal discussions. Lisse, like many other participants, pointed out that the "real political stuff" and "agenda setting" went on in the Subcommittee. Lisse was not entirely satisfied with Dawson's representation of environmental interests, and since Kakida was not formally assigned to the Subcommittee nor did "he force his way on as he could have done, no environmental chips were played" in this critical forum.

Lisse felt the environmental community might have been more effective if more organizations had attended the meetings and tried to voice their concerns, but there was never any effort to do so. However, even if the environmental community had pulled together, the process would still have worked against them in some ways. Lisse did not feel that negotiation skills were equal among all Committee members, whereas in an effective consensus process the skill levels should be equal. Better negotiation skills gave some public members an edge over others, thus, participation by some public members was hindered. In addition, the level of commitment to the process—toward obtaining a win/win solution through compromise—was unequal. Lisse felt that commitment to the process, or willingness to compromise, could have been equalized through establishing ground rules. It was not spelled out at the outset that participants should be willing to be "somewhat co-opted" in order to facilitate a compromise. As a result, Lisse felt that some participants came into the process with the intention of giving *nothing* away.

Conclusion

Under the influence of a few dedicated persons—individuals who were not satisfied with traditional mechanisms for developing environmental policy—

a unique forum has evolved in Wisconsin. It does not fit a textbook description of a consensus process: a process that stresses open communication and full participation by all members; attempts to equalize skills and power among the participants; requires broad and complete representation from all affected interests; and results in an end product that is 100 percent acceptable to all members. However, the Wisconsin "consensus" process was a departure from traditional legislative politics. It took people out of negotiation situations in which individual lobbyists pressured individual legislators to accept his or her position. Instead, it put lobbyists and legislators together with technical experts and agency personnel to discuss and resolve issues jointly in a more cooperative atmosphere. The resulting "hybrid" process mixed some key principles of a consensus process—group negotiations, an emphasis on cooperation and agreement, and an attempt to achieve effective representation from the affected interest—with traditional characteristics of legislative politics such as behind-the-scenes bargaining, imbalanced power and skill levels among participants, and small closed-group decision-making.

Although a "hybrid" process, the cross between nontraditional and traditional decision-making modes yielded a Committee process that was dominated by traditional politics. Thus, effective participation required a much higher level of political sophistication and awareness than a true consensus process might have. The orientation and underlying forces of the Groundwater Committee were well understood by experienced and influential lobbyists and legislators. However, for public members unfamiliar with legislative decision-making, the Groundwater Committee was a difficult forum in which to operate. These difficulties are best illustrated by the experiences of Citizens for a Better Environment. Terry Kakida was the only formal environmental organization representative on the Committee and yet he never emerged as a primary force. Although a talented scientist and researcher, Kakida's personal and professional skills were not those required by the Committee.

Kakida was not from a highly political organization, nor was he an experienced lobbyist or legislative expert, as were the more influential public members. Munts selected CBE for the organization's technical expertise, yet Kakida entered the Committee with a policy agenda and specific issues he wanted addressed in the bill. Kakida was not successful in seeing his concerns expressed in the Committee decision and, even though he was not totally dissatisfied with the Committee bill, Kakida was forced to vote against the Committee's end product, calling it "an illusion of groundwater protection." Kakida's experiences mirror those of other citizen organizations in similar situations, and by focusing on the experiences of Kakida, the need for political and legislative savvy in the hybrid Committee process can be illustrated.

Terry Kakida was unable to adequately represent CBE's interests for a variety of reasons. Foremost was his unfamiliarity with the subtleties of the legislative process and the Committee's role in that overall process. Since CBE does not lobby, Kakida did not have as strong a sense of the political bargaining and negotiating that is required to influence legislation as did other Committee members.

Munts never promised that the Special Committee would be protected from the traditional politics of legislative development. However, the group discussions and consensus orientation of the Committee may have suggested to some public members that the Special Committee would offer a more hospitable, cooperative environment to develop policy. For example, as a scientist, Kakida felt that the Special Committee should have provided scientists and public health specialists with a broader role in developing groundwater legislation. But as Kakida observed, the Special Committee bill was "definitely a lawyer's bill." The Special Committee was controlled by powerful lobbyists and individuals with a strong legislative/legal orientation.

When the Special Committee proved to be only minimally removed from traditional legislative politics, public members with little experience in or sensitivity to such a process were "left out in the cold." The political sophistication that is acquired from experience was essential to successful participation in the Special Committee. The skills needed included an ability to identify the critical decision networks operating outside of the full Committee and a willingness and ability to tap into these networks. Because Kakida either could not or chose not to push his way onto the primary decision-making forum—the Compensation Subcommittee—when he was not appointed to it, he did not play a strong role in formulating the bill. Although Kakida did not feel that he was disadvantaged by a lack of negotiating skills or political expertise, it would seem unlikely up against seasoned and talented lobbyists in a politically complex situation that Kakida could have been a potent force.

Not only did Kakida's low political profile prevent him from assessing and using the Committee dynamics to his advantage, it also lessened his effectiveness in the overall legislative process. As explained earlier, the small work group that was forged out of the Special Committee process continued to play a critical role in the later stages of legislative development.

Munts expected her Special Committee members to maintain their commitment to developing a groundwater law throughout the legislative process. For Special Committee participants unaccustomed or unable to take on an aggressive role in lobbying and negotiating within the traditional legislative framework, the Special Committee was the end of the line. This limitation was a handicap, since Munts never lost sight of future rounds while orchestrating the Special Committee. She looked for politically powerful and active individuals who would continue to be effective as the bill progressed through the legislature.

Kakida's experiences not only point to the need for political savvy and clout to participate effectively in the hybrid Committee process, they also

illustrate a characteristic of the Committee process that hindered the environmental community as a whole—adequate representation.

Determining and acquiring representation from the various interests in
groundwater was a difficult task for Munts and the Legislative Council.
Although the Committee was merely the first round in developing groundwater legislation, Munts realized she needed representation from the three
primary interests—agriculture, industry, and environmentalists. Obtaining
a representative from the environmentalists was particularly complicated.
As compared with industry, environmental (and to some degree agricultural)
interests are diffused and fragmented. There is no principal actor that can
voice the entire community's concerns. As mentioned earlier, Munts
brought CBE to the Committee primarily for technical expertise. CBE is
not a leadership group within the environmental community and, therefore,
could not easily represent interests broader than their own. Munts had
wanted to bring in a leadership group, Wisconsin's Environmental Decade,
as an environmental, citizen group representative, but the organization
would not participate. It would seem that without Decade there was no
clear leadership group for Munts to call upon. Thus, representation was a
major problem area for environmentalists.

Even though Munts wanted to have an effective environmental-citizen
advocate on the Committee, in general she does not believe that most
environmental groups have the skills or the "staying power" to participate
on a legislative committee. "Citizen environmental groups often do not
have a strong interest in the technical and legal minutiae involved in the
development of a complicated bill," according to Munts. This perception
of the environmental community, combined with her inability to pinpoint
a main representative from the state's various organizations, led Munts to
rely on Thomas Dawson for environmental advocacy during the Committee
process and then solicit participation from environmental groups afterward.
As a result, it took more effort later in the legislative process to obtain
support from the environmental community.

In contrast, James Derouin did not feel that representation should have
been a problem for environmentalists. Derouin feels that Wisconsin environmental groups have substantial political strength and moxie and that
internal fragmentation should not be accepted as a handicap. According to
Derouin, "If we give in to the criticism that the environmental community
is too fragmented and diffuse to effectively participate in a committee process, we will have even greater environmental fragmentation and there will
eventually be no one to deal with—at which point the WMC just won't
deal."

Derouin claimed that much of the criticism surrounding the Committee
and environmental representation is the result of a "stage" environmentalists
are going through. Leadership groups won't agree to *any* legislation because
they "can't sell memberships and sell themselves as 'watchdogs' of the

environment if they appear too conciliatory," claims Derouin. He said, "Environmentalists want to be heroes, even if being a hero may not be the best thing for the state."

Despite these problems, Munts's approach to environmental representation was relatively successful in that it produced a final bill that was supported by the state's major environmental organizations—Decade, the Sierra Club, and Audubon Society—when it left the legislature. The role played by Wisconsin's Environmental Decade was no doubt very instrumental in increasing the environmental community's effectiveness in the overall legislative process. Decade purposely stayed on the outside of the Committee to play the "gadfly" role and offer a critical response to the Committee bill. By remaining active and involved in the Committee process, Decade ensured a role for both themselves and other environmental organizations in subsequent decision-making forums. Specifically, Lisse created the opportunity to work with Munts in amending the bill in the legislature, to help fill in the holes she identified in the Special Committee bill. Her working knowledge of the Committee bill no doubt helped Lisse work to amend the bill in the legislature.

Obviously, Decade did not disadvantage themselves by declining the offer to participate in the Committee. They did not permanently close any doors. Therefore, even though the environmental community was not well represented in the Special Committee, they were able to implement their concerns in the final bill. If environmental organizations had not had access and influence in the legislature, they might have been facing what they saw as inadequate groundwater policy.

The difficulty in obtaining representation could have severely handicapped the environmentalists, especially since the environmental organizations did not build effective coalitions to enable or enhance representation. Both CBE and Decade acted relatively independently in the process, CBE on the inside and Decade on the outside. Unlike Derouin and Cliff, Kakida's voice was not that of the greater community. Formal coalition-building both before and during the Committee process could have enabled Kakida and Lisse to present stronger fronts. The existence of a coalition previous to the Special Committee might have allowed the environmental community to assign a citizen representative to the Committee who could bring a unified environmental voice with him or her and take information back to other organizations. A coalition among environmental groups might also have provided a forum for the groups to discuss issues and strategize.

Of course, it is merely speculation as to whether such formal coalition-building would have been effective. Even though a coalition might have made determining representation easier, if the coalition were internally unsound, a seemingly unified external front may have masked fragmentation among the various groups. This fragmentation could have worked against the environmentalists. As the situation was, Munts was sensitive to the fact that the environmental-citizen community did not have a highly influential role on the Special Committee, thus she was open to their input in her work with the Environmental Resources Committee and the legislature. If the environmental organizations had appeared to pull together, providing a representative for the Special Committee, to only fall apart later on, Munts might not have been as open to environmental influence in the rounds following the Special Committee process. She might not have given the environmentalists a second chance.

The ability to assess the role and probable success of coalition-building to facilitate representation on the Committee is another example of the political sophistication needed for successful participation in this hybrid process. Committee politics were influential both internally and externally. Internally, the Committee process required an understanding of power relationships, an ability to unearth and tap into critical decision networks, and lobbying/negotiating skills. Externally, effective participation required an ability to strategize and assess political options, such as the use of coalitions, deciding whether or not to participate, and developing informal roles outside of the process.

Interviews

Representative Mary Lou Munts, Wisconsin State Legislature	April 16, 1984
Steven Born, University of Wisconsin	March 1984
Roger Cliff, Wisconsin Farm Bureau	April 19, 1984
Thomas Dawson, Wisconsin public intervenor	April 24, 1984
James Derouin, Wisconsin Association of Manufacturers and Commerce	August 20, 1984
Myron Ehrhardt, farmer	March 23, 1984
Terry Kakida, Citizens for a Better Environment	March 11, 1984
Richelle Lisse, Wisconsin's Environmental Decade	March 29, 1984 and May 29, 1984
Mark Patronsky, Wisconsin Legislative Council	April 19, 1984
Bonnie Reese, Wisconsin Legislative Council	March 1984

Draft Case Study Readers
Representative Mary Lou Munts
Terry Kakida
Thomas Dawson

References

Amy, Douglas J. "The Politics of Environmental Mediation." *Ecology Law Quarterly* 2, no. 1 (1983): 3.

Derouin, James G. "The Wisconsin Model: A Consensus Approach to the Resolution of Environmental Issues." *Wisconsin Academy Review* (December 1981).

Wisconsin Legislative Council, Summary of Proceedings, Special Committee on Groundwater Management: April 26, 1982, May 25, 1982, June 29, 1982, July 21, 1982, August 30, 1982, September 29, 1982, November 30, 1982, February 11, 1983, March 25, 1983, and May 16, 1983.

Wisconsin Legislative Council Report No. 25 to the 1983 Legislature, "Legislation Relating to Groundwater Management," August 17, 1983.

Wisconsin Legislative Council Staff, "The New Law Relating to Groundwater Management (1983 Wisconsin Act 410)," Information Memorandum 84–11, July 11, 1984.

5 Conclusion

Julia M. Wondolleck, Nancy J. Manring, and
James E. Crowfoot

"The environmental community was enfranchised in a way they never would have been able to be. We were at the table with the U.S. Army Corps of Engineers and the Denver Water Board with our own experts and our ideas were on the table. We wouldn't have had that opportunity in any other forum."

In these remarks before the 1988 Conservation Foundation National Conference on Environmental Dispute Resolution, Daniel Luecke, a senior scientist with the Environmental Defense Fund (EDF), was clearly pleased with the gains made by his organization through participation in the Denver Metropolitan Water Roundtable, a collaborative effort to resolve that region's long-standing water policy disputes. To illustrate this enfranchisement, he mentioned a meeting he had attended just the day before in which the Denver Water Board was explaining their future plans to the governor of the state of Colorado. In response to a question by the governor about safety issues, the Denver Water Board representative turned to the EDF hydrologist present at the meeting and said, "Lee, correct me if I'm wrong, but this is our understanding of the safety issue. . . ." Luecke believes this acknowledgment both of the environmental community and of its expertise is an indication of the phenomenal change in relationships and the level of respect and trust between traditional adversaries resulting from this dialogue.

Luecke's enthusiasm about this particular EDS experience is not unchecked, however. At the same time that he was describing how much the environmental community potentially gained through the Water Roundtable negotiations, he was also cautioning groups about the inequities he believes are inherent in these processes and the heavy toll they place on a nonprofit group's resources, staff, and other activities, particularly on a group's attention to other pressing issues.

The decision about how to proceed in a conflict situation—whether to heighten the conflict, de-escalate the conflict by exiting or ignoring a situation, or, conversely, to resolve a specific dispute through collaborative interactions—is not a decision to be taken lightly or without analysis by an organization. Each decision has significant consequences not only to an issue but also to the organization and the individuals comprising it.

A significant literature exists on the functions and strategies of conflict in advancing an organization and its objectives. Little analysis has been done, however, that asks how and with what consequence a citizen organization might use processes designed to settle, rather than heighten or avoid, a specific dispute.

This book has examined some of the experiences of citizen groups that have actively promoted and/or participated in both formal and informal EDS processes. While by no means a comprehensive analysis of all likely conflict situations and EDS process characteristics, the analysis contained here does shed light on some of the key questions and issues a citizen organization must address for itself before confidently, or at least knowledgeably, pursuing this path. While the findings should not be construed as predictive, they should give a citizen group perspective on dispute settlement processes and insights into the types of problems and issues they will encounter, ways in which other groups have either successfully or unsuccessfully grappled with these issues and dilemmas, and some ideas for possible actions they might take.

The Benefits and Costs of Participation

As seen in the cases presented throughout this book, there are both advantages and disadvantages to participation in EDS processes for citizen groups.

Citizens may find an alternate dispute settlement process gives them greater power and influence in the decision-making process. They may experience greater access to key decision-makers and important information, and they may be able to influence or control meeting agendas to their advantage.

By participating in EDS processes, citizen groups can gain power in other significant ways. For individuals, it can be an opportunity to develop new skills in areas such as negotiation, communication, active listening, group process, and coalition-building. An NIS participant referred to the process as a "political education." One Fitchburg participant felt that the experience was instrumental in her gaining a position on the Town Council. The situation can empower individuals when they recognize that their input does affect decision-making. Citizens involved with the NIS recognized that their suggestions mattered and carried clout. As a result, they gained confidence and became "pretty feisty."

The confidence, credibility, negotiation skills, and political savvy gained by individual members can translate to greater effectiveness and legitimacy for the group as a whole. Several citizen groups enhanced their image and credibility with public officials by participating in an alternative forum. The citizens involved in the Pig's Eye controversy gained respect and leverage for themselves by participating in the attempted mediation as "statesmen," negotiating in good faith. The success of the Common Ground policy dialogue gained the citizen participants greater legitimacy and respect with key decision-makers and legislators.

Many citizen participants felt that the greater access to decision-makers that they experienced in their particular situations would continue into the future. Many believed that access and influence would be enhanced by their newly established credibility and familiarity with traditional decision-makers. For some, like several of the NIS participants, the alternative dispute resolution process was the first time for the involved citizens to demonstrate their knowledge and abilities to government and agency actors. They felt that the process opened doors between citizens and government and created an ongoing avenue for cooperation between them. Sand Lakes citizen participants felt that their work on the Quiet Area management plan set the precedent for and legitimized citizen involvement in agency planning.

In some cases, not only have the citizens found greater access to decision-makers, but they also have changed the process of decision-making to their advantage. The San Juan citizen participants were able to persuade the Forest Service to change their procedure for notifying the public of impending actions. The San Juan citizens were also able to establish an Advisory Group to monitor the ongoing implementation of agreements and recommendations made by the group. The pressure exerted on the DNR by the Sand Lakes citizen participants caused the DNR to change its customary process of decision-making. The DNR adopted an internal, cross-cutting task force that compelled them to confront the internal differences among divisions. This structural response led to a management plan with a wider base of support within the department.

Perhaps some of the greatest ongoing benefits result from the improved communications and working relationships that grow out of the EDS collaboration. Better communications can create a positive environment for implementation of agreements and for future cooperation on other issues. As mentioned earlier, stereotypes may be dispelled, surprise alliances may be discovered, and new lines of communication may be opened. Participants often have the opportunity to demonstrate not only their competence, but also their reasonableness to traditional opponents. Thus, adversarial relationships may evolve into cooperative ones as formerly opposed groups find new avenues for mutual cooperation. Common Ground citizen participants mentioned that trust among groups increased as a result of the freer discussions, defining of roles, and clarifying of expectations. New lines of communication were established and "old wounds were healed."

In most of the cases analyzed in this book, the EDS process enabled the citizens to address successfully their key issues of concern in a manner that most participants felt was far preferable to the alternative methods of decision-making. For example, citizens felt that the Fitchburg mediation avoided a lengthy court battle that would have caused further delays for residents in need of a safe water system. Likewise, the San Juan and Sand Lakes citizen participants felt that the alternative process enabled them to address their concerns more promptly without the uncertainty, inconvenience, and resource drain of lengthy trials and/or administrative appeals.

The Common Ground and Wisconsin groundwater citizen participants also agreed that the EDS process was a better use of their organizational resources. Citizen participants from both lamented that time, energy, and money had been wasted in the past in endless fighting in committee rooms, with strong legislation consistently being defeated by the extreme factionalism and lack of agreement over the issues.

In the San Juan case, residents were able to stop the proposed road-building and develop a timber-harvesting and road-building plan that protected their interests and investments. They also were able to persuade the Forest Service to develop timber sale proposals that smaller timber companies could bid on, thereby avoiding the problems associated with large timber companies and transient work forces.

The Common Ground consensus project developed strategies to promote soil conservation and wetlands protection (and made some progress on a farmland preservation plan). The legislature passed two out of three of their proposals. Likewise, the NIS project was able to address successfully a number of community issues. Some problems such as traffic light synchronization and police in-house training were remedied even during the process; other positive changes were cited six months after completion.

The Sand Lakes citizen participants were able to expand the Quiet Area by two hundred acres, a snowmobile trail was moved farther north away from the Quiet Area, clear-cut sizes were reduced in the forest management plan, and five additional development leases were changed to nondevelopment.

As noted above, the Fitchburg residents got a new, safe water system and the unexpected bonus of a community park. Although the Wisconsin groundwater effort was more of a mixed success—as political compromises often are—improved groundwater legislation was passed by the legislature.

The group problem-solving techniques employed in most EDS processes enable participants to broaden the range of possible alternatives. Freed from the narrowness and restrictions of a purely legal challenge, solutions can be very creative. In the Fitchburg case, through mediation, the town realized that it did not have to pipe municipal water out to the subdivisions in question and potentially disrupt the area's overall development plan; rather, they could drill individual wells as needed. Mediation also helped uncover creative options for the developer in assisting the affected residents. Being "cash poor," the developer agreed to provide land for well sites and for a park; thus, residents got a new, safe water system and the unexpected but needed parkland. The San Juan participants discovered an innovative way to handle the conflict by developing a solution on the basis of "viewsheds."

Although EDS processes, as seen, potentially offer many advantages to citizen groups, they should never be viewed as a panacea or cure-all. They may be advantageous in some circumstances and a liability in others. It is incumbent upon citizen groups to be able to choose the appropriate process or forum that will best address their issues and protect their interests.

Citizen groups should realize that some of the problems stem from the fact that an EDS process may be a new procedure for all parties. In this sense, citizen groups are not alone in some of the difficulties they face. However, because citizen groups usually have a narrower margin for failure, they may have more to lose than government or industry actors in an unsuccessful alternative process.

Furthermore, because an alternative process demands the active involvement of citizen groups and individual members, citizens may not be able to simply entrust their interests to the hands of experts. Greater participation in decision-making is thus a two-edged sword. Consequently, it is imperative that citizen groups recognize the problems they may face and critically evaluate their abilities before engaging in an EDS process.

Unlike many traditional arenas where problems are handed over to lawyers and judges or agency officials, if a citizen group becomes involved in an EDS process for resolving a conflict, the members will be directly involved in the resolution of the dispute. In the end, citizens' issues may be addressed more promptly and more effectively than in the traditional forums; however, they may have to devote more personal and organizational time to the process.

Citizen groups may have to challenge well-financed, generously staffed government agencies and industries. The representatives from government and industry usually are able to participate in the course of their jobs; for citizens, participation is often an additional commitment outside of work and family responsibilities, and they usually lack the support staffs that government and industry have.

Group problem-solving techniques can be very time-consuming. There are often large amounts of information replete with legal and technical jargon to assimilate. Participants from the Common Ground, Wisconsin groundwater, NIS, Sand Lakes, and San Juan cases all reported the intense time demands as a problem of the alternative process. NIS citizen participants stressed that there were "copious" amounts of information to digest, and that the substantial time commitment may have discouraged other citizens from participating.

Citizen organizations may not have the necessary skills to participate effectively in an EDS process. Lack of effective negotiation and problem-solving skills was cited as a problem by respondents from the Pig's Eye, NIS, Wisconsin groundwater, and Sand Lakes controversies. NIS citizen participants cited lack of familiarity with the process as a stumbling block. They noted that some people simply are not "process" oriented, and that some do not profit from a "learning by doing" approach. They stressed that citizens need to know how to run meetings and be an effective chair, and have good team decision-making skills.

Part of the organizational cost of an alternative process is the time and energy spent to maintain interaction with constituents. Representatives from citizen groups may have to devote their energies not only to participating in the actual problem-solving sessions, but also within their own organizations to maintain group cohesiveness and support for negotiated agreements. Often group members who are not on the problem-solving team do not understand the need for certain compromises and concessions. Thus, the citizen representatives must educate and win over their own supporters in order to preserve their personal credibility within the organization as well as within the alternative process.

Successful participation of citizen organizations in EDS processes often demands the formation of strong coalitions. Managing the coalitions places additional demands on an organization's time, energy, and financial resources. Not only must citizen representatives devote time to problem-solving sessions within their own organizations and within the actual group of disputants, but also with members of other citizen groups in order to maintain the strength and unity of the coalition. For example, in the San Juan dispute, the Vallecito group almost fell apart the first day; they had assumed that they all shared the same interests. When they discovered rifts within the coalition, they had to call an emergency meeting to uncover and clarify their mutual interests, and then develop an acceptable joint strategy.

An alternative process may limit the types and timing of issues that can be addressed. In some cases, the more complex and controversial issues may be left unaddressed. The easier issues are purposely handled first in order to reinforce a sense of success for the group; more difficult issues may repeatedly get pushed back on the agenda. The Common Ground participants purposely limited the areas of discussion in order to facilitate agreement. Only partial progress was made on the more difficult issues of wetlands protection and farmland preservation.

The pressure to reach consensus in an EDS process may cause some participants to lose sight of their original objectives. Citizens may be co-opted by more powerful groups and end up endorsing the activities of adversaries. Citizens may be frustrated by their lack of leverage and political naïveté and may lack access to critical decision networks. In some cases, citizens may have power and influence that they do not realize they possess.

The Findings of Other Researchers

Other researchers of environmental dispute settlement processes have discovered procedural benefits that accrue to participants in the process, regardless of the direct outcome of the process on the issues in dispute. In a comprehensive evaluation of "mediations that failed," Leonard Buckle and Suzanne Thomas-Buckle (1986) found that while a signed, viable agreement may not have been reached, those participating in these processes felt that the mediator's intervention clearly influenced the eventual course of the conflict and the participants' involvement in it. Among other factors, these researchers found that a group's involvement in a formal dispute settlement process helped the groups to clarify their own interests and objectives, to create potential solutions to the dispute, to build their negotiation skills, and, in some instances, to provide a symbolic image of cooperation to other parties, not necessarily present at the table:

> Clients were most interested in learning from mediation about their interests, available options, and, most important, how to negotiate. The parties perceived that this latter skill not only helped resolve the dispute at hand, but also reportedly equipped them to manage other disputes in other arenas. Similarly, some felt that mediation gave them a chance to engage in games and symbolic politics, in particular, using mediation as a delaying tactic or as a forum for portraying themselves as cooperative people. Less central to most of the parties, but still seen as beneficial, are more nearly outcome-oriented contributions of the mediators—the increased fit between the outcomes of the mediation process and the clients needs and a reduction in delay, effort and costs. (1986, 68)

In a study of the negotiated rule-making processes currently being employed by the U.S. Environmental Protection Agency to resolve disputes there, Susskind and McMahon (1985) found that the structure of EDS processes can empower all parties in various ways and constrain the most powerful. They found that while environmental groups were outnumbered and came into the negotiations with what other parties perceived as uncertain power, they were quite capable of holding their own and "exerted considerable influence" over the final agreements.

Susskind and McMahon question the arguments made by some theorists that the most powerful groups in dispute settlement processes will achieve their ends while the less powerful interests are bound to be disappointed. They feel that a number of factors contributed to the "empowering" of the traditionally less-powerful citizen and environmental group representatives in the EPA cases they studied. First, coalitions certainly helped advance the concerns and increase the influence of the less powerful groups. Second, they believe that the process of facilitation itself imposes constraints on the exercise of excessive power by some groups, thereby keeping parties in check and from treating any other party unfairly or trying to co-opt them. Third, the drive toward consensus embodied in these processes as they progress also helps keep parties' behavior in check. Finally, processes that provide some level of common resources to help defray the costs of involvement and to support the research needs of all parties help to empower less powerful groups. The U.S. Environmental Protection Agency (EPA) provides a "resource pool" of up to $50,000 to help cover the costs of participation and technical studies in its Negotiated Rulemaking process. This money is managed by an independent body, the American Arbitration Association, and represents a combination of EPA funds and contributions by private foundations. Similarly, providing training in negotiation and group process skills for those less familiar with these processes can help diminish some inequities that put citizen groups at a disadvantage.

Douglas Amy's (1987) extensive work on the impact of dispute settlement processes in citizen organizations largely disagrees with the conclusions of Susskind and McMahon. Amy stresses the dangers of co-optation, the power of prevailing institutions' understandings and underestimation of environmental problems, and the social inequities involved in these problems and reformist solutions. Amy stresses the importance of organizational power as an absolutely essential ingredient for citizen organizations to achieve environmental change.

Summary

It appears that the EDS processes discussed in this book have the potential for advancing a citizen organization's interests in specific disputes. Realizing this potential, however, requires the knowledgeable and strategic involvement of citizen group participants. The benefits are not blindly received; the difficulties must be strategically confronted and avoided.

Our observations of the plight of citizen organizations both in surviving and, beyond mere survival, in successfully advocating change in support of their interests have spanned two decades. We have been encouraged by both the increasing willingness and increasing sophistication of citizen and environmental group involvement in EDS processes, as one of many different strategies employed in their much broader efforts. Moreover, we genuinely believe that participation in these processes can lead to an increased appreciation of environmental concerns and accommodation of measures to protect our environment and natural resources. This larger outcome will be achieved only if groups enter EDS processes knowledgeably, understanding their interests and their options and strategically pursuing them.

Many lessons have been drawn from the cases discussed in this book. Detailed recommendations for specific situations and problems have been suggested throughout the previous chapters. At the organizational level, groups must be mindful of several key questions in choosing whether and how to participate in an EDS process. These were discussed in detail in chapters 3 and 4. Briefly, they include:

What is our goal?

What are the appropriate tactics for achieving this goal?

Is there room for compromise?

What are the potential gains to our organization from participating in the EDS process and what are the likely costs?

Is it appropriate for our organization to shift from an adversarial to a collaborative process?

How will the EDS process mesh with other issues and projects of the organization?

How might we maximize and maintain our different options?

What resources do we need in order to participate effectively?

What resources do we have at our disposal?

How can we acquire additional resources (people, information and expertise, finances)?

Is forming a coalition with other groups an appropriate strategy for us in this specific situation?

Who would most effectively represent our organization in the EDS process?

How will we maintain communication with this representative?

How will we ensure that our organization's membership is kept abreast of the process?

Does our representative need particular training or other specific resources before participating?

How will we ensure that the representative fills these needs?

Citizen groups need to pay attention to more than just their own organizational needs. Additionally, these groups must be mindful of certain aspects of the EDS process itself. Remember, EDS processes, for the most part, are new to everyone. Consequently, citizen groups should actively participate in initiating, structuring, and guiding these processes. Specific process considerations include:

What are the goals of the process?

How will the agenda be set?

What will the structure of the process be?

Does the process need a third party facilitator?

If so, who might best serve this role?

How will agreements be reached (consensus, voting, majority rule)?

Should the media be involved? If so, how?

Who will be participating in the process? Is there anyone else who should be involved who has not been contacted?

What might we do if some key stakeholders decline participation in the process?

How are we going to ensure that any agreement reached will be implemented as intended?

We would like to conclude this book on a note of encouragement, albeit cautious encouragement, to you, the leaders and members of today's citizen and environmental groups. We are optimistic about the future of EDS processes in advancing your environmental agenda. Whether or not our optimism is warranted and EDS processes do prove to be an effective tool for citizen groups, however, depends upon the level of understanding and preparedness with which these processes are pursued.

And, finally, when the agreements have been reached or, alternatively, you have chosen to pursue strategies other than an EDS process, please share your experiences. This book does not contain definitive answers; it merely begins raising the critical questions, distilling the experience of citizen and environmental organizations, and increasing the interaction and the awareness of those citizen groups reading it. Certainly, additional research will, with time, help to clarify and expand this understanding. However, by far the greatest benefit and learning will come from you, and other groups and individuals like you, as you continue to seek enhanced environmental quality for all citizens, sharing your experiences and the lessons learned with each other.

References

Amy, Douglas. *The Politics of Environmental Mediation*. New York: Columbia University Press, 1987.

Buckle, Leonard G., and Suzanne Thomas–Buckle. "Placing Environmental Mediation in Context: Lessons from 'Failed' Mediations." *Environmental Impact Assessment Review* 6 (1986): 55–70.

Susskind, Lawrence, and Gerald McMahon. "The Theory and Practice of Negotiated Rulemaking." *Yale Journal on Regulation* 3, no. 1 (1985): 133–65.

Index

Contributors

Lisa Bardwell recently completed her doctorate in natural resources at the University of Michigan and is pursuing research interests on environmental problem-solving and efficacy.

James Crowfoot is dean and professor in the University of Michigan's School of Natural Resources. He is also a core faculty member of the university's interdisciplinary Program in Conflict Management Alternatives.

Sharon Edgar is a resource specialist with the Resource Recovery Section of the Waste Management Division of the state of Michigan's Department of Natural Resources.

Nancy Manring is an adjunct instructor in political science and program manager for the Community Problem-Solving Program in the Institute for Local Government Administration and Rural Development at Ohio University. She is completing her doctorate in natural resources at the University of Michigan.

Kristen Nelson is doing research in Central America on issues of empowerment involved in farmers' adaptation and use of new technologies. This work is part of her focus on environmental sociology as the core of the Ph.D. program she is completing at the School of Natural Resources, the University of Michigan.

Martha Tableman is program coordinator for the Science and Public Policy Program at the Keystone Center in Keystone, Colorado, where she is involved in efforts to facilitate the resolution of environmental disputes. She recently completed her doctorate in natural resources at the University of Michigan.

Julia Wondolleck is an adjunct assistant professor in the University of Michigan's School of Natural Resources, where she teaches courses in natural resource conflict management and negotiation skills building. She is the author of *Public Lands Conflict and Resolution: Managing National Forest Disputes* (New York: Plenum, 1988).

Also Available from Island Press

Ancient Forests of the Pacific Northwest
By Elliott A. Norse

Better Trout Habitat: A Guide to Stream Restoration and Management
By Christopher J. Hunter

The Challenge of Global Warming
Edited by Dean Edwin Abrahamson

Coastal Alert: Ecosystems, Energy, and Offshore Oil Drilling
By Dwight Holing

The Complete Guide to Environmental Careers
The CEIP Fund

Creating Successful Communities: A Guidebook for Growth Management Strategies
By Michael A. Mantell, Stephen F. Harper, and Luther Propst

Crossroads: Environmental Priorities for the Future
Edited by Peter Borrelli

Economics of Protected Areas
By John A. Dixon and Paul B. Sherman

Environmental Restoration: Science and Strategies for Restoring the Earth
Edited by John J. Berger

Fighting Toxics: A Manual for Protecting Your Family, Community, and Workplace
By Gary Cohen and John O'Connor

Hazardous Waste from Small Quantity Generators
By Seymour I. Schwartz and Wendy B. Pratt

Holistic Resource Management Workbook
By Alan Savory

In Praise of Nature
Edited and with essays by Stephanie Mills

Natural Resources for the 21st Century
Edited by R. Neil Sampson and Dwight Hair

The New York Environment Book
By Eric A. Goldstein and Mark A. Izeman

Overtapped Oasis: Reform or Revolution for Western Water
By Marc Reisner and Sarah Bates

Permaculture: A Practical Guide for a Sustainable Future
By Bill Mollison

The Poisoned Well: New Strategies for Groundwater Protection
Edited by Eric Jorgensen

Race to Save the Tropics: Ecology and Economics for a Sustainable Future
Edited by Robert Goodland

Recycling and Incineration: Evaluating the Choices
By Richard A. Denison and John Ruston

Resource Guide for Creating Successful Communities
By Michael A. Mantell, Stephen F. Harper, and Luther Propst

Rivers at Risk: The Concerned Citizen's Guide to Hydropower
By John D. Echeverria, Pope Barrow, and Richard Roos-Collins

Rush to Burn: Solving America's Garbage Crisis?
From *Newsday*

Shading Our Cities: A Resource Guide for Urban and Community Forests
Edited by Gary Moll and Sara Ebenreck

War on Waste: Can America Win Its Battle With Garbage?
By Louis Blumberg and Robert Gottlieb

Wetland Creation and Restoration: The Status of the Science
Edited by Mary E. Kentula and Jon A. Kusler

Wildlife and Habitats in Managed Landscapes
Edited by Jon E. Rodiek and Eric G. Bolen

Wildlife of the Florida Keys: A Natural History
By James D. Lazell, Jr.

For a complete catalog of Island Press publications, please write:
    Island Press
    Box 7
    Covelo, CA 95428

or call: 1-800-828-1302